More Praise for *Dialogue Gap*

"As someone who spent 50 years managing people, I wish I had read this book long ago. Peter provides us with a detailed description of the difference between negotiation and communication; he makes us realize that in times of crisis, dialogue is always the solution and the very essence of teamwork."

—Jean Marchand
Chairman and Founder, Universitas Trust Funds of Canada
Chairman and Founder, Educaid, educational assistance fund

"Peter has been a passionate proponent and champion of effective dialogue for many years, and his latest book should be considered an essential reference tool for anyone looking to take their negotiations, mediation, and dialogue to the next level."

—Peter R. Morgan
Former police hostage negotiator and
Head of the Police Negotiation Cadre
Hong Kong Police

"I value how Peter Nixon has covered dialogue in his book and have already adopted a dialogue-based behavior that has led to a healthier, more productive working environment."

—Dr. Hayat Abdulla Maarafi
Executive Director, Qatar Debate
Member of Qatar Foundation

"I share Peter's passion for promoting and, indeed, pointing the way on how to achieve meaningful dialogue. In business as in the global community we now live in, it all comes down to transparency and open sharing of thoughts."

—John Crawford, JP
Chairman, International Quality Education Limited
Hong Kong

"Effective dialogue and negotiation in business are the only way to remain on top of your competition. I thank Peter for letting me understand the skill and the art of effective negotiation."

—Irfan Muneer
Sales Director, Din Group of Industries
Karachi, Pakistan

"Effective dialogue is needed to help congregational life; dialogue training is needed for clergy and church leaders, and dialogue is essential if the church is to remain an instrument of transformation in the world of the twenty-first century."

—Father Mark Rogers
Discovery Bay Church
Hong Kong

"This is a must-read book for all who want to understand the art of conversation and the virtue of listening."

—Therese Necio-Ortega
Marketing and corporate communications specialist
Principal, TNO Link Concepts Consultancy Ltd
Hong Kong

"I fully endorse the fact that dialogue is the key process in making real change happen within teams and organizations."

—Joanne Davis
Managing Director, Eventworks Ltd
Hong Kong

"It is only through dialogue and understanding that we will ever create peaceful hearts and minds."

—The Very Reverend Diane Nancekivell
Chair, Kids4Peace USA
Vermont, United States

"Peter Nixon's Optimal Outcomes dialogue road map is my new talisman (defined as 'to initiate into the mysteries') of optimal outcomes."

—Denis Vaillancourt
Founder and Managing Director, Securicom Solutions
Vancouver, Canada

Dialogue Gap

Dialogue Gap

*Why Communication
Isn't Enough and What
We Can Do About It, Fast*

Peter Nixon

WILEY

John Wiley & Sons Singapore Pte. Ltd.

Other Wiley Editorial Offices

John Wiley & Sons, 111 River Street, Hoboken, NJ 07030, USA

John Wiley & Sons, The Atrium, Southern Gate, Chichester, West Sussex, P019 8SQ, United Kingdom

John Wiley & Sons (Canada) Ltd., 5353 Dundas Street West, Suite 400, Toronto, Ontario, M9B 6HB, Canada

John Wiley & Sons Australia Ltd., 42 McDougall Street, Milton, Queensland 4064, Australia

Wiley-VCH, Boschstrasse 12, D-69469 Weinheim, Germany

ISBN 978−1−118−15783−1 (Hardback)
ISBN 978−1−118−15784−8 (ePDF)
ISBN 978−1−118−15785−5 (Mobi)
ISBN 978−1−118−15786−2 (ePub)

Typeset in 11.5/14pt Bembo-Roman by MPS Limited, a Macmillan Company, Chennai, India.
Printed in Singapore by Markono Print Media.

10 9 8 7 6 5 4 3 2 1

Despite the fact that optimal outcomes are derived through dialogue,
we often endure dialogue gaps @ work, @ home, and in society.
This book is dedicated to those of you who suffer
the negative effects of dialogue gaps whether they are caused
by others or by you. If you know a dialogue gap
that needs improving, offer the stakeholders this book
and engage them in dialogue for a better world.
Be a dialogue leader—the solution is in the dialogue.

—Peter Nixon

Contents

Introduction

What Is Dialogue Gap?

Only praying and wishing for a world without problems is unrealistic. We must learn from our sad experiences and promote the spirit of dialogue.

—14th Dalai Lama, 2009[1]

We believe that there is a greater need than ever for leaders to meet and genuinely "think together" the real meaning of dialogue. Only through creating such opportunities can there be any hope of building the shared understanding and coordinated innovative action that the world desperately needs.

—2001 letter penned by senior leaders from BP, Hewlett-Packard, Intel, Shell, Visteon[2]

To open yourself to begin to understand the theory behind dialogue is to open yourself up to the forces that make human endeavours effective or not. Once you are aware of these forces, you can no longer simply blame people for situations that don't work out and you can begin to set up conversations that will engender better results.

—William Isaacs, 1999[3]

The world is in crisis. Everywhere we turn we are confronted with unprecedented problems be they economic, environmental, social, or health related. To survive the twenty-first century we need to rediscover how to dialogue not just to live peaceably and sustainably on this planet, but also to lead our organizations through the turbulence and into a successful future. Communicating better isn't enough. We need to innovate and find ways to do things differently. This requires effective dialogue at work, at home, and in society.

This book explores the gap between the quality of the dialogues we have and the quality of the dialogues we need to survive and thrive in the twenty-first century. I call this gap *the dialogue gap*. In this book I explore the causes and implications of dialogue gap; how to improve our dialogues to reduce the negative effects of dialogue gap in our lives; how to assess, practice, and sustain improved dialogue; and finally, I share my vision for a dialogic future.

Dialogue is the only important human skill that we don't train people how to do effectively. Many of us have studied breathing, sleeping, eating, walking, but nowhere in the academic or corporate curriculums will you find lessons on how to dialogue. Is it any wonder that the world is in the poor state that it is?

"Clearly we need to rethink the old approaches to governing the global economy," say Tapscott and Williams, authors of *MacroWikinomics*.[4]

The world is still a beautiful place full of promise and opportunity and new solutions are being developed through the global collaboration of passionate like-minded people who are connecting through the Internet and in person to share ideas and think together. The Global Redesign Initiative of the World Economic Forum (WEF) is just one of hundreds of groups around the world trying to stimulate dialogue toward creating a sustainable future.[5] Klaus Schwab, founder of WEF, suggests that the old ways of solving problems "through traditional negotiation processes characterized by the defense of national interests are inadequate in the face of critical global challenges."[6]

In dialogue, we change through mutual appreciation, sympathy, and empathy. This is not the easiest method of human communication, but it is the most fruitful. That is why dialogue is the most meaningful path to negotiating a new global civilization based on the contributions of all past human civilizations.

—Majid Tehranian[7]

The 2010 IBM CEO Survey revealed that complexity in business today is rising but CEO ability to deal with it is doubtful. Likewise creativity is considered the most important skill of CEO's today; co-creating products and services with customers is defining success and the most dexterous leaders are producing the best results.[8] What do I consider to be the common thread between all these findings? A leader's ability to dialogue effectively will help him or her handle complexity at the speed it arises, harness the creative ideas of people around him or her, co-create with others, and remain dexterous to deal with change. Why is dialogue not therefore included in corporate curriculums and business schools everywhere? I think it is only a matter of time.

The Clarity of Expatriation

Important insights arise from periods of reflection assisted by trained observation, input from a wide variety of perspectives and compassion to understand differences. Things we know and take for granted today were once unimaginable. Discovery of new information is often made easier by people encountering situations from a completely different mind-set and whose resulting detachment allow them to see things as they really are.

Growing up in the French Canadian city of Montreal in the 1960s and 1970s is incredibly different from my current life in Hong Kong where I have lived since moving here a few months after the fall of the Wall in Eastern Europe and the Tiananmen Square massacre in Beijing in 1989. In many respects the insights I offer in this book arise from my being displaced and therefore detached, a feeling typical of expatriates everywhere, and yet I am compassionately interested in and professionally trained to analyze life in my new surroundings.

We have now entered a stage of history during which "dialogue" is becoming as necessary as "life" and "peace." In fact, dialogue may be the only means by which we can guarantee life and peace.
—Majid Tehranian[9]

Many readers may consider the existence of dialogue gap as obvious but I consider it so important that I have diverted my work, encompassed its full importance and do all I can to share the implications of my findings and how to achieve optimal outcomes with groups around the world through writing, speaking, consulting, training, and coaching.

My main observation, that ***the solution is in the dialogue***, highlights a crisis of our time because I have observed that we don't dialogue when we should and even when we do dialogue the quality and quantity of our dialogue falls significantly short of what is needed as demonstrated by the growing number of intractable problems in the world today. My observation that the solution is in the dialogue results largely from my having had the opportunity (voluntarily) to radically change my "lifeworlds" more significantly than most people in their

career.[10] These changes have forced me to reconcile the glaring differences these colliding lifeworlds brought to my attention. In the following chapters you learn about what I call dialogue, where dialogue gap originates, and what we can do to improve dialogue both personally and organizationally. I am passionate about our need to improve dialogue and I believe that if we don't improve dialogue quickly the long-term prospects for civilized life on earth are limited.

Although I discuss dialogue issues @ home and @ large, the main application of this book is aimed at helping with dialogues @ work. Toward the end of this chapter you will find a list of dialogue gaps at work describing where they appear and what optimal outcomes look like when dialogue leaders step in to make this a reality. Similar lists exist for situations at home and in society but the ways to resolve these are largely the same and the rest of this book offers solutions available to all three environments. What principally makes the difference in all these environments is your ability to effectively lead the dialogue.

What You Will Discover in This Book

This book is my dialogue with you. The book is divided into three parts of three chapters each. Part I introduces the details of the book, key definitions, dialogue gap including how dialogue gap arose and its implications @ work, @ home, and @ large in society.

Part II provides solutions to overcome or reduce dialogue gap and goes into detail about getting the right people to dialogue on the right issues in the right way and at the right time and space, all elements of what I call the dialogue puzzle.

Part III focuses on dialogue leadership and helps you identify behaviors and processes to improve and sustain dialogue both personally and inside your organization.

Sprinkled throughout the book are quotations from leading thinkers, past and present, whose contributions to our dialogue here are both an inspiration and a guide for us as dialogue leaders. Also included with each chapter are a few short case scenarios drawn from my client work to provide you with live examples of where effective dialogue or the effects of dialogue gap had an important impact on the outcomes for the organization.

How Dialogue Gap Arose

The purpose of dialogue is none other than pursuit of truth.
—Montaigne[11]

Chapter 1 discusses the origin of dialogue gap and defines the terms used throughout the rest of this book. It provides a useful overview of my observations on dialogue. After reading Chapter 2 I suggest you jump around the book to engage in the aspects of dialogue you want to go deeper into. Chapters 3 to 5 explore the dialogue puzzle and suggest that optimal outcomes are achieved when dialogue among the right people (the stakeholders) is managed effectively to cover the right issues in the right way, at the right time, and in the right space. The chapters explore each piece of the puzzle in order.

Implications of Dialogue Gap

One of the most important differences my changing lifeworlds exposed for me is one that I share with many of you, too, especially the older and normally paper-based readers of this book. If you commenced your career before the 1990s you had the chance to work and live for a time before the advent of computers. Now, however, you find yourself living in a world where it is hard even to imagine a day without heavy reliance on computers, cell phones, and the Internet. If, on the other hand, you commenced your career in the 1990s, it is likely that the Internet world we live in today is all you have ever known and you might well be reading this book in its digital format.

Those of us who experienced an analogue youth (i.e., no computers) and are now experiencing a digital adulthood (lots of computers) will relate to and agree with the problems arising from what I refer to as ***the digital tipping point***, the point after which we spend more than half our time digitally rather than personally connected with other people on a daily basis.[12] Many of us passed our digital tipping point many years ago.

Another colliding pair of lifeworlds compares the first 25 years of my life in which family, community, and work challenges were answered by getting together to talk, discuss, debate, and work out a way forward together. If there were no challenges to resolve, then family, friends, and colleagues would meet anyway to swap stories, tell jokes, and simply enjoy each other's company. I was most impressed by the people who told the best stories, wove the best arguments, and asked the smartest questions. I respected the expression "people will know how smart you are by the questions you ask." These same people often seemed to be the community leaders for whom we all held respect.

Since the advent of digital communication, my life, like many of you reading this book, has involved much less dialogue and much more communication. We now send and receive hundreds of messages daily but find ourselves seldom if ever sitting around engaged in dialogue.

I define communication as exchanging information and I define dialogue as thinking together.

Communication and dialogue are important and closely related but not the same nor should they be used for the same situations. Sadly today many people communicate when they should dialogue; for example, people send e-mail when they should talk face to face. And to make matters worse, we are spending less and less time in dialogue so our dialogue skills are diminishing.

So perhaps, if we could this morning have a dialogue on whatever subject you want, bearing in mind that without this quality of affection, care, love, and compassion, we merely play with words, remain superficial, antagonistic, assertive, dogmatic, and so on. It remains merely verbal; it has no depth, no quality, no perfume.

—J. Krishnamurti[13]

Chapter 2 explores various examples of life beyond the digital tipping point causing problems at work, at home, and in society. It looks at situations where Dialogue Gap creates problems that didn't even exist 10 years ago.

Moving from my life in Canada to my life in Hong Kong meant leaving a North American culture that values speaking up, making a difference, and leading change to a Confucian culture, which values letting others speak first, not rising above the crowd, and avoiding conflict if possible. These differences motivated my exploration of cross-cultural differences in negotiation and how to achieve optimal outcomes in our world today. My cross-cultural observations together with practical ways to improve negotiated outcomes are described in my first book *Negotiation: Mastering Business in Asia* (John Wiley & Sons, 2005).[14]

My international work in negotiation has created another collision of lifeworlds for me. I started my career auditing with the large international firm called Coopers & Lybrand (now called PwC and the world's largest accounting firm). I first worked for the firm in Montreal and then moved to Geneva and onto Hong Kong. My audit career gave me a professional license to walk into major multinational companies around the world and uncover what made them successful. I was deeply interested in this work and chose to use my international audit skills to build a practice helping multinationals negotiate optimal outcomes for their businesses.

I offered a rare combination of skills in a rapidly growing marketplace (Asia Pacific) and business opportunities were good, so thus began a decade of extensive work and travel participating in exciting cross-cultural commercial and change management negotiations taking place during the rise of China and India. My travels took me to the United States, Europe, the Caribbean, the Middle East, and throughout the Asia Pacific region from the north in Japan and Korea through China and the ASEAN countries down to Australia and from Pakistan and India in the west all the way to Taiwan in the east and everything in between.

Whereas my audit and early negotiation work was largely focused on the financial aspects of corporations, the more I gained experience and became known in the field, the more I was invited into situations that involved social, environmental, and economic issues of great importance. At the same time I came to realize that in many situations my negotiation clients were simply looking to increase their happiness and reduce their suffering (a basic Buddhist belief). At this point my colliding lifeworlds resulted in two additional observations:

1. Despite clients communicating more than ever, by leveraging the Internet and all it offered multinational corporations, companies were still not achieving optimal outcomes This realization led to my recognizing that communication and dialogue were not the same and that my Star Negotiator model, described in my negotiation book, needed tweaking to suggest that **Star Negotiators** *dialogue* **rather than** *communicate* **effectively**.[15]
2. My second and related observation is that **optimal outcomes** (as defined by Nobel Prize–winning John Nash as the point at which no one party can achieve more in a negotiation without another party losing something) **can only be achieved using dialogue (not communication)**.

How to Get the Right People Talking about the Right Issues

Part II picks up where my book on negotiation left off. In Part II I explore specifically how to get the right people talking about the right issues in the right way and at the right time and space. Chapter 3 combines people and issues because they are hard to separate and given different people have different perspectives and issues of importance based on their role and background. In Chapter 4 I explore the factors involved in getting the stakeholders into dialogue and how to identify and classify their issues.

How to Dialogue in the Right Way

Another observation that resulted from my colliding lifeworlds came when I combined my external consulting with my internal career of board membership and senior executive coaching. Once the challenges of implementing change became more fully understood so, too, did the solutions I offered my clients, family, and friends. These insights form the basis of Chapter 4 where I describe dialogue leadership behaviors in detail. When used effectively these behaviors enable you to rebuild dialogue and optimize solutions at home, at work, and in society.

How to Dialogue in the Right Time and Space

Chapter 5 reminds us that achieving optimal outcomes also requires managing the time and space aspects of the situations you or your organization find yourselves in. I delve briefly into these factors because they are important and because the cases shared in this book often point to problems in these areas.

How to Assess and Practice Better Dialogue

Part 3 of this book focuses on you as a dialogue leader and provides valuable tips to begin achieving optimal outcomes. Chapter 6 offers dialogue assessments that I use with clients at both the personal and organizational level to try and help them identify where they are going wrong and what they need to do to rebuild effective dialogue into their organizations and lives. Readers will find the list of dialogue blockers valuable when checking what is hindering their own dialogue skills. Most of these "dialogue blockers" were provided by our clients over many years of working with them to improve their outcomes.

The essence of dialogue lies in prompting the meeting of hearts and minds.
—Daisaku Ikeda[16]

Chapter 7, **Sustaining Dialogue,** explores dialogue theories, approaches, methods, and processes to maintain effective dialogue especially when facing the challenging situations that life throws at us. Although many of these processes are known to facilitators, they are lesser known to the business world and the general public and seldom are they lined up and compared as I attempt to do here.

The "keeper" for me [from Alan Stewart's presentation] was the wonderful notion that every time we talk openly with another human being, a third joint-level of consciousness is created, from the best of both of us. When we argue or debate, we actually seek to block the other's contribution and limit potential solutions or suggestions, limiting world consciousness.

—David Catherine Palin-Brinkworth[17]

Chapter 8, Dialogic Leadership, introduces a concept I call *Potentialism* and that itself arises from another collision of my lifeworlds. Like most people my age, I grew up in the city in which I was born and, apart from a trip to the World Boy Scout Jamboree in Lillehammer, Norway, and a scholarship year at the University of Alberta, for 27 years I lived where I grew up, in the province of Quebec in Canada. Since leaving Montreal, however, to work in Geneva in 1988, at about the same time PCs were becoming fully present in companies around the world, I have worked, lived, and traveled internationally. Whereas the first half of my life was local, the second half of my life has been global. As a result of this changed lifeworld my perspectives have given rise to what I refer to as *Potentialism.*

International travel helped me see the most beautiful things the world has to offer but also exposed me to the most wretched things. I have witnessed firsthand the extremes of wealth and poverty, sickness and health, education and ignorance, pristine nature and extreme environmental degradation, happiness and depression, peace and war, faith and desperation, life and death.

My travels, professional training, and colliding lifeworlds have given me the detached yet compassionate role of a reflective practitioner and I feel obliged to share my observations and suggested solutions with you here in this book. Many of you are fellow travelers with whom I have learned many of these things. Some of you have preceded or followed me on some of the paths I have taken and have as a result witnessed similar things. Some of you long to change your own lifeworlds to widen your understanding of the world in which we live. Some of you are content where you are and have no goal to change or expand your world preferring simply to make your existing world a better place. Regardless of where you are or what direction you are moving I encourage you to accept my concept of Potentialism—*"we all have a duty to realize our potential while helping others realize theirs."*

Chapter 8 discusses how we might realize our potential through a dialogic future. I touch on some of the negative implications that will arise if we don't improve dialogue (some of which we can already see today in the social, economic, and environmental crisis that we face around the world) and the positive results that can be achieved if we learn to dialogue more effectively as leaders.

I conclude this book by encouraging you and other readers to use the ideas and experience shared in these pages as the beginning of your own **dialogue on dialogue** together with the people you share your lives with, at home, at work, and in society. I encourage local, national, and world leaders to set an example and to use this book to remind people that we need to improve dialogue effectiveness if we are to resolve the ever increasing challenges of our globalized, interdependent, and fragile twenty-first century. Finally I encourage parents, teachers, and trainers everywhere to use this book as a resource to teach our young people and train our workforce to use dialogue to realize their personal and organizational potential while helping others realize theirs.

One thing science and religion agree on today is that we have plenty of problems awaiting us in the future. Knowing the solution is in the dialogue and knowing that leaders like you aim to make a positive difference, I join the majority around the world who in faith and hope, believe we can realize our potential while living an environmentally sustainable, socially just, and spiritually fulfilling human existence on earth.[18]

The 21st Century is the Century of Dialogue.
—14th Dalai Lama[19]

The World in Turmoil

As I put a wrap on the writing of this book, evidence of Dialogue Gap is rumbling through the Middle East and North Africa and sending jitters through autocratic leaders in China and beyond. In Japan questions are being asked about the quality of dialogue that placed nuclear reactors on top of known geological fault lines and close to shore in reach of tsunami waves.

People today are connected and communicate like never before. Using communication tools like Twitter and Facebook we create communities to share information and occasionally inspire assemblies in person in spaces like Tahrir Square in Cairo to dialogue and enact change @ work, @ home, and in society.

The purpose of this book is to highlight how our overreliance on communication (defined as the exchange of information) that has diminished our ability to dialogue (defined as productively thinking together) leading to suboptimal outcomes at work, at home, and in society.

I suggest that the quality of dialogue is diminishing at a time when the need for effective dialogue is greater than ever before. The short-coming between the quality of the dialogues we have and the quality of the dialogues we need is what I call Dialogue Gap. I believe dialogue gaps are growing for most of us because our dialogue skills are diminishing and because we spend less and less time in dialogue, preferring instead to communicate using our favorite communication gadgets such as "smart" phones, e-mail, and the Internet.

In studies carried out in 2011, 10 percent of Hong Kong teens qualify as being addicted to the Internet while in the United States 4 percent of teens have problematic internet use.[20] In the U.S. study, teens who reported an irresistible urge to be online and tension when they weren't, also reported being more likely to be depressed, aggressive, and use drugs.[21] In Hong Kong 82 percent of those surveyed use the Internet to interact with other people or check on them through social networks, chat rooms, and message boards. Of those considered addicted, symptoms include avoiding face-to-face contact with people other than via Internet messaging.

Leadership—Dialogue versus Autocracy

Noticeable perpetrators of dialogue gap today are those leaders who prefer the command and control culture of the twentieth century—those who repeatedly remind us that it is "my way or the highway," "take it or leave it," "you are either with us or you are against us." This dualistic thinking typical of autocratic leadership was successful when followers had incomplete information and a need for direction, but the world has changed. Now people access information freely and instantly over the Internet and via mobile phones and self-organize to achieve their common goals. Successful leaders today need to master dialogue to quickly understand the situation and agree on the best way forward. It is only in this way that you will achieve optimal outcomes in the complex environments in which we work today.

The only way forward is for the government and opposition to engage in a dialogue, and you can't have a real dialogue when parts of the peaceful opposition are in jail. The government must create the conditions for dialogue, and the opposition must participate to forge a just future for all. . . . Such open discourse is important even if what is said does not square with our worldview. . . . That is the choice that must be made—a choice between hate and hope; between the shackles of the past and the promise of the future. It's a choice that must be made by leaders and by the people, and it's a choice that will define the future.
—Excerpt from U.S. President Obama's
Mideast Speech, May 19, 2011

Although societal dialogues get the most coverage in the media, dialogue @ work has the biggest impact on us economically while dialogues at home seem closest to our hearts. This book examines dialogue in all three settings: work, home, and society, but focuses primarily on dialogues @ work.

We need to improve the quality of our dialogue if we are to achieve optimal outcomes; however, when leaders suggest dialogue be used to address problems they do so assuming that the people involved know what dialogue means and how to dialogue effectively. But dialogue has all but disappeared from the workplace and we don't teach dialogue in schools so how can we expect people to respond effectively?

As you read in Part I of this book, life in the digital era is forcing us to communicate digitally more than ever before. As we spend more and more time communicating we are spending less and less time conversing. As a result our dialogue skills are diminishing. When we do choose to dialogue our diminished dialogue skills lead to more conflict further reducing our desire to choose dialogue when decision making and the cycle continues until we find ourselves with a gap between the quality of dialogues we have and the quality of dialogues we need. Faced with dialogue gap what do we do? Rather than work things out, we change suppliers, change employers, change our spouse, or move to a new community. In many situations it is not just a dialogue gap, it is a gaping black hole where no one talks to each other and conflict is rife. Sound familiar? This book is for you.

LEADING ORGANIZATIONS

| D | C | B | A | 0 | 1 | 2 | 3 | 4 |

TO OVERCOME PROBLEMS   TO CREATE PROBLEMS

"The times they are a changin'."

Thoughts from Vaclav Havel, former president of the Czech Republic and one of the key opposition leaders involved in the 1989 peaceful "velvet revolution" that led to the break-up of Czechoslovakia, seem applicable today:

I think there are good reasons for suggesting that the modern age has ended. Today, many things indicate that we are going through a transitional period, when it seems that something is on the way out and something else is painfully being born. It is as if something were crumbling, decaying and exhausting itself, while something else, still indistinct, were arising from the rubble.

—Vaclav Havel[22]

The people power that split Czechoslovakia into two countries (the Czech Republic and Slovakia) is now also having its effects in countries like Tunisia and Egypt. Effective dialogue leadership in these countries is contrasted with the autocratic leadership and violence in countries like Yemen, Syria, Iran, Libya, and China.

Open dialogue and exchange among people at the citizen level will have to form the undercurrent of all international efforts for constructive change.

—Daisaku Ikeda[23]

Dialogic leaders recognize the difference between communication (sending information) and dialogue (thinking together), and use effective dialogue to achieve optimal outcomes in the situations they face. Autocratic leaders are normally juxtaposed against democratic leaders but there are many democratic leaders who are not dialogic. Expressing yourself by voting doesn't mean you will ever be asked your opinion by the person you voted for or that your opinion, if solicited, will ever be incorporated into creating optimal outcomes. Dialogic leaders know they need your input and that of all stakeholders if they are to achieve optimal outcomes.

In my experience (and an area ripe for academic proof) dialogic leaders @ work engage employees better, sell more, resolve conflicts faster, manage projects more efficiently, achieve better value for money, innovate, and stay ahead of the competition. Less effective leaders fall short of achieving optimal outcomes and find it near impossible to sustain results over time. Dialogic leaders @ home enjoy happier environments, happier relationships, and better health. Dialogic leaders @ large in society enjoy sustained political office, more resilient economies, more sustainable environments, and less conflict.

Dialogic leaders need not be liberal and charismatic; in fact, many I know are conservative and introverted. Dialogic leaders are those who know optimal outcomes are achieved by getting the key stakeholders to dialogue on the right issues in the right way and at the right time and space. Each of these concepts is explored in a practical way in this book along with specific behaviors, tools, and suggestions to help you become more dialogic.

Most leaders lead how they were led and since dialogic leaders have been relatively rare in the past it is normal that the more common form of leadership—especially that espoused in the West—is the decisive take it or leave it style of leadership that aims for short-term wins over sustainable longer-term optimal outcomes. For better or worse the interdependence and complexity of the world today requires dialogic leadership and fast.

Now, more than ever, we must reach out in a further effort to understand each other and engage in genuine dialogue.

—Daisaku Ikeda[24]

Conversation versus Dialogue

Many ask about the difference between conversation and dialogue. It is perhaps only a matter of semantics as both words function as nouns (dialogue, conversation) and verbs (to dialogue or to converse). Although we converse in dialogue, a conversation and a dialogue are not exactly the same. I differentiate the two nouns by looking at the outcome. Conversation and dialogue are both based on conversing, but conversations (as I see most people using the term today) tend to be primarily for answering questions of a social or interpersonal nature whereas dialogue tends to be used primarily for answering questions of a commercial or political nature. The following explanation further differentiates the nouns in question.

Conversation

- Purpose: Commonly used to answer questions of an interpersonal or social nature.
- Participants: Whoever comes are the right people.
- Starting time: Whenever you start is the right time.
- Finish time: Conversation ends when people have to depart or when they lose interest.
- Outcome: Whatever happens is the only thing that could have.
- Space: It is important to create a hospitable space.

- Subject: Topic of interest common to participants.
- Derivative value: The Gems: Stories, insights, shared discoveries, friendships, happiness, better awareness of issues, perspectives, possible solutions, further questions, reduced stress, improved health, referrals, and so on.

Dialogue

- Purpose: Commonly used to answer questions of a commercial or political nature.
- Participants: It is important that all key stakeholders contribute their perspectives.
- Starting time: It is a process decision when best to start the dialogue depending on several factors including who is available and what outcome you aim to achieve.
- Finish time: Dialogue ends when objective is met, question is answered, or people give up.
- Outcome: An answer to the question or a better understanding of the question, which might lead to more dialogue.
- Space: You can select and create space based on the outcome you aim to achieve knowing that stakeholders, issues, and other factors have a dynamic influence on space.
- Subject: Challenge or problem common to stakeholders.
- Derivative value: The Gems: Stories, insights, shared discoveries, friendships, happiness, better awareness of issues, perspectives, possible solutions, further questions, reduced stress, improved health, referrals, and so on.

Eight Steps to Dialogue

As the following useful box graphic demonstrates, I suggest that there are eight steps to dialogue. Knowing this allows us to teach and train people to become dialogic leaders and helps us to identify what is missing when people call for dialogue to resolve problems and find answers.

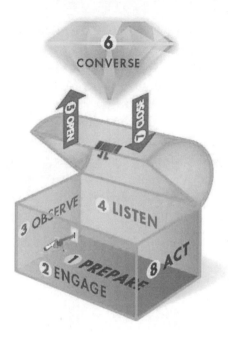

Step 1—Prepare for Dialogue

Wisdom suggests that 80 percent of the outcome of a dialogue depends on the preparation. The best preparation that I can suggest is to walk through the dialogue puzzle outlined in this book following what I affectionately call my Rx6,—the right outcome requires you to get the right people to dialogue on the right issues (Chapter 3) in the right way (Chapter 4) and at the right time and in the right space (Chapter 5).

Step 2—Engage the Stakeholders

You can engage people in a number of ways. The typical ones include asking them a question or telling them something that interests them. You can also send a message through silence, body language, third parties, or through the media. The topic of engagement is taken up in many ways today but especially in sales, service, and employee engagement. Whenever you engage stakeholders in matters of importance to them they will respond. Engagement is addressed throughout this book and is based on the understanding that engagement is the only way we can optimize outcomes for everyone. You will notice, however, that engagement is only one of eight steps. In organizations today many people wonder why making a presentation or sending a memo doesn't lead to change. As you will learn, this is because the solution is in the whole dialogue, not solely in the PowerPoint presentation. I like the analogy of the farmer who plants seeds in the audience during the engagement stage for later nurturing and harvesting through the dialogue process. Clients wonder how this engagement step differs from the later Step 5, which is to open the dialogue. Essentially what you are doing at Step 2 is still communication—sending messages or planting seeds that will later be developed through dialogue.

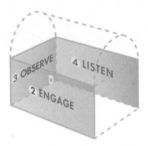

Step 3— Observe

Although Telepresence and other high-definition video conferencing systems are beginning to make up for the disadvantages caused when we are not physically together, dialogue (as opposed to communication), to be effective, needs people to see each other and preferably to be physically together. When you are together you can watch the body language and facial expressions to substantiate the verbal messages you are absorbing through listening. Readers interested in improving their observational skills are encouraged to consider Chapter 4 as well as researching some of the references by Dr. Paul Ekman and others included in this book.

Step 4—Listen

Once you have communicated a message to the stakeholders, you have to listen to know how it has been received and how they have responded. Your deep listening at this stage is crucial for deciding how you will want to open the dialogue. In this book we cover listening as part of absorbing messages (Chapter 4).

Step 5 — Open Dialogue

When we open from communication into dialogue we symbolically open the box or open the door to receive the jewels of reward that can accrue through dialogue. These rewards are not accessible through communication alone and many leaders fail to understand this. It is not enough to send and receive information you need to stop sending messages and instead begin conversing together. In the farming anecdote, this is the stage during which you add sunlight to others' ideas by asking questions. When observing dialogues you can always spot the moment when the talking at each other ends and someone asks an open-ended question (usually beginning with what or how) thus shedding light onto the other; for example, "What do you think?" or "How do you feel about the plans as presented?"

Step 6 — Converse

When farmers are nurturing their seedlings they protect them from harm and make sure that they get sufficient light, nutrients, and water in order to emerge into their full potential. The same can be said of conversing in dialogue. Dialogue experts know that successful outcomes don't just happen by chance. There are some specific things they do to ensure success. One acronym I find useful when conversing is FILL, which reminds us to do the following:

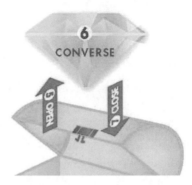

Here are some other useful reminders of what happens when we converse in dialogue.

- What we do when conversing in dialogue.
- We welcome and introduce people to each other as we would friends in our home.
- We introduce the purpose or question.
- We collaborate in an open friendly format.
- We build ideas together with enthusiasm.
- We develop ideas rather than try to score points or persuade others.
- We harness the collective intelligence of the group.
- We enlarge each other's vision.
- We express our mind and heart (thoughts and feelings).
- We listen to understand and to identify deeper questions, which further our dialogue.

How to converse in dialogue:

- We interact with curiosity rather than telling.
- We notice and honor the emotional underpinnings of others and our own responses.
- We recognize that right and wrong, winning and losing are irrelevant.
- We welcome diversity of opinion as the wellspring of creativity.
- We sustain openness to creativity.
- We appreciate the value of interdependency.
- We recognize and acknowledge blind spots in our own perspectives without losing face.

- Whenever we treat each other well good things happen.
- We assemble stakeholders to stimulate each other in an interactive live setting.
- We invite people into the dialogue to share their perspectives at key junctures and whenever they feel moved to do so.
- We link ideas and disparate perspectives.

It is important that we remember that dialogue requires more than just being good at conversing. Being effective also requires being good at the other steps listed here.

Step 7—Close the Dialogue

Effective dialogue leaders do some specific things when drawing dialogues to a close. They reward the openness of the participants by thanking them and then agreeing to take the next steps together with others present. It is not enough to have had a good dialogue. If change is to happen, specific follow-up needs to be agreed on and locked into place. As part of this follow-up it is also useful to agree on when we will meet again to report back on the things we have agreed to do together.

Step 8—Act

I suggest that part of dialogue is not just talk but also action and it is important that stakeholders act to achieve both quick wins (to keep motivation high) as well as the long-term plans agreed on together. In moving from dialogue into action it is important that people stick to the priorities that have been agreed on together. Priorities change with the situation, so it is important that the action steps be flexible enough to respond to the evolving horizon and whenever necessary, people need to reengage in dialogue when changes necessitate new plans. It is also important that stakeholders stay in touch with each other because long periods of silence or simple communication can lead to demotivation and disengagement.

The Results of Dialogue

The jewels of dialogue are many and unpredictable except to say that if you don't engage in dialogue you can't possibly achieve the jewels that await you. Some of the things we know about the results of dialogue include:

- Dialogue is an iterative process like archaeology where digging, finding jewels, surfacing, and polishing the jewels leads people to find even more jewels.
- Ideas emerge and are revealed through dialogue, like uncut diamonds needing finishing.
- Ideas sometimes emerge two to three at a time, like gems stuck together in the mud, and need to be treated separately in their own right to be fully understood.
- Sometimes what emerges from dialogue is not an answer to a question but a better definition of the problem or more questions thereby allowing for further dialogue.
- Dialogue helps polish ideas to reveal their inherent potential.
- Ideas emerge in a haphazard way, not in a linear or prioritized way, and dialogic processes need to accommodate this reality.
- Emerging ideas or thoughts become the key that opens the door to other ideas and thoughts.

What Does Dialogue Gap Look Like @ Work?

Although every situation is different, the following list of dialogue gap scenarios, drawn from one of my clients in Asia, is typical of problems being faced by many organizations today. The list is typical of the growing dialogue gap because 20 years ago the list would include relatively harder more conflictual situations, but today the situations are relatively easier but equally difficult for managers to resolve in our new era of dialogue gap.

Sample dialogue gap scenarios:

- You are a project leader who is leading a cross-team initiative. You want another team to support a critical part of the project but you know that team has many assignments on hand already.
- Your boss would like you to take up a new assignment but you are already up to your throat. How to say no to your boss.
- Your boss has assigned a project to both you and your peer and expects the two of you to work out how you will collaborate to complete the project together.
- A member of another team calls you asking and expecting you and your team to take up a task but which is not entirely your responsibility from your perspective.
- You are working with an external supplier. This is the first time you work with this supplier and you have to make sure that the supplier can meet the deadline and that its deliverables are good quality.
- You are a project leader and you have to gain extra resources and budget from your boss/top decision makers.
- When you are working with your peers in your department or across departments day-to-day, you have to handle a negative response (no) or disagreement arising from some of them.
- You are leading a team of five persons. Two of them are emotional and unwilling to assume extra responsibilities. This creates negative impact on the other three team members. You need to maintain respectful control of your team and get commitment from all five members toward work.
- How do you negotiate with a customer who asks for a lower price or better terms when he or she claims to have been offered a better price or better terms by your competitors?

Examples of Dialogue Gap and the Optimal Outcomes That Await You

The following table provides a tangible list of the problems caused by dialogue gap and the optimal outcomes available to organizations today. The list is derived from our client work and highlights the situations where effective dialogue can make the most important contributions to improving the outcomes of the organization and the people involved.

Audience	Where Dialogue Gap Appears	Negative Impact of Dialogue Gap	Dialogue Leader's Possible Optimal Outcomes
Negotiation	Negotiation meetings	Get less for yourself while other party gets less, too	Reach best possible outcome
Project management	Project team meetings	Projects late, below spec., over budget, high project team turnover	Award-winning projects delivered on time and on budget
IT services	User take up and interface	Conflict, frustration, waste, unused applications, complaints	Users delighted and applications give competitive advantage to organization
Talent management	Performance appraisal meetings	Poor-quality feedback, lose good people, disconnect between needs and training, lack of feedback	Talent continues to grow and develop in line with needs of organization and changing competitive environment
Entrepreneurship	Getting new ideas off the ground	Missed opportunities, lost opportunities, poor implementation, lost motivation	Successful launch and profitable business
Business development	Commercial sales meetings	Client needs not uncovered or understood	Win business, gain referrals, lock out competition
Sales	Consumer sales	Customer buys something they don't need or which doesn't match their requirements	Get exactly what you need at the best price
Sourcing	Vendor meetings	Don't get best value for money, miss learning about how else vendor can help you achieve your objectives	Vendors give you competitive advantage and best total cost of ownership

Audience	Where Dialogue Gap Appears	Negative Impact of Dialogue Gap	Dialogue Leader's Possible Optimal Outcomes
Sourcing	User meetings	Users' needs not fully understood, procurement not allowed to follow its process	Best supply available at best price—minimize waste of resources
Auditing	Audit interviews	Don't uncover control weaknesses or gather the information you need from auditee	Strong effective control systems working throughout the period
Investigations	Investigative interviews	Don't get truthful, complete, and accurate information	Resolve problems quickly and effectively
Compliance	Compliance meetings	Unclear if compliance requirements are being met and if not why not, lack of commitment to improve	Constructive agreement about goals and how they will be achieved
Partnerships	Partner meetings	Key issues not discussed or lead to conflict and demotivated or departed partners	Successful enthusiastic leadership attracting clients and associates
Education	Senior leadership and teacher meetings	Lack of inspired input leading to poor curriculum design and fulfillment and poor use of resources	Self-supporting group that leads itself and the students to achieve more in a productive environment
Health care	Patient–physician dialogues	Not all symptoms and implications are identified or understood leading to less than optimal care and treatment decisions	Optimal health-care provision at lowest cost possible
Health care	Medical referrals	Lack of patient history known or shared hampering optimal decisions on care and treatment	Full disclosure provided on a timely basis leading to best health care provision possible

(Continued)

Audience	Where Dialogue Gap Appears	Negative Impact of Dialogue Gap	Dialogue Leader's Possible Optimal Outcomes
Research and development	Research collaboration	Synergies are not apparent or achievable	Breakthrough ideas achieved quickly and effectively
Community governance	Town meetings	Every topic seen as a fight, exchange of partisan votes without targeting what's best for community	All issues aired and best decision achieved regardless of political affiliations
Corporate governance	Board meetings	Lack of debate on tough issues, lack of input from some stakeholders, poor decision making, waste of time	Optimal, enforceable decisions, no breaking of ranks after meetings, innovative, competitive, visionary
Political governance	Meetings with government	Passing the buck, no decision, unclear responsibility	Effective consultation with all stakeholders then decision agreed on and reported accordingly—not seeking agreement from all rather consultation of all
Customer service	Customer interactions	Unmet expectations, omitted input on how to improve, lose customer to competitor	Effective handling of inquiries, service breaches, collection and forwarding of input to people who can use it, sustained customer and sales
Membership organizations	Membership sales	Declining number of members and less use of membership	Thriving organization
Trade and investment promotion	Road show presentations	Unclear how help can be extended, what needs really are, unable to see beyond wants	Productive sustainable partnership

Audience	Where Dialogue Gap Appears	Negative Impact of Dialogue Gap	Dialogue Leader's Possible Optimal Outcomes
Legal disputes	Litigation, mediation, arbitration	Irreparable relationship damage, nonrecovery of assets, injustice inflicted	Justice achieved, parties accept settlement
Event management	Event planning and execution meetings	Lack of cooperation and input when it is needed	Great event run angst-free with hair left in your head
Fund-raising	Request for donations	People ignore you, give less than you need, don't refer others, don't care for your charity or cause	Enthusiastic supporter who cares for your cause and does all they can to support your efforts
Religion	Regular gatherings	One-way communication, little idea about the needs of the congregation	Rapidly growing congregation of people who minister and support each other
Budgeting	Budget meetings	Turf wars, hidden fat in budget, variances minimized to hide questions, focus of conversation on wrong topics	Attention paid to material items and debate and dialogue results in best allocation of budget
Recruitment	Job interviews	People fill jobs rather than match talent opportunity to fulfill potential, job hopping to bump up salary	Attract best fit candidate who thrives in position and contributes significantly to organization
Management oversight	Management meetings	Agenda doesn't allocate time against priority issues and dialogue doesn't lead to valuable output, waste of time, unnecessary oversight, getting in the way	Wider, higher level perspective improves local focus and additional experience points out issues less experienced people might overlook

(Continued)

Audience	Where Dialogue Gap Appears	Negative Impact of Dialogue Gap	Dialogue Leader's Possible Optimal Outcomes
Teamwork	Team meetings	Some members don't contribute while others over-contribute leading to suboptimal outcomes	Effective input and process
Design and innovation	Brainstorming and creative sessions	Routine contributions, little new or original or out-of-the-box breakthrough thinking	Breakthrough ideas shaped to fit current situations that lead to significant improvements
Manufacturing, logistics, supply chain	Process updates	Historical reporting rather than dialogue on how might we improve things, ignoring elephant in the room	Tackle priority issues in constructive way leading to optimal outcomes
Corporate finance	Client road shows	Present products rather than listen to needs of client and tailor remarks to how solutions can be created	Financial solutions tailored to needs and wants of client while still producing profitable arrangements for creator
Liquidation	Asset sales	Liquidated assets without regard to real value	Best possible deal for all concerned taking into account all the issues, not only speed and price of liquidation
Traders	Buy-sell meetings	Focus on closing rather than on total cost of ownership and other issues beyond the traders interests	Transactions create value in excess of the short-term profits resulting from the deal

Dialogue Cases for Consideration

I provide case examples at the end of most chapters to enable you to link the concepts discussed to real-life situations that affect us on a daily basis at work, at home, and in society. As you become more attuned to reflecting on the quality of the dialogue in your life, you can begin applying the tips provided in these pages to improve the outcomes in your life and organization.

Trade Dialogues

David, one of Canada's **leading Ambassadors in Asia,** is often sought out for help and advice in trade-related matters. He related to me that one of his favorite tactics is to suggest that "If I was in your shoes I would be thinking this." David says this for two reasons: To share his thoughts and more importantly, to prompt the other party to reveal what they themselves are thinking about the particular topic. In so doing David and the other party inch slowly toward optimal outcomes by better understanding each other's needs.

Conflict Dialogues

Emiko Okada-san is a **Hiroshima bomb survivor** who works tirelessly to rid the world of nuclear bombs. On July 4, 2008, I was privileged to have a private dialogue with her at the Hiroshima Peace Park. I asked what she recommended people do differently to improve dialogue today. "Without doubt, trust each other," was her reply. Initially people might take this as naive given corruption is rife in many parts of the world (see www.ijustpaidabribe.com), but when you think more deeply you realize that if trust was present then dialogue would be more truthful and it would be easier to achieve a positive outcome more quickly.

Corporate Governance Dialogues
As one of the authors of the **public sector corporate governance** guide for Hong Kong, it was clear that senior leadership of these bodies needed guidance as to the issues affecting their governance and how to make improvements. By publishing guidance of this nature professional bodies generate dialogue on issues of importance with people who are in a position to make a difference. Although complaints remain that change is slow and publications of this nature have little impact, indeed the behavior changes from ignorance, not knowing what to do, to avoidance—not doing what should be done. The solution then is in the dialogue. http://app1.hkicpa.org.hk/publications/corporategovernanceguides/eframework_guide.pdf.

Justice Dialogues
Commencing in 2009 **civil justice reform** in Hong Kong has forced litigants filing in Hong Kong's district and high courts to also file a mediation certificate explaining whether the party is willing to attempt mediation and if not, why not. The reforms were introduced to speed up dispute resolution and clear the courts of long overdue and legally less significant cases. Experience in jurisdictions where mediation has become a forced option has all been positive. What do mediators do? Get the stakeholders to dialogue the important issues realizing that some concession making and taking is necessary to resolve the dispute and move on.

Health Care Dialogues
The book *Who Killed the Queen? The Story of a Community Hospital and How to Fix Public Healthcare* (Holly Dressel, McGill–Queens Press, 2008, www.whokilledthequeen.com/) provides a substantial case for the importance of dialogue in

hospitals today. During the 100-year history of this small community hospital in Montreal it constantly outshone its bigger and better funded rivals around the world simply because it flourished in a culture of dialogue and egalitarianism, which is sadly uncommon in the health care field today. What were some of its accomplishments before finally closing its doors in 1995?

- The progressive support, training, and treatment of nurses uncommon.
- World-renowned breakthroughs in anaesthesia.
- Early adoption of X-ray technology.
- Leading work in ENT.
- The first Chinese women doctor hired in Canada in 1949.
- The first ICU in Canada.
- Breakthroughs in laparoscopic and laser surgery.
- First use of preoperative antibiotics.
- Best primary and secondary teaching hospital in Canada.
- The most efficient hospital in Quebec.
- The fastest changeover time of any hospital operating theater in the world.
- The first accredited mammography service in Canada.
- Widely considered the best community hospital in Quebec.

The book explains why this little hospital flourished, why it closed, and why it remains today a perfect example of how public health care should be delivered around the world.

Bottom line: We have never had better meetings, never done less work in preparation, never needed less entertainment (because people are engaged with each other), never had a better return rate, and never been closer to "living our values." But we will keep learning.

I conclude by inviting you to continue our dialogue on dialogue. I direct you to existing and future blogs, wikis, forums, and workshops where you can continue to engage with other dialogue leaders and achieve optimal outcomes @ work, @ home, and @ large in society. Leveraging social media enables you to engage in dialogue with other readers around the world on this crucially important topic for the twenty-first century—the solution is in the dialogue. I look forward to conversing with you.

—Peter Nixon
Peter.Nixon@PotentialDialogue.com

Notes

1. His Holiness the 14th Dalai Lama speaking at a memorial in Okinawa, Japan (November 2009) commemorating the 150,000 soldiers who died during the 82-day battle in 1945.

2. From *The Marblehead Letter*, 2001, www.solonline.org.

3. William Isaacs, *Dialogue and the Art of Thinking Together* (New York: Doubleday/Currency, 1999), 71.

4. Don Tapscott and Anthony D. Williams, *MacroWikinomics: Rebooting Business and the World* (New York: Portfolio Penguin, 2010).

5. www.weforum.org/issues/global-redesign-initiative.

6. Tapscott and Williams, *MacroWikinomics*.

7. Daisaku Ikeda and Majid Tehranian, *Global Civilization* (London: British Academic Press, 2004), xvi.

8. www-935.ibm.com/services/us/ceo/ceostudy2010/index.html.

9. Ikeda and Tehranian, *Global Civilization*, 8.

10. The concept of lifeworlds comes to us from philosophy and sociology and refers to the fact that what we consider self-evident or given results largely from the world in which we live our day-to-day lives. In order to help people see things differently we must first understand how their lifeworlds influence the way they see the world. The phenomenon we experience shape us so understanding the phenomenology of situations is part of the success of good dialogists. Our globally interconnected world is full of colliding lifeworlds and dialogue is needed to help transition our new reality toward optimal outcomes. Readers interested in learning more about lifeworlds and phenomenology might wish to read *Crisis of European Sciences* (1936) by Edmond Husserl.

11. As quoted in Ikeda and Tehranian, *Global Civilization*, 12.

12. I credit Nicholas Carr, author of *The Shallows* (Atlantic Books, 2010) for recognizing the idea of an analogue youth and digital adulthood. In his book, Carr identifies how the Internet is changing the way we think, read,

and remember. My suggestion that life beyond the digital tipping point creates a dialogue gap into which we are all falling at the moment is yet another example of the impact of the Internet and related gadgetry on life in the twenty-first century.

13. *Can Humanity Change?* (Boston: Shambhala Publications, 2003), 219.

14. Peter Nixon, *Negotiation: Mastering Business in Asia* (Singapore: John Wiley & Sons), 2005.

15. The Star Negotiator Model was originally derived using dialogue by asking my clients in Asia who were the best negotiators and what attributes made them successful. The answers resulted in the following five attributes which I remember easily as Dialogue (originally Communication) TIPS:

    Star Negotiators:

    1. Manage **Dialogue** Effectively (the first version of the model used communication instead of dialogue)

    2. Use **T**actics Strategically

    3. Control **I**nformation Wisely

    4. Understand **P**eople Fully

    5. Facilitate **S**ituations Productively

16. Ikeda and Tehranian, *Global Civilization*, 12.

17. As quoted in Alan Stewart, *The Conversing Company Its Culture, Power and Potential,* 2nd edition (Adelaide: Multimind Solutions, 2009).

18. Creating an environmentally sustainable, socially just, and spiritually fulfilling human presence on earth is the goal of a group called the Pachamama Alliance. For further details see www.awakeningthedreamer.org.

19. Panel discussion with His Holiness the 14th Dalai Lama, Washington, DC, October 2009. Recordings available at www.mindandlife.org.

20. Hong Kong study was reported in the *South China Morning Post* on May 28, 2011. Research was conducted by the Hong Kong Playground Association.

21. Yale University study as reported by Reuters on May 20, 2011, www.asiaone.com.sg.

22. As quoted in Ikeda and Majid, *Global Civilization*, 133.

23. Ikeda and Tehranian, *Global Civilization*, 174.

24. Ibid.

Part I

DIALOGUE GAP

Chapter 1

How Dialogue Gap Arose

We need to continue dialogue with our customers and consider making changes depending on their needs.

—*Atsushi Saito, President, Tokyo Stock Exchange*[1]

Malaise of the New Millennium—A Call to Arms

In the 1960s I spent summers as a boy living in an old converted ice house built to store ice for refrigeration through the hot summer months in the Laurentian mountains north of Montreal. By the 1960s electricity had done away with the need for an icehouse and it had been converted into a living space, still with walls a foot thick and a door so low adults regularly hit their heads on the way in.

Typical of most boys in their preteens my imagination was in over-drive at night living in the forest at the side of Lac des Iles. I often found myself staring at the ceiling wondering what those strange noises were beyond the safety of my bed. Mosquitoes make recognizable sounds as do moths hitting the screen, but when squirrels scratch at the wood or bats wriggle around inside the roof the sounds fill your imagination with more sinister creatures and you find your senses moving into overdrive. You begin seeing and hearing more than you normally would.[2] It isn't that your senses improve but rather your presence and your attention forces out everything else until all you are noticing is that which you are focused on or in my case, scared about.

With senses fully activated and now wide awake the scratching sound had stopped so I focused my attention on the ceiling and how, despite contours caused by squirrel holes and water damage (caused by ice forming on the roof through the long deep winter followed by its annual retreat as temperatures returned above freezing in the spring), the roof still managed to somehow come together seamlessly with the walls. As I looked closer I saw that the walls and ceilings didn't connect seamlessly at all, they just appeared to do so because the gaps between the walls were hidden with *quarter round*, wooden molding that my grandfather's carpenter loved to use to hide just about everything. As I looked around I realized that quarter round was used to hide every seam in every wall, as well as the floors, the steps, the windows, everywhere. When my grandfather's carpenter saw a gap he knew it needed quarter round.

Much like my grandfather's carpenter, when I fly around the world and listen to the problems people lay out in front of me, problems caused when two sides come together but don't quite connect or even worse collide, I find that the solution to their differences can be found in dialogue. Dialogue to me is like quarter round was to my grandfather's carpenter. But where quarter round simply hides the problem and leaves you with the impression that all is well (especially when everything is painted the same color), dialogue goes further and aims to rectify the problem by creating a lasting and hopefully optimal outcome for all the stakeholders involved.

My grandfather's carpenter looked after most of the homeowners in the "Paroisse St-Emile" and used the building materials available locally to build and repair whatever was requested. Back then, if you looked more deeply at the local supply chain you would have seen two completely different cultures coming together. Our carpenter and his team were born and raised locally and had little formal education; however, he could converse with my grandfather, a surgeon who had lied about his age to fight at Vimy in WWI and who after the war had requested his cottage be built on the shores of the same lake where he grew up as a boy and played with his brothers before the start of the "Great War."

After electricity arrived at the cottage in the 1950s the little ice-house was converted into a small chalet. In the 1960s, as Kennedy spoke of the Cold War, that little cottage and others like it sprinkled on neighboring lakes and mountainsides throughout the Laurentian Shield, which spans the U.S.-Canada border, seemed totally removed from the rest of the world. This false sense of security is still felt today and while the local carpenter and the international surgeon were able to dialogue sufficiently well together to satisfy both customer and supplier, the quarter round was needed to cover the gaps.

Today, as Atsushi Saito, president of the Tokyo Stock Exchange, states,

> We can no longer pretend to hide our differences if we are to compete globally. We need to continuously dialogue with customers and as their needs evolve our services need to evolve as well. Knowing how to change our services cannot be predicted, the solution results from within the dialogue itself.

Dialogue is not only needed to keep abreast of evolving customer needs, it is also needed to keep abreast of the rapidly changing world in which we live. Indeed dialogue is the fastest way to keep up-to-date and is needed now more than ever before.

Today central bankers have to take decisions in an environment marked by a degree of uncertainty in an economic and financial sphere that seems to me largely unprecedented. The acceleration of major advances in science and technology (not only information technology), the ensuing structural transformations or our economies, the ever-growing complexity of our finance and the overall process of globalisation are itself creating a multidimensional acceleration of change.

—Claude Trichet, European Central Bank Chief [3]

Unlike the dialogue between my grandfather and his carpenter nearly a century ago, today we are expected to dialogue across cultures effectively and instantly just to stay in business. A tall order, given we are all born into local cultures with local awareness and need to build from there.

Patricia and Mireille—Intergenerational Dialogue

Patricia, a beautiful and fit 87-year-old grandmother, has attentively been listening to one of my travel stories when her face turns grave and she says, "Peter, I want to share something I am very concerned about." Seeing Patricia has turned serious and wondering what she is about to share I focus on her with all my attention. "My granddaughter doesn't talk to me. She comes to visit but when she does we watch TV or more often now she just sits on her laptop doing Facebook with her friends." Patricia goes on, her eyes changing to reveal traces of a much younger girl. "When I was the age of my granddaughter I used to be able to talk to my grandmother for hours. I could talk to her about just about anything, subjects I'd be embarrassed to share with my mother seemed to be so comfortable with her. And my grandmother would tell me things of her life that seemed so important for me to learn. Wisdom was transmitted that way and many of life's most important lessons I attribute to having learned from my grandmother." But suddenly Patricia turned serious again. "That's the problem, if my granddaughter doesn't care to engage with me how will she learn those things that were so important for me to learn at her age? I'm concerned she can't engage with anyone. My son tells me that's just the way she is but I hear similar reactions about their granddaughters from my friends. What can I do to engage my granddaughter in dialogue? I'm 87 and who knows how long I'll be around."

Patricia's call to arms—"**What can I do to engage my granddaughter in dialogue**?"—is the rallying cry of our age. People who started their careers before the 1990s onslaught of e-mail and Internet surfing detect a problem but the definition of that problem is only becoming apparent and few people have figured out what to do about it. The problem that Patricia has so effectively identified is also a generational issue because people who have commenced their career in the 1990s or later are communicating faster and more effectively than ever before so they don't understand what people like Patricia are talking about when they flag existing problems. Some see the older, pre-Internet generation as dinosaurs who just need to get a Facebook account and begin instant messaging.

Patricia's life isn't busy. At 87 she curls in the winter and lawn bowls in the summer. The morning paper arrives at her door and her family visits for special occasions. Patricia has a lot of time to reflect and be 100 percent present when her granddaughter visits. Patricia spotted something social scientists are only now coming to recognize. I call it the Digital Tipping Point.

Digital Tipping Point

In Patricia's granddaughter's case the changes were gradual. She became more introverted, spent more and more time connected with friends online and as she visited her grandmother had less and less interest in talking with her or asking her questions. The phenomenon is not new. People who watch a lot of television believe their favorite TV personalities are actually their friends. Some people report that when they visit family members who have passed their digital tipping point watching TV, it seems their family members know more about their favorite TV stars (who are actually strangers) and express more interest in their lives than they do about their real family members sitting right in front of them.

A person has passed their digital tipping point when they spend more than half their time communicating with people digitally rather than in person. Once past the digital tipping point things change.[4]

Boys and PC games are another example of the effects of the digital tipping point. The *New Straits Times* in Kuala Lumpur ran a story entitled "Gamers Gone Wild—children as young as 12 stay out all night to play games at cybercafés."[5] Although the expressed concern in this article was about youth becoming "so addicted they don't care about eating and sleeping . . . mingling with adults who gamble, have cybersex as well as download pornography," my real concern is the opportunity cost of these young people spending hour after hour glued to their digital monitors rather than interacting with human beings. Over time they lose any of the interpersonal skills they might have developed and in due course become less attractive to employers, teachers, and friends.

The digital tipping point doesn't stop with boys. One study on the effects of cell phones and teenage girls in Hong Kong found a strong correlation between a loss of self-esteem and the number of hours they spent digitally connected, for example, texting friends.[6]

Several studies in the United States are finding damaging effects of overuse of digital connections. The Pew Research Center found that one in three teenagers in the United States send more than 100 text messages per day, that girls were better connected than boys, and that 69 percent of youth enjoy having their cell phones to overcome boredom.[7] Again I think we are partly missing the point with this research. When youth exchange texts or play a game on their cell phones when bored they are missing the multitude of opportunities to connect with the people around them. Over time this has a negative impact on their behavior making them less comfortable connecting with other people.[8]

It is common nowadays to watch people sit aside each other in a restaurant, coffee shop, bus, or train and instead of talking to each other they stare intently into the tiny screens on their cell phones to send and receive messages with people they are not physically with. This new phenomenon, to ignore the real people we are with in favor of the digital people at the end of a wireless connection, is creating more implications than most people recognize. We have never been connected with as many people as we are today while at the same time being more isolated and unable to dialogue.

One study out of the United States suggests that digital media use is increasing and that 11- to 18-year-olds have already reached their digital tipping point of more than half their waking hours digitally connected.[9] This is unprecedented and we are only now beginning to understand the implications.

Many of us spend 8 to 12 hours at the office only to come home and check personal e-mail, surf the Web, or watch TV. If that sounds like your life at the moment then you are already long past your own digital tipping point because your digital home life comes after what my clients report is easily two to three if not six hours a day glued to their computers "doing their job" at work. Assuming you sleep eight hours then you are already spending more than half your waking hours digitally rather than personally connected with others.

Some people are addicted to their digital connections. Addiction to social networking, e-mail, online gambling, and pornography is contributing to short-term smiles and long-term frowns. All this isolated online time takes away from being with people and this gradual diminishment of connected time has led to a change in people's feelings, work, and skills.

Life Beyond the Digital Tipping Point

Life in our new digital era is different. We have become more sedentary than ever before and this is leading to terrible obesity and related diseases.[10] Life beyond our digital tipping point is leading to changes in how we think, what we feel, how we work, and what we are good at.

How We Think

Nicholas Carr in his 2010 best seller *The Shallows: How the Internet Is Changing the Way We Think, Read and Remember,* provides a convincing argument through reference to numerous research studies stretching back to the start of the computer that show how the Internet is diminishing our ability to reason and remember complex ideas. Carr suggests that our reliance on the Internet to store and return to us with just a few clicks more information than we can possibly consume, is freeing our brains to become better at multitasking and rapid response. Since the beginning of time our inventions have changed us:

- The invention of printed books eliminated our tradition of dialogic transmission of knowledge.
- The invention of clocks eliminated our ability to know time by looking at the sun.
- The invention of the compass eliminated our ability to find our way by looking at the sky.
- The invention of the Internet is eliminating our ability to think deeply and remember extensive volumes of information.

What use is an encyclopedic mind when all you need is to Google for information? What is considered important today is not knowing more than your competitor but being better able to mine and access the information you need, in a format you can use and at a time when you need it. Carr suggests the change in how we are using our brains, as I describe it, from storing and conceptualizing information to retrieving and reporting information, is changing the way our brains are designed to work and thereby making it harder than ever to do things like dialogue to solve the problems we face today. Just when we need to dialogue the most it would appear that our Internet behaviors are causing changes to our brain that make it increasingly difficult to dialogue effectively. In other words, there is uncontested proof that the more we communicate the more we lose our ability to dialogue. Life beyond our Digital Tipping Point is creating an increasingly large dialogue gap and the implications are only now becoming apparent. Our growing Internet use is diminishing our ability to pay attention, connect disparate pieces of information to form a coherent understanding, and interact with others to negotiate, resolve problems, and create new solutions to the new problems we are facing in our interconnected and overburdened world. Says Carr:

> The mental functions that are losing the *survival of the busiest* brain cell battle are those that support calm, linear thought, the ones we use in traversing a lengthy narrative or an involved argument, the ones we draw on when we reflect on our experiences or contemplate an outward or inward phenomenon . . . the net is . . . diminishing our ability to know, in depth, a subject for ourselves, to construct within our own minds the rich and idiosyncratic set of connections that give rise to a singular intelligence.[11]

It is only in recent years that we have been able to study the brain in depth by using magnetic resonance imaging and other techniques that we have been able to understand the evolving influences of repeated behavior on brain functions. Neuroplasticity suggests that the inner workings of our brains are constantly re-creating themselves in response to how we use our brain. Carr's book provides a good collection of the current research into the Internet's effects on our brains, especially the continuous interruptions and intrusions into our psyches created by pop-up advertisements, banners, constant e-mail, news feeds, social networks, and hyperlinks. In the next chapter I attempt to list some of the effects that are known to exist but here is a glimpse:

An experiment at the University of Southern California,

> Indicates the more distracted we become, the less able we are to experience the subtlest most distinctively human forms of empathy, compassion and other emotions. For some kinds of thoughts, especially moral decision-making about other people's social and psychological situations, we need to allow for adequate time and reflection. . . . If things are happening too fast you may not ever fully experience emotions about other people's psychological states.[12]

What We Feel

The constant spread of digital communication deeper and deeper into our lives is leading to feelings of isolation, stress, and unhappiness. In Matthieu Ricard's *Happiness* he writes for nearly 300 pages on the sources of unhappiness and how to go about changing perspectives to cultivate a more wholesome compassion and happiness.[13] Of course, much of what it takes to change perspective is dialogue. Dialogues that connect you with yourself and with others include dialogues between:

- Our emotions and our intelligence
- Our self and our soul/spirit
- Actions and priorities
- Friend and foe
- Parent and child
- Teacher and student
- Partner and you
- Colleague and you
- Supplier and client/customer
- Boss and employee
- Buyer and seller

Throughout this book there are examples of dialogues and because dialogue is so important it is amazing that we have never been taught in school or received training at work on how to conduct dialogues effectively either with ourselves or with others. Given the state of the world today it seems long overdue that we learn to dialogue effectively.

How We Work

At work the digital tipping point is also having significant effect. One of the most prevalent topics for human resource professionals today is **employee engagement**. How to engage an employee? Talk to them. How to motivate someone? Talk to them to find out what motivates them and then respond accordingly. Engagement isn't difficult but if you hire a smart employee, sit him or her in a cubicle and connect them only via Internet to colleagues, clients, and suppliers, it won't take long before they too feel isolated, frustrated, and unhappy. Sadly this recipe for disengagement describes most offices today.

When people pass their digital tipping point there is also a drop in **efficiency**. People arrive at work eager to impress their boss, customers, and colleagues. They take their instructions and get on with the job. Meanwhile, because we work in dynamic environments something changes but no one tells the employee so they continue to do as they think best only to complete the project and realize what has been done is no longer needed, or worse, sets the team and project back.

Entire projects can be completed without any impact. In one example, I was hired to study a client's operations and make suggestions for improvements. A small team interviewed all the key stakeholders and made a report to the chairman for him to review with his board and take actions accordingly. Sometimes consultants are used as an excuse for the board members to say they made changes because the consultant suggested it when in fact it was their idea all along. This was not the case here. Four years after submitting my report I learned that nothing had been done. In this case the chairman decided to leave behind a blueprint for after he was gone so the next chairman would know what to do, which might make sense but he didn't tell anyone and the report went unnoticed by his replacement for four years. Not surprisingly many of the recommendations remain unfulfilled even today.

Another problem I am witnessing on the far side of the digital tipping point is the loss of tolerance. I see this because as a negotiation consultant and mediator when I am requested to step into conflict situations and work them out I notice that many of the internal conflicts result from one or more of the employees not recognizing conditions changing and no one in the department or company or on the project has told them of the changes; nor have they otherwise discovered the change because they seldom if ever dialogue with others involved. The fact that conditions were changing and a shift was inevitable are understood but without the awareness that comes with personal contact the changes come as a surprise, often at the last minute after anything more can be done, causing obvious disruption, angst, and sometimes anger. And sometimes these situations also lead to **intolerance** and mutual dislike between colleagues.

What We Are Good At

My many years in negotiation reveal a declining ability of people to negotiate, solve problems together, and resolve conflict.[14] Why? The far side of the digital tipping point is a place where people get to only after falling out of practice with conversing with other people and without regular practice the harder applications of dialogue like negotiation, problem solving, and conflict resolution fall out of reach of most amateurs.

Throughout the book the case studies will reveal various aspects of the challenges involved in achieving optimal outcomes through dialogue. One of the problems the case studies substantiate is what I have coined as *dialogue gap*.

Dialogue Gap *exists where the quality of the dialogue we have is less than that needed to achieve optimal outcomes in the situations we face.*

How We Learn

Dialogue gap is also getting worse simply because people don't see as much of it today and because leaders tend to learn from others: If they don't see their boss using dialogue why would they? Likewise, if people watch bad dialogue they won't want to repeat it and instead choose autocratic divide-and-conquer methods of decision making.

Dialogue gap is a real problem in companies and society today and is fairly well demonstrated in the case scenarios included in this book. I describe dialogue gap and its implications in the next chapter to make the case for needing to improve dialogue everywhere if we are to survive in the humane civilization that Socrates and others have alluded to.

Dialogue Triggers

Before proceeding it is worthwhile to reflect for a moment on the many things that may trigger dialogue to take place. Dialogue triggers include situations like the:

- Need to buy or sell something.
- Need for change such as to improve, resolve, inform, motivate, influence.
- Need to negotiate, lead, parent.
- Need to love, help, care, teach.
- Need to solve, audit, assess, evaluate, appraise.

When the dialogue trigger goes off and the resultant dialogue skills, spaces, or systems are absent or inadequate the resulting outcome will vary from less than optimal to bad. Each of the case studies addresses dialogue gaps in their own way. You might recognize problems similar to the ones you face and hopefully by considering what was done or what might have been done, collect a few ideas to optimize your own outcomes, reduce the dialogue gap you are facing, or turn around a situation confronting you today.

This book is presented in a way that allows you to read it in any order. If it is applications you are looking for then scan the pages for case studies and read those relevant to you. If you are looking to improve your dialogue skills you can start there. If you are wondering about how to sustain dialogue or connect with people facing similar situations to you or if you are looking for people to help you solve some of the dialogue challenges that you are facing then you might prefer to follow the links mentioned in the chapter on sustaining dialogue.

This book and its related website are designed to promote effective dialogue at work, at home, and in society. They are designed to rally the growing dialogic community globally. People who understand the world today understand the only way we are going to survive the twenty-first century is if we learn to optimize our outcomes, minimize the negative effects of our consumer societies, and learn to live together on this wonderfully finite planet, the third planet from the sun.

From Accountant to Dialogist

Most everyone I work with asks me the same question: How did you switch from being an auditor in the world's largest accounting firm to being an international speaker and consultant in negotiation and dialogue? People ask me this question for different reasons. Some people don't see any connection between the two occupations. Some want to understand the career path one takes to become a specialist in this area. Some people want to know how to garner enough courage to make a change in their own careers. Some are simply curious because there are few people who have made such a change.

To understand my own enlightenment you need to understand my background. I came from a family intricately linked to health care and the helping professions but graduated with a business degree in the midst of the greedy 1980s when Canadian business graduates looked to emulate people like Conrad Black and other icons of the Canadian Establishment. The height of the recession, however, meant that earning a professional degree provided an assured job and in Canada becoming a chartered accountant is one of the most respected professional designations of all. I wanted to find out what made some organizations succeed where others failed, so I chose to become an auditor and use my professional license to go inside the biggest corporations in the world to find the answers. My career as auditor took me inside boardrooms from Montreal to Geneva and then Hong Kong where I landed in 1989 just after the Tiananmen Square massacre. By this time the world was changing. The Cold War had just ended with the breaking open of the Berlin Wall, the Internet was beginning to connect the world as never before, and China was in its ascendancy.

By the time I landed in Hong Kong what separated the good and bad organizations was not the numbers, as I had thought, but rather the people. For the next five years working with behavioral scientists Drs. David West and Robin Stuart-Kotze, we led my employer to develop and restructure its talent to effectively capitalize on the growth of the Hong Kong and China markets. The more I learned about leadership and management development the more I realized that what successful organizations really did well was to align their people to work toward agreed goals.

The problem is that few organizations properly identify or agree on the right goals. If they do agree they struggle to realize these goals because their staff, suppliers, and clients don't necessarily share the same goals. It appeared to me that what really made the difference was the ability to negotiate well.

I set out to conquer the subject of negotiation so that my clients could benefit from the solutions they really needed. Work flowed in from around the world and in due course I began to realize that everyone said the best negotiators were in Asia, but all the negotiation models we followed were Western. I then set out to identify what people in Asia thought constituted a star negotiator and my findings resulted in the now internationally popular Star Negotiator Workshop. The workshop details and client experiences were eventually published in *Negotiation, Mastering Business in Asia*.[15]

The Star Negotiator model described in the book refers to five essential attributes common to successful negotiators. These attributes are easily remembered as communication tips. The five attributes are:

1. Communication—Manage Communication Effectively
2. Tactics—Use Tactics Strategically
3. Information—Control Information Wisely
4. People—Understand People Fully
5. Situation—Facilitate Situations Productively

As a result of the book on negotiation my client work and international travel intensified. As I delved even deeper into what made some organizations more successful than others I became stuck on the idea

that if the solution was in the dialogue, why didn't people talk and why didn't people listen? It is believed that important information will reveal itself only when you ask the right question and over time the answer became the entirely new concept, at least to me, that communication was not the problem but rather dialogue was the problem and that the two were not the same. Whereas communication was about talking and listening, even when this was present negotiations were still not achieving optimal outcomes. Furthermore conflict was still rising and clients were increasingly asking me to resolve situations that were not really negotiation requiring concession making and taking but rather difficult situations requiring dialogue.

I then set out to read all I could to understand fully about dialogue so I could help my clients. Little is written on the subject of dialogue and perhaps that is indicative of the problem—not enough attention has been put on the need to understand dialogue because until reaching the digital tipping point, dialogue had been a human gift passed down from generation to generation through personal contact, stories, teaching, and experience sharing by family members, elders, mentors, teachers, priests, and so on. Dialogue is an obvious underpinning of community.

Once I realized the crucial difference between communication and dialogue I updated the Star Negotiator model to reflect this realization and changed Manage Communication Effectively to read Manage Dialogue Effectively. When communication tips became dialogue tips something else significant changed.

When I began walking into clients' offices talking about dialogue, the situations I was being asked to consider became much wider, more complicated, and many would say much more important than the commercial buy/sell and change management negotiations I had been addressing in the past.

Now I found myself walking into boardrooms around the world and listening to directors and senior managers as they shared with me the difficult dialogues (many of which are referred to in this book) they were facing. People asked about personal dialogues like marriage, parenting, and career development. In Jeddah our dialogue focused on the treatment of women in Saudi Arabia. In Pakistan and India dialogue moved quickly to resolving the Kashmir dispute, the U.S. war, and competing with China. In Bahrain dialogue focused on winning the business lost by Dubai after their near economic collapse. In Kolkata we discussed economic growth with a human face to lift the impoverished people of Bengal, the same people for whom Mother Teresa had toiled with her Sisters of Mercy and had even won a Nobel prize. In Washington we discussed the appalling rate of drop-outs in the education sector in the United States where a secondary student drops out of the system every 11 seconds! In Shanghai and Beijing dialogue focused on the Olympics, why the uprising in Tibet was significant and how to solve the Tibet situation that has lasted for so long. In Boston dialogue centered on defense issues in the Middle East, in Toronto we explored environmental activism, and the list of dialogues continues.

By focusing on several of the big dialogues taking place today I hope to help you:

- Recognize the difference between communication and dialogue.
- Learn how to create and sustain effective dialogue yourselves.
- Identify how to achieve optimal outcomes in your lives and organizations.
- Connect with others trying to achieve optimal outcomes through dialogue so that we might all enjoy a sustainable future where we can realize our full potential while helping others realize their potential, too.

Before moving onto the details of dialogue and the rest of this book I should point out one more important change that this path has brought upon me. Years ago I set out to conquer the business world and get rich as this seemed to be the generally accepted thing to do—then. As my career developed and I toured the world I always kept my eyes open. I began noticing people everywhere shared the same goal of increasing happiness and decreasing suffering. Some people defined happiness as owning a fighter jet in the United Kingdom (really), others defined happiness as having a home strong enough to withstand annual typhoons (Philippines). Suffering for some was a significant loss in their investment portfolio while for others it was no access to health care or permanent environmental degradation.

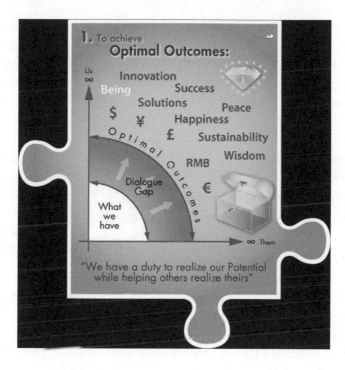

The second thing all these dialogues brought me was the realization that we are all interconnected and that one man's happiness is another man's sadness. For example, the profits of the China fund investor are earned at the expense of the low-paid factory worker and polluted environment in China. This interconnectedness is not just about the haves and have nots, it is also about the reality that we cannot air condition our flats without warming the planet and we cannot drive our SUVs to the beach without drilling offshore for oil and risking oil washing onto the sand we are sunning ourselves on. Everything is interconnected.

The realizations arising from working the world of dialogue at the turn of the millennium is further addressed toward the end of this book when I share ideas about a dialogic future—a future where we can all realize our potential while helping others realize their potential. A future that will call on us to have compassion for those who suffer and to use our wisdom to resolve the problems we face. If the twenty-first century has one benefit to mankind it is the forced realization that we can no longer live the dream that we are somehow immune to the problems of every other living creature on earth.

As we have seen, disease can spread instantly around the world, global warming is affecting us all, terrorism in a rich community comes from poverty in a poor community, competition is global, best practices can change overnight, technology is forever evolving how we work. In all these situations the solution is in the dialogue and we need to relearn how to dialogue to survive the twenty-first century.

A dialogue is something more of a common participation, in which we are not playing a game against each other, but with each other.
In a dialogue, everybody wins.
In dialogue nobody is trying to win. Everybody wins if anybody wins.
—David Bohm[16]

Optimal Outcomes

When I talk about optimal outcomes I am referring to the Nobel Prize–winning economics of Dr. John Nash. Nash's work was immortalized in the 2001 movie *A Beautiful Mind*, directed by Ron Howard and featuring Russell Crowe. Nash's work in Governing Dynamics suggested that an equilibrium point can be reached where it is no longer possible for one party to get more from a negotiation without another party losing something. This is what I define as an optimal outcome and anything short of this is suboptimal. In the popular language of negotiation, getting to yes is easy but achieving optimal outcomes is hard work. Sadly, many of the situations that we encounter on a daily basis achieve far less than optimal outcomes and I sense things are getting worse.

Nash's work left us inspired to aim for optimal outcomes but didn't help too much in how to achieve them. In my experience optimal outcomes can only be achieved through dialogue. The only way stakeholders can define and identify mutual value is through dialogue and the only way they can achieve the outcomes that derive the value they are after is through dialogue. The solution is in the dialogue. The more effective our dialogue the more likely we will achieve optimal outcomes.

Working through your own discomfort and continuing forward in the spirit of dialogue will open people's minds to see that a different way of working together may be possible.
—Linda Ellinor and Glenna Gerard[17]

Effective dialogue requires the right people to talk about the right issues in the right way and at the right time and place. This sounds formulaic but it is comprehensive, incorporates cultural differences, and inherently makes sense to people everywhere.

Right People—By this I am referring specifically to key stakeholders. In many situations when deals break down or negotiations go wrong it is because a group of stakeholders have been omitted from the process. By omitting key stakeholders you also limit the access to the key issues that need to be considered in order to create optimal lasting agreements.

We need the capability of forming a network with "dialogue inside."
—William Isaacs[18]

To ensure that your dialogues are effective you'll need to ensure that all key stakeholders are effectively represented in your dialogues. Effective representation is a problem because some representatives are more effective than others, some representatives are effective but are excluded at key points, and some groups have no representation at all. A classic example of excluding a key stakeholder was when the federal and provincial leaders in Canada attempted to amend the Canadian Constitution in a round of dialogues in 1987 that came to be known as the Meech Lake Accord. This accord ultimately failed because the agreement was crafted without the involvement at a critical juncture of one of the key stakeholders, the Premier of Quebec. The Accord was meant at least in part to ensure Canada would remain whole and not lose its French province to separation but by excluding the French Premier at a key point in the dialogue the deal was eventually lost. Fortunately the province has yet to separate from Canada but the Constitution changes have yet to be agreed and an optimal outcome was never achieved.

There is no truth or wisdom without compassion.

—David Kaczynski[19]

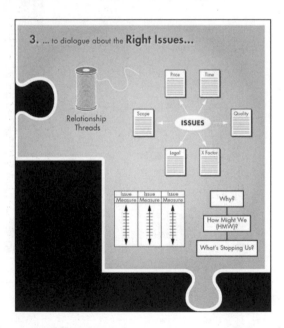

Right Issues—Effective dialogue must ensure that the key issues are tabled, understood, and discussed in a way that addresses the risk and opportunity inherent in each of them. Getting the right issues onto the agenda is not always easy especially knowing that people like to avoid issues they don't understand or that will cause conflict. It is also a problem when issues are raised but the people involved don't fully understand the issues or their implications either when taken individually or when combined with others.

In order to move through that eye of the needle, we must look at old issues in new ways and bring our real selves *into the situation.*
—C. Otto Scharmer[20]

The chief legal counsel for one of my banking clients did a good job helping the bank's procurement team understand contracts by explaining the different clauses and then dividing them into three categories:

1. Issues they could negotiate on their own.
2. Issues that would require legal input if the vendor wanted to change the standard bank clause.
3. Issues that definitely required legal input.

By helping the bank procurement team better understand the issues, the chief legal counsel was able to speed up the contract process while alleviating unnecessary work for his legal team so they could focus exclusively on the high risk and legally complicated issues only.

Human beings create and share knowledge through conversation. It behooves us to heighten our abilities on this score.

—William Isaacs[21]

Right Way—There are a number of ways to manage dialogue and this book will explore some of the more useful dialogue skills, spaces, and systems that are available for you to use as the situation warrants. Professional dialogists understand that different processes or methodologies work better in different situations. I will attempt as best I can to give you insights to the options you have available and when these will be most appropriate for use. Examples of different systems available include using third parties like facilitators or following methodologies like challenge mapping, which get everyone involved and contributing to common challenges.[22]

Dialogue holds the potential to enable us to perceive and use our ignorance because it helps us to reflect in ways we would not on our own.

—William Isaacs[23]

Right Time—When we look at the timing of dialogues there are really three factors of importance: start, duration, and deadline. Dialogues should commence when people are ready to talk and listen. If you start before people are ready they won't participate and if you start too late you'll have to deal with anger or disappointment before you even proceed to the next stage.

Similarly the duration needs to be balanced because those who are satisfied will want to cut things off and move on while those who feel there is still value to be gained will want to keep things going. It is also problematic in situations where, like North Korea, the people involved believe that as long as they have a platform for dialogue they hold influence but once the dialogue is resolved they will be forgotten and the world will move on. North Korea need only look at the East German government to understand their days of dialogue are limited. The only thing we don't know is whether the duration of the Six Party talks about the Korean situation will last months, years, or decades.

Finally the deadline of the dialogue is also important because cutting off dialogue can insult and cause an unraveling of the agreement whereas sometimes keeping things going too long prevents agreement from being achieved. Sales trainers like to use a quick close to prevent analytical buyers from going away and thinking about their purchase because they know that many purchase decisions are made for emotional rather than rational reasons.

My personal view about closing tactics in buying and selling is that a quick close is usually in the interest of only one side of the table and that sooner or later the other side of the table will realize the imbalance and do its best in whatever way possible to rebalance the outcome. If your situation involves long-term relationships I dissuade you from forcing a quick close. An example of attempting to rebalance outcomes is often seen when tenders are won for building contracts based on the lowest bid and then the contractors attempt to win back their lost margins through variation orders during and after the project. This is so prevalent in some parts of the world like Hong Kong that developers include significant percentages (20 to 30 percent) in their budgets to cover eventual variation orders. I worked with one builder that made no money at all building and were it not for their variations they would have been bankrupt. I suggested they weren't builders at all but rather variation experts and indeed their chartered surveying practice was one of the best paid parts of their payroll.

Right Space—The last factor of importance in building effective dialogue is planning where your dialogues should take place. You can for example choose for your location to be more or less formal, comfortable, convenient, or accessible. You can also choose locations and room set-up based on emotional, practical, or intellectual reasons. One classic example often quoted is the selection by the Middle East negotiator to use a venue with a large glass window through which the disputing parties could see children of different nationalities playing in the yard happily together. The underlying message was simple: Wouldn't you like your grandchildren to enjoy a happy future free of racial conflicts like the children playing on the other side of the window?

By its very nature, dialogue encourages people to be curious about the thinking behind conclusions and actions, revealing well-thought-through and incoherent decisions alike.

—Linda Ellinor and Glenna Gerard[24]

Life before and after the Digital Tipping Point

Being digitally connected is relatively very new to humanity and in this new era of instant communication we find ourselves increasingly digitally connected.

The digital tipping point is the point at which we spend more than half our waking hours digitally rather than personally connected with other people.

For many people working today we wake, check our smart phone or BlackBerry for messages, then watch or listen to the news (streamed digitally) while we get ready for work. We commute to work listening to our iPods, car radios, CD players, or talking with people on our cell phones. Once we arrive at work we open up our computers, check our e-mail and stay connected all day only taking breaks occasionally to reconnect with our landlines, cell phones, or to exchange text messages. Coffee breaks have become what some observers call "Crackberry breaks" and the traditional lunch hour for many is now a lunch box at their desk and a chance to surf the Web or manage personal e-mail. After work we commute home in a similar digitally connected way as our commute into work. We arrive home just in time to say hello to the family before our favorite TV program and then call it a day sometimes falling asleep listening to the radio.

Occasionally someplace in between our daily digital connections we might talk to our colleagues or family members in person but not for long because we are so busy being digitally connected to our friends and workmates.

When I describe the digital tipping point in this way it sounds like many of us have already passed our own digital tipping point or live or work with people who have. How are their dialogue skills? Perhaps you'll never find out. How sad. Now consider just a few years ago.

Before the mid-1980s people would wake, share breakfast while chatting about their dreams, their day ahead, or whatever else might be on their mind. During their commute into work they would connect with neighbors or meet new friends and enjoy some light conversation on the way to work. If matters of importance cropped up they were addressed there and then or time was arranged later for personally following up. Coffee breaks were a chance to swap stories, tell jokes, gain a sympathetic ear, or simply catch up with work mates. Lunch hours were often the best part of the day when you could kick back for a full hour or longer and if you were lucky you'd choose a nice restaurant with friends to while away the time meeting old and new acquaintances at yours and nearby tables. Your lunch encounters might give you some really important piece of information to help your daily responsibilities or private life. The commute home was a bit quieter as people relaxed with a book, watched the sunset, or smelled the flowers. Once home many families waited for the breadwinner to arrive and then would all sit together for their evening meal and talk about the highs and lows of their days. By sleep time all the day's problems had been solved, all the opportunities for growth explored and all the preparations made for the next day.

To people born before color TV, microwave ovens, and the advent of the Internet the dialogic life is something we remember with fondness but for people who grew up after the 1970s the life of communication lived beyond the digital tipping point is the new normal.

The problem we face in this book, however, is that the new normal comes with implications. To begin to understand the implications of life beyond the digital tipping point it is important to understand the difference as I describe it between communication and dialogue.

Communication ≠ Dialogue

Communication ≠ Dialogue

Communication is thought of as exchanging information but in the most part it is really sending information to others. The Oxford dictionary actually defines communication as imparting news or the science and practice of transmitting information.[25] Today we send and reply to e-mail, text messages, voice mail, and phone calls. Most of the time we are communicating news, updates, status reports, or simply telling our friends and families what we are doing. Our communications are normally only interrupted by receiving communications from other people.

Whereas communication is about sending information to others, dialogue is different, very different. To understand dialogue today we need to understand a bit of history.

By far the most famous writings on the topic of dialogue are referred to as the Socratic or Platonic Dialogues. The Greek philosopher Socrates lived during the fourth century BCE and became famous for his dialogues on important social issues of the time. Socrates held his dialogues in public and in people's private homes. They were directed at the idea that people should place less emphasis on worldly matters and instead question their values and place primary importance on improving their souls.

We have come to know about Socrates' philosophy through the writings of his followers including Plato, Aristotle, and others.[26] Socrates is considered today one of the biggest influences on Western philosophy. The definition of dialogue (dia-logos) at the time of Socrates suggested a shared knowing, allowing people to govern themselves.[27] Polis, which dates from the same Greek era is what we call politics today but back then polis was a space for dia-logos, which allowed for self-governing. Dialogue was seen as the building block of civilization. Socrates was the first on record to suggest the solution is in the dialogue; but ironically people who disagreed with the values he was espousing at the time decided it was not right that he should be telling others how to live their lives and they conspired to have him tried for impiety, imprisoned, and executed in 399 BCE.

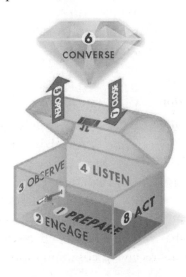

Fast-forward through time and possibly the next most famous contributor to the subject of dialogue was David Bohm, a twentieth-century British quantum physicist who, like Socrates, was considered by his followers to be one of the greatest thinkers of his era and who, also similar to Socrates, fell out with those who disagreed with his views.[28] Bohm was working in the United States contributing to the development of atomic energy but in the anti-communist mind-set of post-WWII United States the political leaders saw him as a threat to U.S. security and forced him to leave behind his work with Einstein and move overseas (clearly a suboptimal outcome). Bohm saw dialogue as a multifaceted process leading to collective thought and in its deepest sense "an invitation to test the viability of traditional definitions of what it means to be human, and collectively to explore the prospect of an enhanced humanity."[29]

Helping connect the philosophical definitions of dialogue given to us by Socrates and Bohm with the reality of the twenty-first century is William Isaacs' *Dialogue—The Art of Thinking Together*. Communication is clearly not thinking together and as such it is clearly not the same as dialogue. Although people accept and recognize that communication is not dialogue, they still confuse dialogue and conversation.

To understand this difference we need to again consider the definition of conversation, which Oxford defines as "an informal exchange of ideas by spoken word."[30] Conversation is in many respects the result of two of more people communicating to each other and as we know, this can happen without any shared understanding or knowing.

Dialogue is more than conversation—it is a thinking together that results in the shared knowing referred to by Socrates and Bohm. In

> *Dialogue is people thinking together to reveal value not otherwise visible on its own.*

practical terms the shared knowing can be demonstrated by an insight, new idea, new perspective, or shared wisdom (what I graphically refer to in this book as jewels), which would not otherwise have been revealed had the people not come together in dialogue.

The rest of this book is devoted to helping you learn to discover value through dialogue at work, at home, and internationally so that as Socrates and Bohm reminded us, we can live an enhanced humanity in civilization on our shared and increasingly fragile earth.

It is useful at this stage to list some of the value that dialogue has derived in our clients once they were shown the way to achieve it. Some of these examples are expanded throughout the book in the case scenarios. For some the jewels of dialogue are financial and for others they are better measured with things like motivation, quality, engagement, and creativity.

Examples of Value Derived from Dialogue

Dialogue Creates Value

Dysfunctional boards get realigned • **Partnerships** talk through pivotal decisions • **Auditors** improve reporting & internal controls • **Negotiators** arrange better deals • **Directors** fulfil their duty of care • **CEO's** know what's really going on • **Chairmen** run better meetings • **Fund managers** time transactions better • **Liquidators** improve recoveries • **Entrepreneurs** make more profit • **Procurement** get better value for $$$ • **Traders** improve margins • **Leaders** make better decisions • **Accountants** cut costs problem free • **COO's** run uninterrupted operations • **Teams** perform better • **Service providers** manage expectations • **Head office** solve local challenges • **CIO's** understand the underlying business • **World leaders** end conflict & poverty • **Account reps** fully know their accounts • **Project managers** keep to programme • **Doctors** improve healthcare • **Architects** meet user requirements • **Developers** build what the market wants • **Manufacturers** produce quality goods • **Recruiters** match positions & candidates • **Compliance officers** stay clean • **Risk managers** spot problems early • **Bankers** reduce their risk & improve returns • **CFO's** manage the financial implications • **Sales executives** increase sales • **Lawyers** address commercial issues

The Solution is in the Dialogue.

To engage our negotiation and dialogue experts contact Negotiate@PotentialDialogue.com

---

Dialogue . . . is more than communication. It is communion in which we are mutually informed, purified, illumined, and reunited to ourselves, to one another, and God.

—Reuel L. Howe[31]

Dialogue in the Headlines

Bahrain King Orders "Dialogue" To End Unrest
          —*Sky News UK*, Saturday, February 19, 2011

In 2009 I published a series of articles on dialogue with the *South China Morning Post* (SCMP) in Hong Kong.[32] I asked if the SCMP could do a search for the use of the word dialogue in their stories from 2004 to 2009 versus 1999 to 2004. As expected, the word dialogue appeared twice as often in the more recent period. Although the word dialogue is being used more often in stories, it is appearing at relatively the same rate in headlines (roughly 10 times per year).

My top 10 favorite dialogue headlines from the SCMP since 1993 include:

1. Dialogue Vital on Issues That Define Our Times (July 2009)
2. Dialogue: The Only Real Way Forward (June 1996)
3. Dialogue: The Only Option (December 2002)
4. Dialogue Opens Better Options (November 1994)
5. Dialogue: The Only Way to Defeat Terrorism (August 2005)
6. So Little Dialogue (July 1994)
7. Waiting for Dialogue (May 1994)
8. Time Ripe for Open Dialogue (June 1996)
9. Time Ripe for Frank Dialogue (April 1996)
10. A Dialogue Requires Equal Footing (November 2003)

In addition to the previous headlines 15 more great dialogue headlines from the SCMP since 1993 include:

1. Minister Mulls Online Dialogue with Protesters (January 2010)
2. Climate Change to Top Agenda at First Sino-U.S. Strategic Dialogue (July 2009)
3. Dialogue in Dark Aims to Enlighten (January 2009)
4. It Takes Two: Finding Dialogue in Unison (July 2007)
5. Dialogue to Pave Way for Closer Ties with Japan (November 2007)
6. Pakistani Leader Urges Taleban Dialogue (March 2007)
7. Dialogue Is the Only Route to Rescue Nepal (January 2006)
8. Dialogue That Makes Sense (November 2004)
9. Dialogue Called For in Workers' Disputes (April 2004)
10. Documents Prove Zhao Wanted Dialogue with Students (June 2001)
11. Overdue Dialogue (May 2001)
12. Kissinger Recommends Dialogue (June 1997)
13. Chance for Real Dialogue Missed (April 1996)
14. Bush Calls for Better Dialogue (January 1996)
15. Dialogue Urged to Cut Crime (November 1994)

The following SCMP caught my attention and I investigated the story.

In the Beginning Was the Dialogue (Oct 2005)

This article reported on the speech in Hong Kong by Professor Robin Alexander where he stressed the importance of dialogue in schools.[33] Alexander defines purposeful dialogue as "much more than good communication skills but requires willingness and skill to engage with minds, ideas and ways of thinking other than our own; it involves the ability to question, listen, reflect, reason, explain, speculate and explore ideas."[34]

Dialogue Headlines in the International News

At the time of writing this book I did an online search for the use of the word dialogue in headlines around the world and in just a few seconds the internet reported back more than 500 instances where the word dialogue appeared in current articles.[35]

Catholics are not willing to accept clergymen who are not recognised by the Pope and it's better for the two sides (Mainland China and Taiwan) to work out their issues through dialogues.
> —Taiwan's Cardinal Paul Shan, as reported
> by Agence France-Presse in Kaohsiung,
> February 21, 2011

Examples of current usage of the word dialogue in news headlines from around the world on one day in August 2010 include:

- Kashmir Dialogues
- Resumption of Dialogue with India Positive Development (sify.com)
- India, Pakistan Unlock Dialogue Process (the *Himalayan Times*)
- China–U.S. Dialogues
- New Achievements Made in Sino–U.S. Strategic, Economic Dialogue (*People's Daily*, English edition)

- A Dialogue of the Mute (Asia Times Online, referring to the wrong people discussing the wrong issues at the wrong time)
- Palestine Dialogues
- Palestinian National Comprehensive Dialogue Postponed (*Xinhua*, English)
- Hezbollah Not Interested in Dialogue with US (Yahoo! news)
- UN Says Dialogue with Israel on Human Rights Is Difficult (*Deutsche Welle*)
- Iranian Dialogues
- Obama Renews Call for Iran Dialogue (CNN.com)
- Iran Letting Chances for Dialogue Slip, Russia Says (*Times* of Malta)
- Iran Nuclear Envoy Calls for Dialogue, Not Sanctions (*Kuwait Times*)
- Healthcare Dialogues
- Dialogue on Animal to Human Transplantation (scoop.co.nz)
- Smart Phone App and Desktop Widget Offers Patient Dialogue Tool for a Complex Cardiovascular Disease (newschannel10.com)
- Afghan War Dialogues
- Pakistan-U.S. Strategic Dialogue: Bridging the Trust Deficit
- U.S. Envoy Tells Afghan Insurgents Dialogue Is Vital (Scotsman.com)
- Forward Movement in Pak-Afghan Dialogue Necessary—Holbrooke (RTT News)
- National Dialogues
- Let Us Be a Nation in Dialogue (mmegi.bw, referring to Botswana sliding backward)
- Bilateral Dialogues
- Cuba and the Virtue of Dialogue (*Havana Times*)
- Multilateral Dialogues
- Indonesia Wants to Spur Two Koreas Dialogue (*Jakarta Globe*)
- Hugo Chavez Calls for Dialogue and Good Relations (Reuters)
- China Says Kosovo Issue Should Be Resolved through Dialogue (*Xinhua*)
- Creative Dialogues
- Artist Hopes to Inspire Dialogue, Giving, with Interactive Exhibit (rgi.com)
- Commercial Dialogues
- Offshore Drilling—All Benefit from Dialogue (*Naples News*)
- Dialogue between PAL and Pilots Not Certain (*Sun Star*, referring to airline pilots strike)
- Despite Lawsuit Board Seeks Dialogue (*Waynesville Daily Guide*)

The environmental and political turmoil in the months since I searched the headlines for use of the word dialogue has caused the word to surface even more than ever before. It is as if world leaders are screaming "Dialogue Gap is preventing us from achieving our full potential." Adding to the previous list, some of the latest headlines include:

- U.S. Prods Saudis to Promote Dialogue in Bahrain (CBS News, March 15, 2011)
- Jordan's King Sets National Dialogue Deadline (Fox News, March 15, 2011)
- Libyan Authorities Appeal for Dialogue with Rebels (*Jerusalem Post*, March 7, 2011)
- Dialogue Disputed in Yemen (CNN World, March 3, 2011)
- Fiery Exchange at Climate Dialogue (SCMP, November 5, 2011)

The preceding sample of headlines reminds us of several important things:

- Use of the word dialogue is global.
- Dialogue is referred to for critical issues regardless of them being related to war, politics, health care, business, or personal.
- Dialogue is valuable in situations where conflict exists or opportunity awaits.
- Some problems seem to persist a long time despite people's best efforts to resolve the conflict.
- We cannot achieve optimal outcomes as long as problems like these still remain outstanding.

I think we all understand the importance of dialogue but have you ever considered the fact that despite its importance we have never taught dialogue skills in school, universities, or in corporate training programs! What other centrally important skill can you name that we rely on every day that we never teach people to do or improve?. We have courses on walking, eating, breathing, communicating, but whatever happened to dialogue? Is it any wonder we have the problems we have given we have never focused on this basic need?

Can you now understand my vision for Dialogue Institutes situated in major markets around the world teaching dialogue and supporting the big dialogues locally to ensure that optimal outcomes are achieved and our humanity and civilization is enhanced? Part of the answer to the absence of dialogue curriculum around the world can be understood by considering two things: culture and language.

All cultures around the world have been built on dialogue and although some cultures are more expressive and some are more introspective, as we start the twenty-first century, in my experience they all have one thing in common—as communication increases dialogue decreases and as a result the basic human gift of dialogue that has been passed down generation to generation since the start of time and that never really required training because it simply happened everywhere, is now in need of preservation and strengthening.[36]

Definition of Dialogue in Other Languages

Every language brings with it a particular focus for things and dialogue is no different. Through our workshops we are always asking for insights as to the local differentiation of the meaning between dialogue and communication. Here are some examples:

Chinese and Japanese (similar)—*Due Hua*. Due Hua means "one to one words" or communication as I define it.

In traditional Confucian culture, where leaders tell followers what to do and followers do it without second-guessing their leaders, dialogue has yet to work its way into daily lexicon.[37]

- Tagalog (primary dialect in the Philippines) **Pangu Ngusab**—to explain ideas also suggests communication rather than dialogue.
- Urdu (spoken widely in Pakistan) **Guftogo** (dialogue) is differentiated from *Muklama*, which means to negotiate and *Batt Cheet*, which means to communicate. Interestingly it seems that exchange of ideas or brainstorm is a closer explanation in Urdu.

Future research could place local languages on a spectrum spanning from communication through conversation and onto dialogue while looking for correlation between a local language's definition and practice of dialogue and the local experience of innovation and peaceful living. My suggestion here is that the more dialogic a culture, the more innovative and less conflictual the culture.

Dialogue Skills

It is through dialogue that man accomplishes the miracle of personhood and community.

—Reuel L. Howe[38]

My 20 years of experience in negotiation and dialogue and my exhaustive reading on the subject of dialogue, conversation, and communication has derived what I consider to be the key skills of good dialogists. These are explained in depth in a later chapter but at this stage you should know that there are five categories of skills, two of which you will recognize as communication skills (voicing and listening or what I refer to as expression and absorbing), and then three more skills, which when added to these two, move you from communication onto dialogue (suspending, presence, and respect).

The five skills of a dialogic leader together spell PRESA (presence, respect, expression, suspending, and absorbing) and to succeed in the world today I suggest we need PRESA. A later chapter goes into great detail on each of these skills but here is a quick introduction to each of the five attributes of good dialogists:

1. **Presence**—We are today better at multitasking than at any time in history but this newfound skill has diminished the value we place upon presence, being 100 percent connected with the person or topic at hand, 100 percent mindful, absent of distractions like other thoughts, interruptions, cell phones, and media. When we have 100 percent presence all our senses are focused on the dialogue at hand, the messages (verbal and nonverbal) being exchanged by the participants in the dialogue, and aware of the emerging value as it begins to reveal itself to those looking for it.
2. **Respect**—Respecting the differences is critically important because this allows for the creation of space in which understanding and knowing can emerge for all parties involved. Absence of respect eliminates dialogue altogether because either one or more of the stakeholders simply shuts down and while communication might appear to be continuing, value can never be revealed.
3. **Expression**—We used to call this voicing but the more we examined it the more we realized that really it is expression and while

some people are comfortable speaking others prefer song, art, dance, prose, poetry, or even eye contact, tears, emotion, and body language. In fact even people who are expressionless are in fact sending some sort of a message worthy of investigation.

4. **Suspending**—All of us have trouble throwing away our conceptions of the world until something better can displace it and many people never update their conceptions of the world because they never make space for another way of seeing the world. We need to suspend our judgments, ego, or whatever else is preventing an opening of space for another worldview to slip in at least long enough for us to consider if our existing view is correct or needs some updating, either shifting to the new view or shifting to some combination of our view and their view creating a third view. Many people never allow the space needed to see things differently thereby preventing themselves the opportunity of growth in humanity and civilization that Socrates and Bohm referred to in their work.

5. **Absorbing**—Just as voicing has grown to expression so has listening grown to become absorbing because messages are taken in by us in so many ways and dialogue is not just a matter of listening but also seeing, feeling, smelling, touching, sensing. Children are great examples of this when they instantly react to things their senses tell them they either like or dislike. It would seem that as we age we become less in tune with our senses and emotions. As Malcolm Gladwell reminds us in his book on gut feelings, if we listen to our stomachs we'll usually end up better off than not.[39]

Dialogue Time and Space

Dialogues take place at a time and space that can either help or hinder the achievement of optimal outcomes. In the chapter on dialogue time and space I address the main issues that affect both of these factors including the importance of the dialogue PATH, which is useful to mention here since readers will wonder where these factors fit into the dialogue puzzle.

- P—Place addresses the issues related to the physical venue where you meet.
- A—Agenda addresses when and how to include dialogue in your meetings.

- T—Trust includes the soft factors needed for people to dialogue together.
- H—Health includes the impact of the dialogue on a stakeholder's head, heart, and soul.

Dialogue Systems

Dialogue systems refer to established methodologies, which create dialogue for the stakeholders involved. Dialogue systems can be led by the stakeholders themselves or by a facilitator who is expert in the system being used. There are many different systems and the goal of this book is to help collect the main systems into one place and describe what conditions or situations warrant their use above other alternatives. The main systems are covered in the chapter on sustaining dialogue.

---

*Dialogue is not just for groups to come to an agreement, engage citizens or make a decision. **Dialogic methods are also used to help groups think faster, more creatively, and more productively** while engaging all the knowledge, wisdom, experience and diversity in the room in an interdisciplinary, intercultural, dynamic manner. . . . **Think how amazing we could be in business, government and community if we could tap into the wisdom and experience in diverse groups in a better way** than linear, presentation-based meetings. It is already happening—my recommendation is to teach these tools and to work with facilitators to raise our capacity to engage each other in discussion, dialogue, interchange and innovation.*

—From a collection of ideas to improve government posted on a website created by the U.S. National Academy of Public Administration, http://opengov.ideascale.com/a/dtd/3872–4049

Potentialism

The underlying philosophies of this book combine to provide a socioeconomic direction for consideration by political leaders in the twenty-first century.

Nash's Nobel Prize—winning economics proves that optimal outcomes are only possible when you focus on what's best for you and the other stakeholders involved. Socrates, Bohm, and others remind us that optimal outcomes are only achieved through dialogue. We have a duty to help people improve their dialogue skills, spaces, and systems so that optimal outcomes can be achieved.

Given the recurrent failures of capitalism and communism witnessed in the twentieth century and given the global acceptance of the fact our human existence on earth is inextricably intertwined and now in jeopardy, I offer the reader and politicians everywhere a new "ism" for the twenty-first century. I call the new "ism" *potentialism* and I define potentialism in this way: It is our duty to realize our potential while helping others realize theirs. This may sound rather basic but it clearly is not. It aims to build on the obvious attractions of both capitalism and socialism without the drawbacks, which inevitably prevent the realization of individual and collective potential.

Potentialism leverages the Pareto Principle and suggests that taxation should be limited to 20 percent of income, CSR outreach by companies and individuals should be able to qualify toward satisfaction of the 20 percent, bureaucracy and inefficiency in the public sector must be eliminated to allow it to operate on the 20 percent allocation, infrastructure must be upgraded everywhere to help realize potential. Examples include:[40]

- Improving public transportation to eliminate human time lost in traffic.
- Improving access to education throughout life so people continue to be useful to others while finding their own gift, calling, or potential.
- Improving diets, exercise, and health care to ensure that people live healthily sufficient to realize their full potential.

How This Book Holds the Space—Real Case Scenarios

Throughout this book are sprinkled real-case scenarios and as you will soon discover—if you have not already—many of these cases do not represent dialogue successes. We want to offer this book itself as a dialogue place where contradictions can be captured and addressed and in so doing demonstrate to you the reality that the solution is in the dialogue and that if we really want to begin achieving optimal outcomes around the world we have to start with the suboptimal outcomes that we are living within our own lives.

Before launching into the rest of this book I also want to offer to you the reader the chance to leave aside the written word and delve into other options also offered with this book. By visiting our website (www.PotentialDialogue.com) you can open dialogue with other readers and in time contact people dealing with dialogues similar to the ones you are grappling with, access video, and sound files.

Once you are comfortable with all that is being offered in this book and its accompanying materials we can meet again in the next chapter, which goes deeper into dialogue gap and its pervasive effects in companies, societies, and the international scene.

Dialogue is the collective way of opening up judgments and assumptions.

—David Bohm[41]

Dialogue Cases for Consideration

Talent Management Dialogues

Thomas, a senior government prosecutor working in Asia, finds himself in a corporate culture that focuses entirely on legal matters to the detriment of managing and developing its human resources. The result? A crisis situation where the department isn't attracting young bright lawyers, turnover of existing staff is high, and succession planning has become problematic. The chief executive position seems to be untenable and has seen rapid turnover making it even more difficult to correct the underlying problems. An outside consultant was recruited from overseas to have a look at how things could be improved and most of the recommendations related to a lack of dialogue inside the department. Although this might well have a significant impact on the quality of justice being achieved, it also has an impact on career development for current prosecutors. Thomas has been given a few performance appraisals several years late and written by people with whom he has had none or very little face-to-face communication at all.

Service Dialogues

In 2009, www.verint.com reported that "global consultancy Bain & Company recently asked 362 companies whether they believed they had delivered a **superior experience to their customers**. Eighty percent of the companies said they had. However, when Bain turned the question around and asked customers whether these companies had provided them with a superior experience, only 8 percent of the companies were flagged as actually having done so." Verint is trying to overcome dialogue gap by leveraging voice analytics and other technology to help its clients learn more from customer dialogues; for example, analyzing voice records in call centers. Verint understands that the solution is in the dialogue and has made a business of helping its clients recognize what they were missing the first time around in dialogue with their customers.

Project Management Dialogues

One of our ASEAN-based **banking clients** asked us to address the following scenarios when working with them to achieve optimal outcomes through dialogue. We worked through the situations applying various approaches, methods, and processes to ensure that each situation best achieved its possible outcomes:

- How to get a hold of data to analyze and report to others when the people from whom we need to get the data either don't understand, don't cooperate, or both.
- How to minimize the problems on project rollout when there exists poor dialogue between country and region and when country and region have conflicting objectives.
- How to manage teleconference dialogues that have multiple stakeholders from several countries and that deal with complex issues and tight deadlines.
- How to push stakeholders to provide timely and accurate information to auditors when the request for information is

new and not easily satisfied due to system limitations, a lack of understanding and ownership, and tight deadlines.

- How to select and run a two-day off-site for the group that satisfies most people's expectations.
- How to engage in dialogue with a colleague of higher rank who doesn't appear to value you or your work but with whom you need to garner cooperation.

Sourcing Dialogues

In working with my clients in Asia we have identified the **top 12 buy-side challenges** making it difficult to achieve optimal outcomes and that require greater training and preparation than used to be the case. These challenges include:

- Business line decides on vendor before negotiating.
- Ownership and accountability of contracts is lost over time.
- Lack data on vendors' relationships with business units and others.
- Deals are done in silos. For example, what has been done before in other parts of the company?
- Dynamic needs keep changing requirements.
- Budget is more important than quality.
- All stakeholders are not included in discussion.
- Too many stakeholders make decision making hard—need a process.
- Business doesn't give the procurement department enough time, usually because it invites procurement too late in the process (see first bullet).
- Business doesn't learn from mistakes.
- Operational impact of contractual arrangements is not previewed.
- Businesspeople don't look far enough ahead into the future because people want it right away.

Sales Dialogues

Working with my professional services clients we have identified the **top sales challenges** preventing achievement of optimal outcomes. These include:

- Lack confidence selling.
- Can't find buyers.
- Can't find buyers with a need to buy.
- Can't choose which opportunities to pursue first.
- Can't easily convert leads into sales.
- Hard to win follow-on business.
- Don't know how to stay in touch when I have nothing new to sell.
- Don't negotiate well.
- Don't handle conflict well.
- Have no time for after-sales service.
- Can't displace favored suppliers despite better solutions.
- Go after low-lying fruit and miss the big orders.

Leadership Dialogues

In *Performance, The Secrets of Successful Behaviour* (Prentice Hall), Dr. **Robin Stuart-Kotze** describes how leadership behavior can block, sustain, or accelerate momentum in an organization. Having worked closely with Robin for a number of years I greatly admire his ability to link the science with the practice of everyday business. In his book he looks into the following behaviors, all linked to dialogue and all having a direct impact on the achievement (or not) of optimal outcomes:

Defensive-aggressive behaviors

- Lose your temper when you get frustrated.
- Make it difficult to challenge your opinions or decisions.
- Openly criticize people's failures.

Conflict-avoidance behaviors
- Go to some lengths to avoid disagreement.
- Give the appearance of agreement to avoid argument.
- Sit on the fence on disputed issues.

Responsibility-avoidance behaviors
- Distance yourself from others' failures.
- Avoid sharing information with others.
- Cut yourself off from people at times.

Notes

1. Atushi Saito, President Tokyo Stock Exchange, *Wall Street Journal*, July 27, 2010, in response to the TSE scrapping lunch breaks to better compete with bourses in India and China.

2. Psychologists call this heightened awareness *flow* and readers interested in focusing their attention might be interested in Mihaly Csikszentmihalyi's writings on the topic.

3. Claude Trichet, European Central Bank Chief in a speech to the U.S. Federal Reserve's Economic Conference, August 2010, as reported in *International Herald Tribune*, September 1, 2010.

4. Tipping point was first coined by Malcolm Gladwell in his book of the same name. In that book he referred to the point at which trends pass from being local to being global. What I am contending is that once people spend more than half their time connected digitally rather than in person, things begin to change and seldom for the better.

5. *New Straits Times*, Malaysia, Streets section, July 17, 2010.

6. Hong Kong YWCA, April 25, 2010.

7. Pew Internet and American Life Project, Pew Research Center, April 20, 2010.

8. Evidence of the growing discomfort of people to connect with strangers is the explosion of networking training, which is now being run in companies everywhere to build their sales, account management, and client service standards.

9. In the report *Generation M2, Media in the Lives of 8–18 Year Olds*, Kaiser Family Foundation, January 2010, the authors find that 11- to 18-year-olds are spending 8 hours per day digitally connected and if they are Black or Hispanic the average soars to nearly 10 hours per day.

10. The U.S. Army study *Too Fat to Fight* reported that between 1995 and 2008 the number of new recruits rejected because they were too fat increased 70 percent. *International Herald Tribune*, September 1, 2010.

11. Nicholas Carr, *The Shallows* (Atlantic Books, 2010).

12. Carr, *The Shallows*. The USC research to which Carr refers in his book is drawn from an article by Carl Marziali, "Nobler Instincts Take Time," USC website, April 14, 2009, http://college.usc.edu/news/stories/547/nobler-instincts-take-time.

13. Matthieu Ricard, *Happiness: A Guide to Developing Life's Most Important Skill* (New York: Little Brown, 2003).

14. Much of my experience is summarized in *Negotiation, Mastering Business in Asia*, Wiley Singapore, 2005.

15. Nixon, *Negotiation, Mastering Business in Asia*.

16. David Bohm, *On Dialogue*, ed. Lee Nichol (London: Routledge, 1996), 7.

17. Linda Ellinor and Glenna Girard, *Dialogue: Rediscover the Transforming Power of Conversation* (New York: John Wiley & Sons, 1998), 173.

18. William Isaacs, *Dialogue and the Art of Thinking Together* (New York: Doubleday/Currency, 1999), 325.

19. As quoted in McLeod, *Mindful Politics*, 108.

20. C. Otto Scharmer, *Theory U* (Cambridge: Society for Organizational Learning, 2007), 178.

21. Isaacs, *Dialogue and the Art of Thinking Together*, 335.

22. Challenge mapping is part of the Simplex Applied Creativity process developed by Dr. Min Basadur of Canada. His approach to creative problem solving can be further explored in his books *The Power of Innovation*, FT Pitman, 1995, and *Simplex, A Flight to Creativity*, Creative Education Foundation, 1994.

23. Isaacs, *Dialogue and the Art of Thinking Together*, 334.

24. Ellinor and Girard, *Dialogue: Rediscover the Transforming Power of Conversation*, 230.

25. *The Concise Oxford Dictionary*, Oxford University Press.

26. Thomas C. Brickhouse and Nicolas D. Smith, *Plato and the Trial of Socrates*, Routledge, 2004.

27. Isaacs, *Dialogue and the Art of Thinking Together*.

28. British scientist David Bohm (1917–1992) was considered by his contemporaries as possibly the greatest quantum physicist of all time and richly deserving of the Nobel Prize. Sadly the suboptimal political dialogues that colored U.S. politics during the post–WWII McCarthy anti-communist era forced Bohm to plead the fifth amendment instead of addressing the congressional inquiries into his left-leaning politics. Having worked with Einstein at

Princeton, Bohm was eventually forced to leave the United States where his ideas had ironically contributed to Oppenheimer's Manhattan Project, which eventually led to the atomic bombs dropped on Hiroshima and Nagasaki. Bohm believed in the socio-therapeutic qualities of dialogue and believed that more people should experience dialogue groups to overcome the isolation and fragmentation of society.

29. Bohm, *On Dialogue*.

30. Ibid.

31. Rueul L. Howe, *The Miracle of Dialogue* (Minneapolis: Seabury Press, 1963), 106.

32. Readers can find the articles at www.scmp.com/classified.

33. www.robinalexander.org.uk/docs/EaDform2.pdf.

34. Katherine Forestier, "In the Beginning Was the Dialogue," *South China Morning Post*, October 22, 2005.

35. www.newslookup.com.

36. I refer the reader here to consider cross-cultural studies by researchers like Gert Hofstede and others who have clearly demonstrated cultural differences between cultures on traits like expressiveness, which affect dialogue. www.geert-hofstede.com/

37. Many commentators on this will refer to the rote learning tradition of Chinese and Asian cultures.

38. Howe, *The Miracle of Dialogue*, 5.

39. Malcolm Gladwell, *Blink: The Power of Thinking without Thinking* (New York: Penguin Books, 2005).

40. Italian researcher Pareto was the first to discover that you get 80 percent of your return from 20 percent of your efforts. Since then the 80/20 rule has been applied to many different situations.

41. Bohm, *On Dialogue*, 53.

Chapter 2

The Implications of Dialogue Gap

The problems of most organizations can be traced directly to their inability to think and talk together, particularly at critical moments.

—William Isaacs

Change Is at Hand

The world is rapidly becoming a much more complicated place to live peacefully and successfully. Economic turmoil, conflict, pollution, disease, overpopulation, climate change, and other challenges are making the need for dialogue greater than ever. At the same time the rapid

Dialogue Gap *exists when the quality of our existing dialogue falls short of what we need to achieve optimal outcomes.*

85

growth and frequent use of digital communication is having a multitude of effects that aren't always positive.

Digital gadgetry like personal computers, smart phones, and televisions are:

- Improving communication but diminishing dialogue.
- Connecting humanity but isolating us in front of our screens.
- Improving multitasking but eliminating presence.
- Providing immediate answers but reducing our ability to think for ourselves; giving access to all stored knowledge but ruining our ability to remember it.

Should we care about these changes? Hasn't mankind always managed to adjust to overcome current challenges? Is there really any need to worry? Given what I see in the organizations I work with around the world I think we need to push back the boundaries on several of these fronts so as to reduce the dialogue gap these changes have created. This chapter provides you with some of the sullen evidence that

City lights hide the stars just as communication devices hide dialogue.
—Peter Nixon

causes me to think we need to reverse the growing dialogue gap before it is too late.

The past few years have included a forecast increase in natural disasters and the debate about whether weather change is real is not compassionate toward the people who have lost their homes to earthquakes, floods, and fires around the world.

The most awful natural disaster currently inflicting itself on a place I have visited is the flooding of the Indus River valley in Pakistan. Monsoon rains have caused flooding that has now affected nearly 20 million people. Not only have their homes been washed down the river, their crops are underwater and waterborne disease is risking the death of more than a million people. The floods took away roads and bridges, and most landing spots for helicopters or planes have remained underwater for far too long.

At the time of writing the floods in Pakistan were occupying the airways and I reflect on three related Indus River dialogues:

Many people involved in the war on terror believe most of the terrorists are being or have been trained in the Madrasas (religious schools) of Pakistan. Is it any surprise that international relief money is slow in coming to Pakistan? Are Western donor countries slow in fronting up cash just because of the recession or are they less concerned about suffering in Pakistan due to its perceived role in the war on terror?

As the floods ravage the Indus Valley there is debate raging in the United States about whether a mosque should be built close to the World Trade Center site where on September 11, 2001, hijackers flew two planes into the Twin Towers. The Twin Towers were not only the tallest buildings in New York City they also (in the minds of the attackers) represented the worst aspects of U.S. capitalism— immorality and greed. The attack, now known as 9/11 (the same numbers used in North America for calling in emergencies to police), left thousands dead and the whole world in shock. 9/11 was the furthest thing from an optimal outcome the world has seen in a long time. As a result of the hatred generated by this attack a large majority of Americans are currently opposed to allowing a mosque to be built near the 9/11 site. Opponents cite several reasons why they are opposed to the building of a mosque on private land near the 9/11 blocks in Lower Manhattan but the main arguments are:

- People see Islam as being related to the attackers (because all of the attackers were Muslim) and don't want the religion represented near the sacred site of 9/11.
- People think building a mosque near the 9/11 site is legal but not at all tasteful given the very hard feelings people continue to nurse years after 9/11.

The third Indus River dialogue that comes to mind is related to a company I consulted in Karachi in 2010. The Pakistani manufacturing company was started by the grandfather in the 1960s and over the past 50 years he and his sons have built a large corporation employing nearly 10,000 people, providing top-quality, ISO-certified products to Western markets. While I was visiting their factory they asked me how to respond to one of their key U.S. accounts that had recently announced to them that despite their long relationship and best value for money the board of directors of the U.S. company would no longer allow sourcing from Pakistan. What should we do they asked? Is this bias? Racism?

The Pakistani situations outlined here highlight several challenges about dialogue:

- It is not easy to see the best way forward in a tough situation.
- When we become angry or harbor ill feelings for someone it is impossible to achieve the best possible outcome.
- It is easy to believe we are not all interconnected.
- Even if we want to engage in dialogue it is not easy to figure out how to do it.

The airline hijackers that flew their planes into the Twin Towers might have thought they were doing the right thing for their cause and that they would go to heaven as martyrs once they died, but their lack of dialogue (it was a surprise attack) and their dreadful choice of tactics not only led to failure but many believe left the situation even worse than existed before. For example, there are even more non-Muslims occupying Muslim territory (one of the terrorists' issues), and there is even more hardship in their ancestral lands (northwest Pakistan and Afghanistan) now than there was 10 years ago when they were plotting their attack.

Western donors who believe donor funds for flood relief to Pakistan might be diverted to fund the Taliban (perceived enemy of the West) or get siphoned off through corruption might be right, but failure to address the poverty that exists in that part of the world also leads to the growth of terrorists and the welcoming of groups like the Taliban that purport to help local people survive and get an education.

U.S. human rights groups that campaign internationally for religious and other human rights and freedoms struggle with the contradiction of restricting the construction of a Muslim mosque within a close proximity of the World Trade Center site.

U.S. corporate buyers who stop sourcing from their best value for money suppliers will struggle to achieve optimal outcomes in their sourcing negotiations with other vendors in other countries with whom they have yet to develop the same trust and relationship history that they have had with their existing supplier in northern Pakistan.

The Solution Is in the Dialogue

In dialogue, people come to the realization that knowledge arises because of the shared experience of a collective. Increasing our effectiveness requires we discover what we do not know, our ignorance, not our knowledge.

—William Isaacs[1]

Whether we are discussing international aid, terrorism, buying practices, or human rights it is normal that we will encounter difficult situations with entrenched views on all sides of the debate. The only way we can work things out for lasting optimal outcomes is if we get the stakeholders to talk about the right issues in the right way and at the right time and place. Believing that the solution is in the dialogue and setting up the dialogue spaces and systems to allow for dialogue to take place lays the foundation for success. Let's consider the common challenges facing the previous situations:

It is not easy to see the best way forward in a tough situation: You need faith sometimes to believe that the solution is in the dialogue but history can give you this faith because if you look at any situation, eventually, once competition, killing, or terrorism exhausted themselves, dialogue is what helped the parties improve on their situation as compared to before.

Truly inspired ideas and actions are more likely to emerge when people enter into inclusive dialogue.

—Deborah L. Flick[2]

When we become angry or harbor ill feelings it is impossible to achieve the best possible outcome.

— Gandhi[3]

HHDL (His Holiness the Dalai Lama) believes that the twenty-first century is the "Century of Dialogue" and that we must develop compassion to realize our potential while helping others realize theirs. Although Gandhi and HHDL didn't comment on Socrates or Nash's Nobel economics it is clear that they are in agreement about one thing—that you must have compassion for your enemies because they are suffering from something that is causing their behavior and if you want to improve the situation you have to address the suffering of your enemy. The only way that you can begin to address the suffering of your enemies properly is to understand their suffering and understanding comes from compassion.

Do not confuse having compassion for your enemy with passivism. If your competitor is attacking you in your markets you need to act fast to protect your business. When Iraq invaded Kuwait the coalition forces reacted with Desert Storm and repelled the attacker to protect the integrity of Kuwait.

Real visions are uncovered, not manufactured.

—Joseph Jaworski[4]

It is easy to believe that we are not all interdependent—until recently it was easy for most people in the world to believe that what happened "over there" would not affect us at home and that throwing garbage "away" actually meant you'd never have to think about it again. The twenty-first century with all the realities of climate change, international trade, terrorism, immigration, and the Internet all collude to help us realize that we are all interconnected. Despite being globally interconnected most people are local and will remain local all of their lives. International secondments, although increased dramatically in the past 30 years, is still a privilege of only a small percentage of people in the world. We need to learn to dialogue with the people we are interconnected with but don't really understand.

Simply put, for our planet to survive we need fundamental change,
both in our behavior and in our underlying outlook with respect to
nature.

—His Holiness the Dalai Lama[5]

Even if we want to engage in dialogue it is not easy to figure out how to do it—the last of the challenges identified previously is addressed in this book because if you agree (a) the solution is in the dialogue and if you manage (b) to regulate your emotions to enhance your situation and have compassion for people suffering around you and (c) if you accept that we are all interconnected, it is still hard to engage in dialogue with people especially on the tough situations outlined in this book, the Big Ds, which are outlined as case scenarios.

What Makes Some People, Families, Organizations, Societies More Successful than Others?

It is not the grandeur of the vision that matters but what it accomplishes.
—Peter Senge, C. Otto Scharmer,
Joseph Jaworski, and Betty Sue Flowers[6]

In my experience people, families, organizations, and societies that dialogue effectively are more successful than those that don't. In other words, where the dialogue gap between the need for dialogue and the skills, spaces, and systems is small you find more success but where the dialogue gap is larger you find less success. Although this should form the basis for future doctoral research there appears to be a direct correlation to effective dialogue and organizational success. The goal is to reduce the dialogue gap by becoming more effective at dialogue, creating dialogue spaces, and using dialogue systems in a coordinated way to achieve optimal outcomes in the situation you face in your personal, work, community, or national life.

People with good dialogue skills are found to succeed better, live longer, and be happier.[7] Families with good dialogue skills seem to have better lasting marriages and raise more balanced kids. References to these findings are sprinkled throughout the book and tend to enlarge the subject matter beyond what readers might have previously thought about the importance of dialogue and how it differs from simple communication.

It's the one thing that helps people make savvy decisions that, in turn, lead to smart actions.

—Kerry Patterson, Joseph Grenny,
Ron McMillan, and Al Switzler[8]

Most of the case scenarios in this book attest that teams and organizations stumble when the dialogue gap grows but speed up again when the dialogue gap reduces. Although it is natural to always have some dialogue gap (e.g., new situations need time for stakeholders to react) the best organizations over time are those that have been able to sustain the most effective dialogue over time.[9]

The best societies are also those that sustain the smallest dialogue gaps with their constituent groups and public sector corporate governance is dedicated to improving this dialogue. Socrates stressed that it is not democracy (i.e., one man one vote) that leads to success but rather civilized dialogue (thinking together) that allows the stakeholders to understand the issues and take optimal decisions good for all.

How Dialogue Gap Arose

In Chapter 1 I discussed the difference between communication and dialogue and considered the impact of living beyond our digital tipping points. If you are still reading that's good because there is more news to report on the impact of the digital tipping point and dialogue gap at home, at work, in our communities, and internationally.

Historically we have been best at confronting known problems only once we have recognized them. I believe that it will be the same with dialogue gap now that this book is highlighting the problem. If indeed the problem has not been identified until now it is because the dialogue gap snuck up on us while we were focused on other things.

During the past few decades communication tools have become more interesting to use to the point that today many of us spend more than half our waking hours using e-mail, texting, on the Internet, and watching television. In the groups I work with people spend on average 2.5 hours a day just reading e-mail at work. Many report this number to be much higher and more like four hours a day. You hear things like "it takes me all morning to clear my in-tray." If people work five days a week, 2.5 to 4 hours per day on e-mail equates to 12 to 20 hours per week spent communicating whereas before the Internet era launched (early 1990s or late 1980s depending where in the world you were working), this time would be equivalent to one to three work days per week would have typically been spent in dialogue with colleagues, customers, suppliers resolving issues, creating value, making connections.

Similarly at home before the advent of the Internet, longer working hours, slower commutes, and television, families would sit and eat together in the evenings and dialogue.

Sadly, both at work and at home, as communication hours grew, dialogue hours shrank. With less time spent in dialogue or watching others in dialogue our dialogue skills have diminished. Nowadays when dialogue is needed (e.g., in negotiation, problem solving, performance management) the effectiveness is diminished or even in some cases where people are well past their digital tipping point, nonexistent.

Another aspect of the "communication age" is that dialogue spaces have diminished and dialogue systems have been replaced by communication systems and branded communication products like Facebook, Sharepoint, YouTube, and PowerPoint.

Although our dialogue skills, spaces, and systems have receded over the past 20 years our need for dialogue has been rapidly increasing. As our need for dialogue has increased we have tried to address this with more communication, for example, e-mail. Whereas 10 years ago people might have to handle one e-mail every few minutes, now many executives tell me that they get sometimes one e-mail per minute (spam included) on a busy day. To cope with the increase in communication we have gone mobile so now we can write and respond to e-mail on our phones while commuting, walking dogs, playing with our kids, or eating with our spouse. The same is true with text messages.

Clearly, increased communication is not the solution—the solution is in the dialogue. Executives who are today peaking at 300 e-mails per day are realizing that this is not the way to go and they are calling for dialogue. The need for dialogue is not only coming from our impossibility of keeping up with our communication devices. It is also the nature of the world in the twenty-first century that requires dialogue.

The world today is much more complicated than before. In every industry—banking, commerce, health care, education, science, manufacturing, logistics, travel, F&B, tourism—our local markets are affected by what happens in the far reaches of the world. The Internet has meant that information is instantly available. Stock markets and currencies react instantly to developments globally. At the same time we are dealing with unprecedented issues like climate change and massive human migration, unstable economies, and fast-spreading viruses.

To survive the twenty-first century we need dialogue because it is the most effective way to achieve the optimal outcomes we need to survive humanly together on this third planet from the sun. Dialogue is uniquely available to us as human beings and has been so basic to our existence that it is as if we didn't even notice. Now we need to regain our ability to dialogue simply to survive. It is not in looking at a website or sending an e-mail that many of our problems will be solved today. It is in getting the stakeholders to talk about the right issues in the right way and at the right time and place that we will begin to overcome the problems we are facing.

> *There is nothing more powerful than an idea whose time has come.*
> —Victor Hugo[10]

Socratic Dialogues and Life in the Twenty-First Century

Socrates might have had a leading influence on Western thought, but there are not many places in education today where you see anything resembling dialogue. Instead teachers teach curriculum,[11] kids memorize information communicated to them through books, lectures, and websites but few seem to be able to talk about what they know or how it relates to the world today.[12]

To shrink the dialogue gap we need to reintroduce dialogue skills training in schools (probably at the teenage years, around 15 years of age) and in organizations. We need teachers who teach dialogue skills, classrooms that create dialogue spaces, and teachers who are trained and follow dialogue systems tackling the difficult dialogues faced by teenagers. Teachers are not only helping teenagers come to terms with the challenges they are facing at this stage of their lives, they are also creating young adults with the dialogue skills needed to continue to learn in universities and then enter the work force more confident and better able to deal with the dialogue gaps, which will be turning up more often until we reverse the trend of declining dialogue in our societies, organizations, and families.

At work we need trainers who help executives rebuild their dialogue skills and are helping to reduce conflict, optimize outcomes, strengthen relationships and more. We need to see more training and teaching in this all-important area.

If you are not already convinced of the importance to rebuild dialogue in our schools and organizations you might appreciate learning more about the negative effects of dialogue gap and life beyond the digital tipping point.

How the Internet is affecting our brains and identities? It's easier to act your way into a new way of thinking, than to think your way into a new way of acting.
   —Richard T. Pascale, Jerry Sternin, and Monique Sternin[13]

Nicolas Carr, former executive editor of the *Harvard Business Review* and author of the current best seller *The Shallows* is alarmed by the pervasive effect that digital life is having on how we think and remember and, as a result, who we are as humans.[14] In his text (pages 125–141) Carr reports a long list of implications the Internet is having on us. One of the findings he identifies is that we prefer skimming to reading, so here is a list of some of the implications that I consider to have the most important implications for dialogue and decision making (the most important from the list for me are in **bold**):

- When our brains become overloaded by too much incoming information "we're unable to retain the information or to draw connections with the information already stored in our long-term memory . . . **our ability to learn suffers and our understanding remains shallow.**" One of my coaching clients, a senior banker in Singapore, readily admits that he struggles to stay focused today because the constant distractions have reduced his ability to focus and concentrate. Bloomberg screens, BlackBerry messages, e-mail, and constant interruptions make life near impossible for senior decision makers.
- "Distractions become more distracting." "It is not unusual *for office workers* to glance at their in-box 30 to 40 times every hour."
- Long-standing research proves that "frequent interruptions scatter our thoughts, weaken our memory and make us tense and

anxious. The more complex the train of thought we're involved in, the greater the impairment the distractions cause." "Every time we shift our attention our brain has to reorient itself further taxing our mental resources." How many readers have found the new flash advertisements and pop-ups on their computer screens draining their hours away at work. Professionals needing to complete timesheets can't identify anymore where hours have disappeared to during the day.

- "As we reach the limits of our working memory **it becomes harder to distinguish relevant information from irrelevant information**, signal from noise. We become mindless consumers of data." Hopefully most readers of this book will not be facing the problem themselves but certainly if you have sat and tried to help your children complete their homework you will know exactly what this piece of research is stating and we are only now starting to see the impact of these heavily affected youth moving into workforces around the world.

People seem to imagine that if we are all digitally connected, then we would all be in touch, and the great malaise of the age—the isolation, pace, disconnection that many of us feel—would be allayed.

—William Isaacs[15]

- "Using the Internet . . . can impede deep learning and thinking." "Research continues to show that people who read linear text comprehend more, remember more and learn more than those who read text peppered with *(hyper)* links." How many readers find it better to turn off the computer and read a book.
- Following links on the Internet from site to site "substantially increases readers' cognitive load and hence weakens their ability to comprehend and retain what their reading."
- Tests of reader comprehension "declined as the number of links increased." The ongoing debate about digital books still seems to fall in favor of static print as being a better medium for deep learning and thinking (different than browsing).

As a general rule, the electronic medium constricts and degrades the essential senses of sight, smell, touch, and feel through which humans bond with each other.
—Richard T. Pascale, Jerry Sternin, and Monique Sternin[16]

- "The division of attention demanded by multimedia further strains our cognitive abilities diminishing our learning and weakening our understanding."
- "The internet wasn't built by educators to optimize learning. It presents information not in a carefully balanced way but as a concentration-fragmenting mishmash."
- "Switching between the two tasks short-circuited their understanding: they got the job done but they lost its meaning."
- **"Learning facts and concepts will be worse if you learn them while you're distracted."** (This has significant implications for BlackBerrys and PCs in meetings as I point out later in this chapter.)
- The constant stream of new data on the web "vastly overvalues what happens to us right now . . . we crave the new even though we know the new is more often trivial than essential."
- People seem to read only 18 percent of the words online and less than 10 percent of page views last beyond two minutes. "How do readers read on-line, they don't."
- "In most countries people spend 19 to 27 seconds per page."
- "It almost seems that they go online to avoid reading in the traditional sense."
- "I find that my patience with reading long documents is decreasing. I want to skip ahead to the end of long articles." "Skimming is becoming our dominant mode of reading."
- "We are evolving from being cultivators of personal knowledge to being hunters and gatherers in the electronic data forest."
- "Young people had significantly increased the speed with which they could shift their visual focus among different images and tasks."
- "Many of us are developing neural circuitry that is customized for rapid and incisive spurts of directed attention."

- **"Improving our ability to multitask actually hampers our ability to think deeply and creatively . . . the more you multitask, the less deliberative you become, the less able to think and reason out a problem . . . you become more likely to rely on conventional ideas and solutions rather than challenging them with original lines of thought."**
- If we train ourselves to become better at multitasking we will improve, "but except in rare circumstance you can train until you are blue in the face and you'd never be as good as if you just focused on one thing at a time."
- "To be everywhere is to be nowhere" (Seneca).
- **"Our new strengths in visual-spatial intelligence go hand in hand with a weakening of our capacities for the kind of deep processing that underpins mindful knowledge acquisition, inductive analysis, critical thinking, imagination and reflection."**
- "We can assume that the neural circuits devoted to scanning, skimming, and multitasking are expanding and strengthening while those used for **reading and thinking deeply, with sustained concentration, are weakening or eroding.**"
- Heavy multitaskers were more easily distracted by irrelevant environmental stimuli, **had significantly less control over the contents of their working memory and were in general less able to maintain their concentration on a particular task.**
- "As we train our minds to multitask online we are training our brains to pay attention to crap."

As the neuroscience research continues we are bound to see more evidence that life beyond the digital gap is having profound changes on the way we process information and make decisions and that we risk growing dialogue gap everywhere if we don't find ways to respond to this evolution. This book is written in response to the problems I have encountered in my clients' organizations, which seem to mirror problems being uncovered everywhere. What follows is an assortment of examples of the effects of dialogue gap and life beyond our digital tipping points at home, at work, and in society.

Dialogue Gap @ Home

Managing your wealth starts the way it continues. With a dialogue.
— UBS Wealth Management advertisement

Digital Tipping Point Bad for Eyesight

A study of two- to six-year-olds carried out in Hong Kong has found that watching TV in a moving vehicle, playing video games, or using computers for long periods of time has led to a 40 percent increase in nearsightedness among children.[17]

Digital Tipping Point Bad for Your Brain

I often share the gym with busy executives conscientiously burning off the calories and preparing for a lengthy and relatively immobile day at the office. We weren't built to sit idly at the office in front of computers. Obesity and related diseases are a well-known problem so time at the gym is a great idea.

Some people at the gym love to get on their stationary bikes or the treadmill where they can watch the news while keeping an eye on their smart phone. Sadly research is now telling us that although the exercise might be good for our hearts, the multitude of digital inputs are bad for our brains. Not surprisingly our brains can be overloaded just like computers and if we don't allow time for our brains to process all the information and experiences on a daily basis we can actually diminish our mental abilities.[18]

If Passing the Digital Tipping Point Is Bad for Teenagers, What Is It Doing at Work?

Research has shown that compared to the lightest digital users, 47 percent of the heaviest users of digital gadgets in schools in the United States scored grades of **C or lower**, reported being sad or bored more often, got into trouble more often, did not get along as well with parents, and were not happy at school.[19]

Although the research can't determine if the use of digital gadgets causes the problem or increased use results from these underlying conditions, one thing certain is that problems aren't being solved as long as heavy use continues.

Teenage Need for Connection Is Filled with Digital Gadgets

If you have visited Hong Kong you know that people here love technology and digital communication devices and that they have more than most people in the world. In a 2010 study of 12,000 Asian youth aged 8 to 24, Hong Kong youth topped all categories for use of digital gadgets:[20]

- Eighty-seven percent of Hong Kong respondents owned a mobile phone followed by Singapore and South Korea at 85 percent. But for the 12- to 14-year-old age group in Hong Kong the coverage was as high at 93 percent.
- Sixty-six percent own desktop computers (twice the regional average).
- Fifty percent own digital çameras (versus regional average of 17 percent).
- Forty percent own handheld video games.
- Twenty-five percent own TV game consoles.

In the same study Hong Kong teenagers also ranked first in Asia (Asia must certainly be first in the world) for the number of digital gadgets per person (**4.1**, double the average) and for the number of hours spent connected to either television or the Internet (**20.4 hours per day**, 6 hours more than the average).

Susanna Lam Fung-san, Synovate Research Director for Hong Kong was quoted as saying, "Hong Kong youth find communication plays an important role in their lives." The study found that:

- Sixty-three percent of Hong Kong youth use social networking.
- Fifty-six percent blog (regional average 39 percent).
- Forty-seven percent participate in forums and discussion groups.
- Sixty-nine percent e-mail (regional average 53 percent).

What are youth doing on the Internet in Hong Kong? The research indicates they are mostly searching for information and listening to music and some readers will be happy to know that 47 percent of the surfing youth in Hong Kong read newspapers online.

Narrowing Dialogue Gap Can Reduce Stress

Once people rediscover the art of talking together, they do not go back.
— Peter M. Senge[21]

An interesting study by the Royal Society found that girls who dialogued with their mothers before a stressful presentation in class were significantly less stressed (as measured by levels of cortisol stress hormone) as compared to those girls who did not have a chance to talk with their mothers at all.

Researchers were intrigued to learn that oxytocin (referred to by the researchers as the love hormone because it is closely linked with emotional bonding) increased within 15 minutes of talking to their mothers and that the effect lasted for as long as one hour. No apparent difference was found between dialogue in person or over the phone.[22]

Smart Phones Interrupt Parenting

A recent Canadian newspaper article suggests that "a generation of kids is being neglected in favour of electronic devices."[23] This article points to the reality that as the number of texts and e-mail has ballooned, parents have responded by bringing their work home and focusing on their smart phones when they would have otherwise been focused on their children.

The article makes reference to current research that suggests children of parents who ignore them in favor of their digital communication devices suffer from feelings of hurt, jealousy, and competition but don't want to show their feelings to their parents for fear it will lead to worse feelings for either side.[24]

The same article makes reference to "engaged parenting," which suggests that parents who dialogue with their children more often enable children to have a larger vocabulary.

In the language of dialogue the difference between distracted and engaged parenting is really the attribute of dialogue. Children, like pets, know when you are present and when you are not and the quality of early childhood learning has been found to be directly linked to the quality of dialogue with the people looking after the children.[25]

Dialogue Gap @ Work

Years ago I noticed the more virtual we become the more we need face to face encounters . . . it's not what you say but how you say it and there's no substitute for face to face dialogue.

—Jeff Pulver[26]

Ineffective Trade Show Dialogues—The Situation

In April 2009, during the height of the recession, I visited the Gifts & Premiums Show in Hong Kong. This annual trade fair is a meeting place for buyers and sellers from around the world and in many respects is just the same as the hundreds of other major shows and fairs that you find in cities like Las Vegas, Frankfurt, Guangzhou, and Mumbai.

I attend many trade shows to keep abreast of the markets, products, and to meet clients. In April 2009 I attended this show with a specific purpose, to get quotations for some specific products that I was considering having produced for client engagements.

I met with dozens of suppliers and with those showing a good match to what I wanted. I explained my needs, designs, budget, and so on. I exchanged business cards with all the suppliers and after qualifying them focused on 17 suppliers who committed to reverting to me with their quotations after the show was finished and once they had returned to their home countries.

The vendors were from Hong Kong, China, Philippines, and Taiwan. Now well over a year later not one of the suppliers has bothered to even reply. One of the suppliers put me on their mailing list and I redirected their mail into my spam filter.

A few months after the show I began asking buyers and traders I know in Asia if it is a fact that 100 percent of the suppliers do not reply. They all laughed and said yes this is normal. Paying for a booth at a show and sending a small team of people overseas to sit in the booth and dialogue with prospective customers costs a lot of money, so it seems only natural that they should follow-up, but no, this does not seem to be the case—so what is wrong?

Ineffective Trade Show Dialogues — The Solution

Readers who attend these shows know the routine. Sellers sit in their booths amid hundreds of booths sometimes in dozens of halls and try to attract you into their booth to meet you. In exchange for a free pen or key chain or something similar you enter their booth and exchange cards. If there is a real interest the vendors staple your card to a page in their note book and mark down a few notes about your specific interest. As a buyer you take the vendors card and possibly make notes of your own and then you go your separate ways.

In those short few minutes the buyers and sellers communicate but seldom if ever dialogue. Few buyers and sellers even know how to dialogue in these situations and seldom does the booth provide for a dialogue space suitable for dialogue. The system established at trade fairs is destined to failure if buyers and sellers can't find a way to move beyond communication and into dialogue.

The more successful buyers and sellers arrange for a follow-up discussion, possibly over a drink or meal or even through a factory visit. The problem with the current situation is that the quality of the dialogue at first encounter limits both parties to follow-up. Buyers might meet and then completely overlook quality suppliers that can take them to the next level while sellers might have their best client walk in and out of their booth and never even know it.

The secret in these trade fair dialogues is for the stakeholders involved to learn to dialogue more effectively. In the height of the recession, at one of the biggest shows in the world, buyers and sellers were connecting but not engaging. As we outline in our workshops called "The DNA of Sales & Sourcing," buyers and sellers have to plan, connect, dialogue, record, and follow up. In the experience of everyone I talk to, the industry is full of people who plan and connect but then don't dialogue so they can't possibly record the right information and that results in a recurring complaint of buyers—the sellers don't follow up.

Smart Phones and Corporate Governance

The attending leaders brought "an extraordinary concentration of power, but their meetings don't seem to produce anything."

—Abba Eban[27]

Dialogue gap is also appearing in the boardroom as older directors less prone to using communication devices hand over to younger directors who themselves are plugged in constantly to e-mail and the Internet.

Dr. David Beatty, a leading expert in corporate governance, has gone so far as to say that, "boards should ban the use of BlackBerrys, iPhones, and all other e-mail-enabled wireless devices in their meetings. The distractions they create are inevitably leading to bad decisions."[28]

Beatty goes even further suggesting that, "failing to ban such devices may, in principle, represent a breach of a board's fiduciary duties to shareholders." The same article makes reference to research on split-attention and points to research showing people talking on cell phones while driving have more rear-ended collisions than people legally drunk.

Dialogue and Employee Engagement

Readers who have attended company sessions where they are briefed on the current strategy or direction of the organization might consider themselves lucky because from my experience most employees don't even get briefings like these. In organizations suffering from little or no communication of strategy, employees can be excused from thinking they are being treated like mushrooms, kept in the dark and covered with s★★t.

My advice to executives is that you don't only want to brief your employees, you also want to engage them in dialogue because your employees are key stakeholders in making your plans work. Not only might your plans be slightly off and need some correction (sometimes plans are wholly off the mark and only inviting dialogue with stakeholders will tell you that) you also need to engage commitment from your staff to make your plans work.

Dialogue makes your plans their plans.[29] Communication will tell your employees what your plans are and how they fit in but only dialogue will get them committed to helping you and the company.

"Death by PowerPoint"

A funny reality in offices today is "Death by PowerPoint." What this refers to is the common practice in (communication) meetings today of

turning off the lights, turning on the PowerPoint presentation and proceeding to put everyone to sleep in the audience. The practice of using
PowerPoint presentation software started when it was released in 1987
and has grown exponentially ever since. Now children learn how to
use it in schools.

The use of PowerPoint highlights five major problems in meetings
today:

1. Some topics need dialogue, not communication.
2. Humans don't think in a linear way but PowerPoint slides limit the
   communicator to proceed in the prearranged order of their slides.
3. When questions arise during a presentation and dialogue begins to
   appear most presenters cut off the dialogue to complete their slide
   deck thereby eliminating the transformative value inherent in the
   meeting.
4. Some topics are so multifaceted it is impossible to simplify these
   into a few words per slide.
5. Some managers consider sharing of a slide pack as communicating
   but as we have learned it isn't effective and certainly doesn't come
   close to dialogue at all.

In early 2010 the international press picked up an interesting story
about PowerPoint and the U.S. military when former U.S. General
Stanley McChrystal, who as head of U.S. and Nato forces in Afghanistan
at the time, referred to a complicated PowerPoint slide he was shown by
saying, "When we understand that slide we'll have won the war."[30]

The New York Times story quoted other U.S. military on the subject
of PowerPoint including:

"PowerPoint makes us stupid."[31]

"It's dangerous because it can create the illusion of understanding and the illusion of control."[32]

U.S. commanders point to real concerns that the largely one-way and
ineffectual PowerPoint presentations stifle dialogue, critical thinking,
and thoughtful decision making. Is it possible that lack of dialogue
could be life threatening in Afghanistan? Certainly.

Further research dug up by the New York Times and reported in
the same article points to ineffective delegation in the U.S. military

resulting from the belief that giving someone a slide deck is equivalent to effective delegation. I have seen similar behavior repeatedly in my private sector clients. I'm sure this has happened or will happen to you—you received a PowerPoint slide deck from the sender believing this is all you needed to proceed on a project, limited, if any, verbal communication and certainly no dialogue.

Reportedly, at the start of the U.S. invasion of Iraq in 2003, U.S. Lieutenant General David McKiernan was frustrated at the lack of dialogue when pushing for specific instructions from General Tommy Franks, U.S. Commander in the Persian Gulf at the time, as to how he wanted to conduct the invasion. Instead McKiernan was given the slide deck that Franks had shown (did they communicate or dialogue) Donald Rumsfeld, then U.S. Secretary of Defense.

Offensive E-Mail Is a Sign of Dialogue Gap

Profane or rude abrupt e-mail is a sign of ineffective communication and since dialogue grows out of effective communication profane, rude, and offensive e-mail is certainly a lead indicator of dialogue gap.

The *Wall Street Journal* ran an interesting story about financial institutions trying to clean up the use of profane language in the e-mail of their employees. To do so they employ software that reads the e-mail before allowing them to be sent. If bad words are picked up by the scanner the sender is given a pop up warning message.

In this article the *Wall Street Journal* quotes a few interesting examples:

Citibank told employees "recent headlines involving inappropriate emails are an important reminder to think before writing and read before sending."

Bloomberg scans e-mail for 70 words and phrases deemed profane and not acceptable on their servers. They make the same software available to clients using their terminals.

Merrill Lynch had their reputation smeared when one of their analysts used an acronym (POS) in a private e-mail to describe a stock he was promoting to the public as a piece of sh★t. The analyst in question accepted a lifetime ban from the industry as a result.

Kendall Coffey, a U.S. lawyer quoted in the story suggests that cleaning up e-mail communication "seems to be an unlearnable lesson" despite "case after case of email disaster reported in newspapers or media."

Dialogue Gap Prevents the Value of Board Diversity

Good corporate governance suggests that appointing members to the board who come from diverse backgrounds and represent the various stakeholder groups should lead to better decision making through improved representation. The thinking is that diversity will allow for challenging prevailing ideas and thereby lead to more innovation, outside of the box thinking, and better governance.

A report in the *Wall Street Journal* suggests that diversity isn't always useful. Despite the value of diversity:

> The truth is people often feel baffled, threatened or even annoyed by persons with views and backgrounds very different from their own. The result is that when directors are appointed because their views or backgrounds are different, they often are isolated and ignored. Constructive disagreements spill over into personal battles . . . to unlock the benefits (of diversity) boards must learn to work with colleagues who were selected not because they fit in by because they don't.[33]

The article's authors point to seven main reasons why diversity doesn't work. Their list sounds familiar to most dysfunctional groups and with some amendment to their descriptions I outline the main problems here:

1. **First impressions reinforce preconceived notions.** For example "typical accountant" making it hard for the new person on the scene to change perceptions later.
2. **First impressions last.** As we all know it is near impossible to overcome the first impressions we make on others and this is true at the board level, too.
3. **Cultural differences are noted but not accepted.** Existing groups have a culture of their own as dictated by the majority of the existing members and when someone new arrives with a different way of behaving due to cultural differences (e.g., quick

to challenge versus slowly suggesting alternatives) the newcomer is normally expected to adapt their behavior or find themselves increasingly excluded from the in group.

4. **Colleagues reinforce opinions.** Once opinions are formed people validate these with colleagues and if others share the same opinion it serves as validation their opinion must be right. This is especially dangerous when the majority are in fact wrong.

5. **Behavior begets behavior.** When someone is perceived as difficult the interactions with him or her become more forced and challenging thereby reflecting and strengthening the difficult behavior found to exist in the first place.

6. **False impressions can spread like viruses.** If a few people develop and then spread negative views of others this can easily develop to a point where the group itself becomes dysfunctional and unable to right itself. This is especially true where meetings are infrequent, formal, and seldom accompanied with informal get-togethers where misconceptions can be corrected.

7. **Opposing groups can develop.** When two groups end up forming, the "us versus them" attitude develops and warring between the two groups can easily devolve into lose-lose outcomes.

To overcome the preceding problems I suggest improving dialogue skills, spaces, and systems and devote most of the rest of this book to this aim. The authors of the *Wall Street Journal* article referred to here have additional suggestions:

- Choose board members carefully (look for the ones with better dialogue skills).
- Assist newcomers (people lose interest early on through first impressions).
- Encourage people not to give in to get along (sometimes it takes time to change minds, including our own).
- Encourage initial dissent (improvements only come from challenging the status quo or current thinking).
- Share the role of devil's advocate (it is a lonely role to play over time and best seen as a process role rather than as one or two personalities).
- Review the role of chairman (in the end it is the role of the chair to make sure dialogue is effective).

Dialogue Gap Prevents Board Effectiveness

What we do in private does impact how we perform in public. How we think does affect how we talk. And how we talk together definitively determines our effectiveness. Indeed, it could be said that all great failures in practical and professional life stem from parallel failures in this single domain of conversation. The problems that even the most practical organizations have—in improving their performance and obtaining the results they desire—can be traced directly to their inability to think and talk together, particularly at critical moments.

—William Isaacs[34]

Research into board effectiveness in the United Kingdom has led the Australian School of Business to develop training programs for boards, citing "boards were not working together effectively, often as a result of unclear communication, responsibility or undefined strategy" and "if those issues aren't sorted out at the top level they cause major ineffi ciency, confusion and poor outcomes throughout the organization."[35]

The UK study found that two-thirds of board members and top executive teams are inhibited when communicating with one another and about half are not clear about their roles and responsibilities.[36]

Most efforts to bring about change do not fail because of a lack of good intentions or noble aspirations, but because their leaders fail to fully see the reality they face—and act.

—C. Otto Scharmer[37]

Dialogue Gap Lost Toyota a Lot of Money

The massive recall of cars that Toyota suffered in 2009 to 2010 due to incorrect acceleration of their vehicles could have been much less costly had a culture of dialogue been present when problems began to surface to Toyota authorities in Japan.

One report suggested that Toyota's approach to domestic complaints was **"If something smells put a lid on it."** It would appear that the culture in Japan has been to protect the companies over consumers.[38]

Dialogue Gap in Society

The most important work in the new economy is creating conversations.

—Alan Webber[39]

The Occupy Wall Street movement that has spread around the world in the past year is testament to the Dialogue Gap that exists in society today. This movement involves people of all descriptions assembling to engage in dialogue about problems faced by the world today (but the subjects of which seem absent from the mainstream agendas of today's leaders). The outcome of these dialogues is not yet clear, and absent from the dialogue are the stakeholders the occupiers are mainly complaining about. While the watching world awaits a communication of the aims of the occupiers, their dialogue is bound to generate valuable outcomes that will eventually work their way into the policies and governance structures guiding our societies around the world; and when they do, we will thank the Occupiers for their willingness to engage in the dialogue at a time when most of the world was simply looking on in disbelief.

Is Dialogue Gap Creating More Whistle-Blowers?

There have been many high-profile cases of employees complaining about their employers in the past few years and I wonder if it isn't related to the issue of dialogue gap.[40] It makes sense in organizations with diminished dialogue that problematic situations would engender silence (conflict avoidance), attempted correction (put down when managers don't know how to handle it), and eventually whistle-blowing once employees have been either ignored too long or pushed too far.

The United States has enacted the Whistleblowing Protection Action (1989) because it realized that optimal outcomes can only be achieved if people are allowed to express their views, and in situations where this is being prevented from happening then protection is needed. There are many situations where employees were fired, downgraded, or reassigned for speaking up so although it might make sense that the solution is in the dialogue it is not always obvious how to empower people to speak up.

In China two recent cases of whistle-blowers have recently returned to the news. Wu Li Hong blew the whistle on pollution affecting Tai Lake because it was the source of water for millions of inhabitants and an important tourist attraction. Wu was recently released from three years in jail for "extortion." Zhao Lian Hai, whose baby died from tainted milk (baby milk was found to be laced with poison) has been **in custody since 2009 for "provoking quarrels and making trouble."**[41]

China and other countries will never achieve optimal outcomes for their societies if they insist on squashing freedom of expression which is one of the five keys to effective dialogue (PRESA—presence, respect, expression, suspend, absorb/listen).

> *People are living ever more apart, despite being ever more connected.*
>
> —Jigmi Thinley[42]

Dialogue Gap Being Filled by PC Games with Ill Effect

When not engaged in dialogue (rarely), young people today are instead filling their waking hours playing computer games. Evidence of this social change is abundant.[43]

China

China is said to have 33 million teenage Internet addicts (14 percent of young people) and mainland authorities are struggling to figure out what exactly to do about it. Groups have been offering desperate parents options such as "electro-shock therapy, surgery, medicines and physical drills to cure" Internet addition.[44]

Korea

I love Korea, the people, the culture, the food, and as a negotiator the fascination with the six-party talks that continue 50 years since the truce was called in the Korean War that has divided the nation and left up to 1 million families split between North and South. What many readers may not know is that Korea's number one cultural export is PC games (US$1.5 billion last year with exports going mostly to China and other Asian nations), that millions of Koreans (kids and adults) are addicted to PC games, and that the industry is creating good and bad effects for Korean society.

In 2009 more than 900,000 teenagers in Korea were deemed Internet addicts and although this is down from previous years thanks to government counseling programs the number of addicts in the twenties and thirties is climbing to well over 975,000 last year. Most popular among these players are the MMORPG's (massively multi-player online role-playing games) where people can form alliances and wage battles that can last for days. These games cause people to feel they are connected and engaged but in fact it is causing them to move deeply beyond their digital tipping point and problems are arising in Korean society that are a foretaste of what can be expected elsewhere.

There have been several reports of people physically attacking others in revenge for their avatars or bots being killed online.

People trade weapons for battle online and the value of these negotiations is now in excess of US$1.2 billion.

Nonstop gamers have been known to eat at their PCs and stay sometimes for days. One 32-year-old man even dropped dead at his PC after playing nonstop through a long weekend.

One married couple who fed an online baby for hours playing PC games returned home after a 12-hour gaming session to find their actual daughter shriveled with malnutrition and suffering from neglect.

Dialogue Can Ease Conflict

New Zealand Associate Professor Ian MacDuff from Singapore Management University reminds us that, "a little dialogue can do much to diffuse conflict."[45] MacDuff has experience getting former enemies to dialogue after the war is over. In reference to his experience in Yugoslavia he suggests that "dialogue means encouraging individuals to share their views in critical yet constructive and collaborative ways."

MacDuff's experience and knowledge of dialogue aligns him with Socrates when he talks about the importance of civic literacy. "Lack of experience and trust in the exploration of opinion and reflection can affect the dialogue process." As we saw earlier in this book Socrates expressed that humane civilization requires effective dialogue. MacDuff is helping students in Singapore learn to engage in dialogue more effectively. Some of MacDuff's favorite questions to open dialogue include:

- What is really at the heart of the matter for you?
- What questions of genuine curiosity or inquiry do you have for me?
- What has been your personal experience in this area, which has led you to the views you have?

Irrational Thinking Needs Dialogue

Sharon Begley reports in *Newsweek* some of the problems that can arise when dialogue gap prevents the clear understanding needed to achieve optimal solutions and as a result conflicts arise.[46] One problem a lack of dialogue causes is confirmation bias—selectively seeing and recalling evidence that supports your beliefs; for example, invading Iraq to free it from the weapons of mass destruction, which after many years of war have still not been found to exist.

Another example Begley gives is what she refers to as logic puzzles where one proves that something is not always true by looking for exceptions—for example, penguins don't fly so not all birds fly. Although this is correct, Begley points to research that shows truth of this kind is not as persuasive so people prefer to push their always true arguments even if when correct because they sound more convincing.

Faulty logic as referred to previously can also be a result of motivated reasoning whereby we purposefully look for evidence to boost our claims and devalue the counterarguments.

Another common irrational stance we find causing conflicts today and for which dialogue can easily put an end to if people suspend their judgments is what Begley refers to as the sunk-cost fallacy. This argument suggests that because we have already invested so much it is best to carry on rather than cut our losses and exit right away. This argument finds money being poured into failed companies and projects long after they are known failures in some ways to respect those leaders before us who have done the same.

Dialogue Gap Leads to Collective Madness

I was caught by the IHT headline "Going Mad in Herds: America's National Lunacy" in which author Maureen Dowd talks about our ability to collectively do or think stupid things.[47] She refers to the large percentage of Americans who think President Obama is a Muslim when the facts argue otherwise.

Lunacy of this nature occurs when dialogue loses elements of respect or suspension of judgment or when key stakeholders are not present in the dialogue. This lack of clarity leads the participants in the dialogue to convince each other of their incomplete views and motivates them to run off and do something not very smart or convince others of the same fallacies.

Dowd quotes nineteenth-century Scottish journalist Charles Mackay, **"Men, it has been well said, think in herds; it will be seen that they go mad in herds, while they only recover their senses slowly, one by one."**[48]

In consideration of how people twist the facts in a dialogue to achieve their own goals (this cannot achieve optimal outcomes because it selfishly ignores the other party's needs) Dowd quotes Daniel Patrick Moynihan **"Everyone is entitled to his own opinions but not his own facts."**

Dialogue Gap and Terrorism

On August 23, 2010, a disgruntled Manila police officer who had been fired from his post hijacked a bus of Hong Kong tourists and demanded he be reinstated. As reported at the time, his firing from the police was the result of a situation where he was implicated in a crime that was far from resolved in a satisfactory way, and because he was not being listened to, like so many people before him, he was forced (at least in his own mind) to take extreme measures to force his superiors to engage in dialogue. Sadly the lack of dialogue that started this mess continued through the whole drama and into the aftermath.

During the siege, the hostage taker was in full "communication" with the police who were trying to resolve the situation. Unfortunately "dialogue" was absent and although the hostage taker made repeated demands (e.g., reinstate my record, reinstate my compensation and benefits, release my brother) his demands were never expanded on (according to the released transcripts) but were instead countered with police demands (e.g., calm down, release the hostages).

The absence of dialogue skills and the absence of dialogue space led to a poor outcome. In terms of dialogue space, along with millions of viewers around the world the hostage taker could see everything unfolding on television from inside the bus, including the police grabbing, handcuffing, and hauling away his brother, which seems to have been the final straw that caused the hostage taker to kill eight hostages on the bus before himself being killed.

Hostage situations when managed well exemplify effective dialogue, which can even lead the hostages and negotiators to feel compassion for the terrorist despite the impending danger. The compassion arises out of the dialogue once they understand the events and misfortune causing the terrorist to take hostages in the first place.[49]

The lack of dialogue that caused the Manila Bus Hostage situation and the resulting death of eight hostages has ironically led to a significant amount of dialogue (and communication) between Hong Kong and the Philippines at the personal, government, and police levels to ensure that the underlying causes that resulted in the unnecessary deaths of the hostages are properly addressed and revenge attacks (verbal and physical) are minimized.

Dialogue Gap and Parliamentary Effectiveness

When Socrates shared his passionate views that eventually got him into trouble all those years ago his basic point was that civil society needed effective dialogue to enable its existence. Parliament is where this dialogue took place in Socrates' day and where it still takes place today, so it is interesting to note that improvements are needed in the quality of dialogue.

When I joined a group of Canada's leading entrepreneurs on a tour of the Canadian Parliament in Ottawa I couldn't resist asking our tour guide if the government ever assesses the quality of dialogue in the House and Senate. Everyone in my group laughed because all they see on C-span and other televised parliamentary debates is mudslinging and at best communication but seldom dialogue. How can a country run itself effectively if dialogue is absent where it is needed most?

Research into the quality of dialogue in the Canadian parlia-mentary system found, "The House of Commons had lost its forum quality and was no longer the place in which meaningful debate occurred."[50] "Citizens expect a greater voice and inclusion in public deliberation . . . but is currently underwhelmed by the existing regime of consultation and engagement." Citizens "do not expect their advice to be taken at all times rather they want to be told how their advice was used." One of the recommendations was to hire "animators" to assist deliberative democracy. Obviously helping improve the dialogue skills of all parliamentarians would be the best place to start.

On March 14, 2008, the Canadian Speaker of the House of Commons, Peter Milliken, whom I had the good fortune of meeting in Hong Kong, implored the members of the House to change their behavior citing, "I do not think it is overly dramatic to say that many of our committees are suffering from a dysfunctional virus that if allowed to propagate unchecked risks preventing members from fulfilling the mandate given to them by their constituents."[51]

In a *Newsweek* article "We the Problem—Washington is working just fine it is us that is broken," the current lack of parliamentary dia-logue is blamed on the selfishness of members of congress who instead of aiming for the best possible outcome for the country are instead wanting to vote for bills that give them something immediately in return for their constituents.[52]

It is impossible to achieve optimal outcomes (like in the health-care debate in the United States) if all the politicos representing the stake-holders in the dialogue are focused exclusively on what's best for them. We touch again on this issue in connection with the need to suspend (judgments, ego, personal interests) in dialogue.

Dialogue Gap in Our Complex Technical Society

Our world today is arguably much more complex than it used to be and dialogue skills, spaces, and systems are needed to handle the pace and complexity of challenges facing us today.

In an interesting article in the *New York Times* David Brooks, reporting on the Gulf Oil disaster in the United States, suggests the following factors (which is supported in his article) contribute to our needing to find a better way to live in "an imponderably complex technical society."[53]

- People have trouble imagining how small failings can combine to lead to catastrophic disasters.
- People have a tendency to get acclimated to risk.
- People have a tendency to place elaborate faith in backup systems and safety devices.
- People have a tendency to match complicated technical systems with complicated governing structures.
- People tend to spread good news and hide bad news.
- People in the same field begin to think alike whether they are in oversight roles or not.

If some or all of the preceding human tendencies are true, and certainly they all make sense in my own experience, we need to reinforce dialogue skills and systems urgently to survive in this increasingly complex world of ours.

In today's increasingly globalized world, with its interconnected economic and environmental challenges, as well as the increasing proximity of peoples and cultures, many factors exert a pressure that tests the limits of our capacity for acceptance of others.
                                        —His Holiness the Dalai Lama[54]

Dialogue Gap and Sexual Transgressions by Church Clergy

Since WWII, despite rising populations, traditional Christian churches in the West receive fewer and fewer parishioners to their weekly Sunday services. In many countries congregations have closed or merged and church buildings are being sold off or abandoned altogether.

The traditional one-way ritualistic and often uninspired church services communicate biblical messages but do little to engage the people, and dialogue is seldom if ever present. Is it any surprise therefore that the growing international list of sexual transgressions by established clergy has been deferred, ignored, or otherwise dismissed by church leadership unless forced otherwise to do something about it?

Although I accept that sin is inherent in man and that mistakes are therefore a natural extension of living, the widespread abuse that has come to the awareness of the international community suggests a real lack of dialogue on a number of topics:

- Within religious groups there has been a lack of dialogue about human sexual urges and how priests might manage this situation where abstinence is considered difficult.
- Within religious orders where transgressions have been uncovered, there appears to have been a lack of effective dialogue about how best to respond to these transgressions given the overwhelmingly negative impact these transgressions have on the victims, the perpetrators, and the rapidly declining brand attractiveness of the church.

There can be no more valuable role for our family of nations than to keep discussing the issues that concern us all.

—Queen Elizabeth II, 2009 Christmas Message

Paul Kennedy, author of *The Rise and Fall of Great Powers* sums up the abhorrent lack of dialogue in the Catholic Church today and hints at its world-leading dialogic traditions by writing "One gets the sense that the Holy Mother Church is not only mishandling the sexual-abuse scandal in a way that would have astonished the great Vatican diplomatic service of the past, but that it has no idea of how to explain itself; how to understand why people outside and inside the Church are so angry and disturbed."[55]

Dialogue Wins Nobel Prize in Economics for Use of Common Pool Resources

If you have read this far into this book you will by now understand my respect for Professor John Nash and his work in Governing Dynamics, which won him a Nobel Prize and on which I place a lot of importance for my work in dialogue.

Readers might not have heard of the first woman to win (and share) the Nobel Prize in Economics (2009), Elinor Ostrom, who basically found that local knowledge is essential to achieving optimal outcomes in environmental and social problems. "There's lots of indigenous knowledge that we need to respect. Simply allowing people to communicate and discuss [I think she means dialogue] about what they can do . . . makes a huge difference."[56]

The King of Bahrain has ordered a start to "dialogue" with all parties in the country, after armed troops opened fire on anti-government protesters in Manama.[57]

Dialogue Wins Nobel Peace Prize for Simply Offering to Dialogue

I was in Washington, DC, across the street from the White House, when in October 2009 it was announced by the Nobel Prize committee that the Peace Prize winner was to be President Obama. As I was awake early and attending a conference in DC I was able to share the news with local conference delegates some of whom reacted with tears of joy and some of whom reacted with astonishment asking what has he done so far?

It appears the Nobel Prize committee was so impressed with Obama's willingness to engage dialogue on some of the most difficult of issues of our time that he became the most deserving recipient for 2009. The Nobel committee hailed, "Obama's vision of and work for a world without nuclear weapons" noting "a new climate," in which "multilateral diplomacy had regained a central position" and notes "dialogue and negotiations are preferred as instruments for resolving even the most difficult international conflicts."[58]

The Nobel committee must have been impressed by President Obama's speech in Cairo, delivered on June 4, 2009, in which he addressed the Muslim world and exemplified all five of the elements of a good dialogist:[59]

1. **Presence**—"I have come here to seek a new beginning between the United States and Muslims around the world."
2. **Respect**—"As the Holy Koran tells us, be conscious of God and speak always the truth."
3. **Expression**—"But I am convinced that in order to move forward we must say openly the things we hold in our hearts and that are too often said only behind closed doors" and later "That is what I will try to do, to speak the truth as best I can, humbled by the task before us and firm in my belief that the interests we share as human beings are far more powerful than the forces that drive us apart."

4. Suspend—"So long as our relationship is defined by our differences we will empower those who sow hatred rather than peace, and who promote conflict rather than cooperation that can help all of our people achieve justice and prosperity. This cycle of suspicion and discord must end."

5. Absorb/Listen—"There must be a sustained effort to listen to each other, to learn from each other; to respect one another and to seek common ground."

Readers will note that for the first time in 20 years direct peace talks resumed between the Israelis and the Palestinians in September 2010. Some say this is in response to a nuclear-armed Iran, but whatever the impetus, the goal is a valuable one and, hopefully, should all the stakeholders be able to remain:

- 100 percent present.
- Respectful.
- Express themselves fully and without malice.
- Suspend their judgments, ego, and self-interests in favor of the greater good.
- Absorb the messages and feelings from all sides in this dispute with the compassion needed to achieve optimal lasting peace.

We will be thankful for a Nobel Prize well earned by the facilitator (Obama) while expecting a shared prize for Israel's Benjamin Netanyahu and the Palestinian Authority's Mahmoud Abbas for resolving this age-old dispute.

Faced with defiant axis of evil foes, the United States is urged to try dialogue.[60]

Dialogue is proving important as the world faces unprecedented problems and readers can only hope that the people promoted and elected to high office are also equally well skilled to dialogue about these problems. In particular we reflect now on our leaders at the IMF and G8 and G20 trying to solve the world's financial turmoil, the leaders at the WTO trying to address trade barriers in our interconnected world, leaders at the UN who are grappling with climate change, border wars, human migration, poverty, and epidemics.

This book is written to share my experience in dialogue, the research and articles I have been lucky enough to find, and hope, because at the heart of every problem we face, large or small, is the hope that the solution is in the dialogue.

In my experience you need only open the box and engage in effective dialogue before you find it improves health and happiness, strengthens organizations and solves problems, increases awareness, improves relationships, and reduces suffering.

The next chapter explores case studies on specific situations faced either by me and my clients or by others with whom I have been associated over the years. The cases tend to highlight more situations of dialogue gap so readers looking for immediate solutions are encouraged to read only those cases related to your situation and then jump ahead to the following chapter where I address how to rebuild dialogue into your life and organization.

Optimal Outcomes—What Jewels Await You When Improvements Are Made?

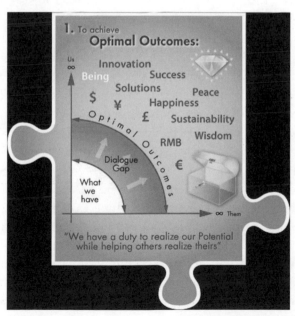

Improved dialogue can bring many benefits including improved health and happiness, strengthened organizations, solved problems, increased awareness, improved relationships, and reduced suffering. The rest of this book outlines how to achieve these jewels that await you in a dialogic future.

Dialogue Cases for Consideration

Community Dialogues

Readers know one of the worst places for dialogue is the condo or **local owners association** that you might be a part of. I was amused to learn that one such association to which I am a member had established a communication committee to establish a system of easy and effective communication between the administration and the owners, as well as between the owners themselves. We were told that once the Internet-based password-protected website was ready we would receive an e-mail with instructions to access it. In the meantime I received an e-mail in Hong Kong asking that I inform our tenant in Canada to move their vehicle, which was inappropriately parked just meters away from the administration office. Why had they not simply gone and spoken with our tenant? What condo and village owner associations need is not more communication but more dialogue.

Organization Development Dialogues

Sometimes what attracts people into a profession (e.g., saving lives or striving for justice) can over time become at odds with what the same people toil for (e.g., getting recognized and promoted). In this case civil servants, responsible for ensuring optimal decisions are made by the courts and the judicial system, are being **prevented by senior management from dialoguing** on crucial issues. People who press the need for dialogue are considered poor performers or troublemakers leading to further deterioration of outcomes. In this context an Optimal Outcome is defined as everyone having contributed their legal perspectives and having heard all substantiated arguments take a decision, which the majority of people agree is or should lead to the optimal outcome. The minority is allowed to feel their opinions are genuinely listened to and respected. This is essential to encourage similar dialogue in future issues. Simple measures of this type of dialogue include:

- Has everyone contributed?
- Are all arguments understood?
- Do the majority of stakeholders agree with and support the outcome?
- Have all views been treated with a degree of respect?

Right People
- Senior management influence corporate culture and determine the quality of effective dialogue.
- Civil servants, especially those trying to make things better can either stick their heads up and risk getting cut down to size or do nothing and assume optimal outcomes are achievable without effective dialogue. In some cases there is no interest in optimal outcomes, merely outcomes that do not require the civil servant taking any direct responsibility.
- Justice recipients, like any customer, typically have no idea how good or bad internal dialogue is in the organization serving them.

- Justice partners get upset when they see their counterparts are unable to fulfill the requirements of justice effectively or efficiently.
- Justice oversight leaders are typically unaware of the reality on the ground and are only aware of what they are told by senior management unless they employ a dialogue system that generates dialogue and reveals the value inherent in the organization. This is especially so for political appointees who may have had none or no recent previous experience working in a large organization.

Right Issues
- Legal or societal correctness of decisions made.
- Support for decisions taken.
- Motivation of civil servants leading to attrition, recruitment problems, and so on.
- Collaboration among colleagues and justice partners.
- Satisfaction of senior management.
- Risk management for oversight leaders.

Right Way
- Inability or unwillingness to express themselves is a problem for everyone and signals a need for dialogue skill training.
- Senior management and civil servants don't dialogue effectively when together and are not often together effectively either for social, business, or professional reasons.
- This group is clearly in need of systems to generate dialogue because individual reports as well as an external report recently completed indicates serious problems arising from a lack of dialogue.
- It appears that the relative lack of effective dialogue means that when attempts are made to dialogue, the differences of opinions raised leads to conflicts and this literally cuts off the dialogue completely until problems escalate to a point where dialogue is again attempted. In short, many of the stakeholders find it unusual to face differences in opinions as normally these are shielded from them as staff seek to avoid

"conflict" at all cost. As these are unusual the messenger is seen as the problem not the issue.

Right Time

There is clearly a problem because the group of people in question does not meet often enough, the meetings themselves seldom last long enough, and the deadlines imposed are often too short reflecting a lack of awareness of the need for dialogue time in order to achieve optimal outcomes.

Asked for information and other relevant information available to the meeting arrangers for some time is not provided until the meeting, or only hours beforehand preventing any real discussion at the meeting.

Members are never asked for dates they would prefer.

Right Space (PATH)

- Place—All of my dialogues with this department have taken place outside the office suggesting there is not safe space inside the department to have a dialogue on the behaviors of this organization.
- Agenda—Typically the departmental meetings are always held at the same meeting place or time. No refreshments are provided despite the meeting generally being held from 5:30 P.M.
- Trusting—Senior management doesn't appear to want to dialogue even when engaged to do so indicating a lack of understanding of the importance of dialogue to achieving optimal outcomes. It evidences a lack of experience and training in dialogue and discussion. They have always done it this way, why change.
- Healthy—Given that dialogue is at the core of justice the apparent lack of willingness is demoralizing to the people, causing them to turn cynical and resign early.
- Clearly the dialogue needs to allow space for professional judgment and legal interpretation; however, the lack of debate suggests that issues are being overlooked in favor of minimizing conflict and speeding decisions.

Expression
Liu Xiao Bo, winner of the 2010 Nobel Peace Prize, is considered by people outside his country as a hero and by political leadership inside his country as a traitor and criminal. In his defense statement read before his jailing several years ago and again on his behalf by Liz Ullman at the Nobel Prize Award Ceremony, Liu wrote "Freedom of expression is the basis of human rights, the source of humanity and the mother of truth. To block freedom of speech is to trample on human rights, to strangle humanity and to suppress the truth. I do not feel guilty for following my constitutional right to freedom of expression, for fulfilling my social responsibility as a Chinese citizen. Even if accused of it, I would have no complaints."

Conflict Dialogues
Contributed by Peter R. Morgan, author of *Critical Issues in Crisis Negotiations* (currently only available to law enforcement personnel), a police hostage negotiator for 24 years and head of the Police Negotiation Cadre, Hong Kong Police, for more than 12 years.

Whether there is any **dialogue in a hostage or crisis situation** very much depends on the subject you're dealing with. In many cases, the subject may well be suffering from emotional or psychological problems and therefore unable to communicate at that time. It is not uncommon for negotiators to talk for several hours with the subject before they finally respond or begin to engage with the negotiator through dialogue. Despite this, negotiators will continue their efforts to engage the subject because until some sort of dialogue is commenced, it is difficult to find out what the problem is and to work toward a peaceful resolution of the crisis.

Dialogue will also allow the negotiator to slow down the incident so that the subject can begin to calm down and become more rational and responsive. With the slowing down of the crisis and by properly containing the incident, law enforcement agencies are then better able to stage-manage the overall response to ensure that necessary and appropriate intervention techniques can be deployed. More importantly, it allows time for the negotiator to develop a relationship with the subject that will hopefully bring about a change in the subject's behavior, eventually leading to a peaceful surrender.

One of the key ways for negotiators to initiate and maintain a constructive and effective dialogue is through active listening. This technique has been the cornerstone of crisis negotiation intervention for many years and has been a key factor in allowing crisis negotiators around the world to develop effective rapport and empathy with the subject even during the most difficult or tense situations as it helps to reduce the panic experienced during the initial crisis so that a semblance of routine can be imposed on the situation. Once the subject feels that the negotiator is genuinely interested in them and is there to help them resolve their problems, they can both work together, through a process of respectful and mutual dialogue, toward a peaceful resolution to the situation.

For example, at 1535 hours on April 27, 1987, a suspect armed with a .22 caliber revolver robbed the Dao Heng bank in Hennessy Road, Wanchai, Hong Kong. Having fired at least one shot, he fled into the street where, after a short chase, he was confronted by uniformed police officers. The suspect then boarded a stationary public light bus (PLB) in an attempt to escape. As none of the persons on board (four adults and two boys) would admit to being the driver, the situation developed into a barricaded hostage incident and police negotiators were called to assist.

Negotiations commenced at 1650 hours, over an hour after the incident began. At first, the subject tried to negotiate through the adult hostage but was convinced that he should talk with the negotiator directly. The subject was also asked to stop waving his gun around because it made everyone feel unsafe. The subject replied that he had no intention of hurting anyone and that he had deliberately fired his gun away from people during the robbery to avoid hitting anyone. He was told that the police knew he did not want to hurt anyone and that was why the police had not taken any forcible action against him.

The subject was not driven by emotional or expressive behavior and seemed well aware of the predicament he was in. The negotiation strategy was very much dialogue oriented, with the negotiator constantly reminding him that he had committed an offense and that he would have to be brought to trial given that the police were not in a position to just let him go. The focus instead was in developing a good level of trust with the subject in order to play down the gravity of the offense committed. This allowed the negotiator to make effective use of various communication and negotiation techniques to reinforce the police interest in peacefully resolving the incident.

Throughout the negotiations, the negotiator was also able to make effective use of active-listening skills throughout the proceedings to elicit a suitable response from the subject. While the use of techniques such as paraphrasing, emotional labeling, and minimal encouragers were effectively used, it was the use of open questions that proved particularly successful in helping to understand what other critical factors were determining the subject's response to the incident.

The use of open questions also brought to light the reason why the subject was so unwilling to surrender, despite indications that he had no real wish to be in his current predicament. As well as the usual concerns about how long his sentence might be, and for which he asked the negotiator to assist in helping to reduce the likely term, it was found that his greatest fear was in being assaulted by the police on surrender because he had "seen that happen in the movies."

By switching at this stage to hypothetical questions, the negotiator was able to solicit from the subject under what conditions he would surrender. Eventually, the subject indicated his willingness to surrender if a senior police officer would sign a written assurance, with copies given to a member of the media, stating that he would be treated fairly on surrender. This arrangement was agreed and, after being handed a letter signed by a senior police officer, the subject surrendered shortly afterward.

Another effective technique used toward the end of the negotiation was building a "golden bridge" in which it is made difficult for the subject to say "No!" Toward the end of the negotiations, the subject was stalling on the surrender because he insisted that a relative be present at the scene. The negotiator made effective use of the golden bridge to overcome this new obstacle, as the following dialogue illustrates:

Negotiator: Have the police been reasonable so far?
Subject: *Yes.*
Negotiator: Are you concerned about the boy (one of the hostages)?
Subject: *Yes.*
Negotiator: Are you concerned about the court's sympathy regarding your case?
Subject: *Yes.*
Negotiator: Do you think it would be in your best interests to surrender now?
Subject: *Yes.*

Epilogue: As a result of this incident, the author received a commendation for teamwork, resourcefulness, and professional ability of a very high order during the negotiation phase of a bank robbery and hostage incident, resulting in the surrender of the culprit and the release of all the hostages.

Political Dialogues

In January 2011 the President of Tunisia simply up and ran away in response to growing conflict about his less than dialogic style of leadership, which was blamed for the nation's poor economic condition and the state of the people today after decades of his rule. U.S. President Obama was quick to voice his support for dialogue when he said, "I condemn and deplore the use of violence against citizens peacefully voicing their opinion in Tunisia, and I applaud the courage and dignity of the Tunisian people. The United States stands with the entire international community in bearing witness to this brave and determined struggle for the universal rights that we must all uphold, and we will long remember the images of the Tunisian people seeking to make their voices heard."

Religious Dialogues

At the **Catholic Bishop's Conference in France** in November 2010 the Pope stated that: "L'Eglise veut dialoguer avec tous dans la recherche de la vérité, mais pour que le dialogue et la communication soient efficaces et féconds, il est nécessaire de se mettre sur la même longueur d'onde dans le cadre de rencontres amicales et sincères" My translation: The Church wants to dialogue with everyone in the search for truth and in order that the dialogue and communication be effective and meaningful it is necessary to be present with each other and to make our meetings friendly and sincere.

Notes

1. William Isaacs, *Dialogue and the Art of Thinking Together* (New York: Doubleday/Currency, 1999), 264.

2. Deborah L. Flick, *From Debate to Dialogue* (Boulder: Orchid Publications, 1998), 47.

3. Gandhi and the present Dalai Lama (referred to here as His Holiness the 14th Dalai Lama or HHDL) are both examples of passive resistance. Gandhi

resisted British rule over India and HHDL is presently resisting (as best he can) Communist Chinese rule over Tibet. It is not surprising that HHDL mentions even today that he has always held great respect for Gandhi, especially the ahimsa values of peaceful resistance.

4. Joseph Jaworski, as quoted in P. Senge, C. O. Scharmer, J. Jaworski, and B. S. Flowers, *Presence* (New York: Doubleday/Currency, 2005), 133.

5. His Holiness the Dalai Lama, *Toward a True Kinship of Faiths* (New York: Doubleday Religion, 2010), 169

6. Peter Senge, C. Otto Scharmer, Joseph Jaworski, and Betty Sue Flowers, *Presence* (New York: Doubleday/Currency, 2005), 139.

7. Dialogue skills as I am presenting them here have not yet been researched as a group of skills by academics but individual aspects of dialogue skills have been researched such as emotional intelligence known as EQ. Readers interested in further information on EQ should look into the works of Daniel Goleman.

8. Kerry Patterson, Joseph Grenny, Ron McMillan, and Al Switzler, *Crucial Conversations: Tools for Talking When Stakes Are High* (New York: McGraw-Hill, 2002), 161.

9. Our thesis—that the best organizations over time are those that sustain the most effective dialogue over time—will be the focus of doctoral research once the parameters of this research are agreed to with a supporting university.

10. Victor Hugo, as quoted in Senge, Scharmer, Jaworski, and Flowers, *Presence*, 131.

11. Readers might be interested in Parker Palmer's book *Courage to Teach* (San Francisco: Jossey-Bass, 1998), which addresses many of the problems faced by teachers today in the United States, but which are replicated in education systems around the world that stress cramming information into kids regardless of learning style, interest, or local situation.

12. Readers are encouraged to listen to the transcripts of the meeting Educating World Citizens hosted by the Mind and Life Institute in Washington, DC in November 2009. Details are available from www.mindandlife.org.

13. Richard T. Pascale, Jerry Sternin, and Monique Sternin, *The Power of Positive Deviance* (Boston: Harvard Business Press, 2010), 38.

14. Nicholas Carr, *The Shallows: How the Internet Is Changing the Way We Think, Read and Remember* (New York: Atlantic Books, 2010).

15. Isaacs, *Dialogue and the Art of Thinking Together*, 388.

16. Pascale, Sternin, and Sternin, *The Power of Positive Deviance*, 184.

17. Chinese University of Hong Kong Department of Ophthalmology and Visual Sciences, as reported in *The Standard* newspaper, August 23, 2010.

18. Loren Frank, assistant professor of physiology at the University of California–San Francisco, points out results of his research that suggests downtime allows the brain to consolidate experience into permanent long-term memories and

that failure to allow for this downtime, for example, (my own) by constantly plugging into digital communication devices the learning process is prevented. This research was reported in the *International Herald Tribune*, August 26, 2010. The article also quotes Dr. Marc Berman, a University of Michigan neuroscientist "People think they are refreshing themselves but they are fatiguing themselves." Another researcher quoted in the story, Harvard Medical School associate clinical professor John Ratey suggests that exercises outside in nature and away from all digital connections gives "more bang for your buck . . . for your mood and working memory."

19. Research conducted by the Kaiser Family Foundation and reported in the *South China Morning Post*, March 29, 2010. Research was conducted in 2008 to 2009 with 2000 students grades 3 to 12. The SCMP ran the article originally reported in the *New York Times*.

20. The study was conducted by market research firm Synovate and was reported in the *Standard* on August 3, 2010. Readers interested in seeing the complete report can click on the following link: www.synovate.com/news/article/2010/08/latest-synovate-survey-shows-young-asians-are-inseparable-from-their-mobiles.html.

21. Peter M. Senge, as quoted in W. Isaacs, *Dialogue and the Art of Thinking Together* (New York: Doubleday/Currency, 1999), xx.

22. "Just a Call or Touch from Mom Can Reduce Stress, Study Says," *Globe and Mail*, May 13, 2010.

23. *Globe and Mail*, June 14, 2010.

24. The research is carried out by Sherry Turkle, director of the Massachusetts Institute of Technology Initiative on Technology and Self. See her new book, *Alone Together: Why We Expect More from Technology and Less from Each Other* (New York: Basic Books, 2011).

25. Betty Hart and Todd Risley, *Meaningful Differences in Everyday Experiences of Young American Children* (Baltimore: Paul H. Brookes, 1995).

26. Tech guru Jeff Pulver, founder of VOIP phone service provider Vonage who in 2010 had 2.5 million subscribers: www.vonage.com.

27. Abba Eban, as quoted in W. Isaacs, *Dialogue and the Art of Thinking Together* (New York: Doubleday/Currency, 1999), 1.

28. *Winter 2010 Progress Report*, Global Corporate Governance Forum, International Finance Corporation. The article reports on the work of David Beatty who is a business professor at the University of Toronto. For further details about Dr. Beatty and related work at the Canadian Coalition for Good Governance, see www.ccgg.ca.

29. Angela Sinickas, U.S.-based researcher and writer contributing to www.melcrum.com, a leading journal in the communication industry, lists the

following important face to face communication factors (what I define in parenthesis as dialogue) important for gaining employee commitment to helping the company succeed:

- Supervisor listens, welcomes questions and feedback (sounds like dialogue to me).
- Access to meetings with senior leaders (sounds like more dialogue with senior leaders).

Sinickas lists several communication factors important for understanding corporate strategy, the employee's role in contributing to that strategy, and his or her satisfaction with the communication, but only dialogue, as she describes it, leads primarily to commitment.

30. The *South China Morning Post* carried this story from the *New York Times* on April 28, 2010. To see the slide, visit www.guardian.co.uk/news/datablog/2010/apr/29/mcchrystal-afghanistan-powerpoint-slide.

31. General James Mattis of the U.S. Marine Corps.

32. U.S. Brigadier General H. R. McMaster.

33. J. F. Manzoni, Paul Strebel, and J. L. Barsoux, "Why Diversity Can Backfire on Company Boards." *Wall Street Journal* in conjunction with *MIT Sloan Management Review*, January 25, 2010.

34. Isaacs, *Dialogue and the Art of Thinking Together*, 3.

35. "Boardroom Skills Get a Tweak," *Australian Financial Review*, July 6, 2009. Quote by Rosemary Howard, head of executive programmes at the Australian School of Business.

36. Studies by Andrew Kakabadse at Cranfied University in the United Kingdom and reported in the *Australian Financial Review* article, July 6, 2009.

37. C. Otto Scharmer, *Theory U* (Cambridge: The Society for Organizational Learning, Inc., 2007), 134.

38. See "In Japan No One Backs the Driver," *International Herald Tribune*, March 2010, 6–7.

39. Alan Webber, as quoted in Isaacs, *Dialogue and the Art of Thinking Together*, 321.

40. Time Magazine Persons of the Year in 2002 were three whistle-blowers recognized for their courageous efforts to shed light on problems at Worldcom, Enron, and the FBI. Since that time there have been thousands more brave whistle-blowers who have had to face the pain between truth and turning a blind eye. In China the world has watched as whistle-blowers on issues including the international SARs epidemic, shoddy school construction in Sichuan that led to a disproportionate number of deaths of school children, and the tainted milk scandal where whistle-blowers typically deal with imprisonment, banishment, then, if lucky, some subsequent form of rehabilitation.

41. Editorial on environmental responsibility, *South China Morning Post*, July 31, 2010.

42. Jigmi Thinley, as quoted in Melvin McLeod, *Mindful Politics* (Boston: Wisdom Publications, 2006), 216.

43. "Tragic Consequences from a Fantasy World—Crimes in South Korea Highlight Issue of Adults Addicted to Online Games," *International Herald Tribune*, May 26, 2010.

44. *South China Morning Post*, February 8, 2011.

45. *The Straits Times*, Singapore, May 26, 2010.

46. Sharon Begley is a science reporter for *Newsweek* and author of *Train Your Mind, Change Your Brain: How a New Science Reveals our Extraordinary Potential to Transform Ourselves* (New York: Ballantine Books, 2007).

47. IHT *International Herald Tribune*, Maureen Dowd, August 23, 2010.

48. *Extraordinary Popular Delusions and the Madness of Crowds* is a popular history of popular folly by Scottish journalist Charles Mackay, first published in 1841 and republished in 2008 by Cosimo.

49. When, as a result of dialogue, hostages develop compassion for their hostage it is called the Stockholm Effect named from research into a five-day bank hostage taking at Kreditbanken in Stockholm in 1973. Dialogue can also result in compassion for the hostages by the hostage taker and this has come to be known as the Lima Effect after research into a hostage-taking event at the Japanese Embassy in Lima, Peru, in 1996 where the abductors released the most important hostages through sympathy.

50. This study was conducted by members of the Canadian House of Commons in 2003 and reported in an internal report entitled *The Parliament We Want*. It was quoted in the article "Parliamentary Reform—Everything Old Is New Again," *Policy Options*, June 2008, Thomas Axworthy, former principal secretary to Prime Minister Pierre Trudeau. A study of this and others can be accessed through the Centre for the Study of Democracy at Queen's University, www.queensu.ca/csd/.

51. Thomas Axworthy, "Parliamentary Reform—Everything Old Is New Again," *Policy Options*, June 2008.

52. Evan Thomas, in *Newsweek*, February 26, 2010.

53. David Brooks, "Drilling for Certainty," the Global Edition of the *New York Times*, May 29–30, 2010.

54. Dalai Lama, *Toward a True Kinship of Faiths*, 38.

55. Paul Kennedy, "The Church Adrift," Global Edition of the *New York Times*, April 14, 2010.

56. "Laureates Show Power of Cooperation," Reuters/AFP/ *Montreal Gazette*, October 13, 2009.

57. *Sky News UK*, Saturday, February 19, 2011.

58. The Nobel Hope Prize, *Wall Street Journal*, October 10–11, 2009.

59. The full text of the speech was published in the *New York Times* on June 4, 2009, and is available at www.nytimes.com.

60. Headline in *International Herald Tribune*, October 28–29, 2006.

Part II

DIALOGUE SOLUTIONS

Chapter 3

How to Get the Right People to Dialogue on the Right Issues

In [dialogue] comes the realization that we are not our point of view, that the shared identity we have had is not what we thought, and that we can together see more than we might have on our own.

—*William Isaacs*[1]

Stakeholders

In every dialogue it is normal to have two or more stakeholders. By stakeholder I refer to people who have a stake in the dialogue because (a) they will be responsible for the outcome of the dialogue, (b) they

will be affected directly or indirectly by the outcome of the dialogue, or (c) their exclusion from the dialogue will cause those who are involved to arrive at a less than optimal outcome.

Stakeholders, either as individuals or as representatives of stakeholder groups, bring their respective issues or perspectives on common issues to the dialogue. One of the most common causes of suboptimal outcomes is the exclusion (through oversight or intent) of one or more of the stakeholders. Exclusion of stakeholders is like preparing a toxic drink for others and then downing it yourself because what you are preparing is problems for yourself for later.

> *Problems can never be solved with the same mind that created them.*
>
> —Albert Einstein[2]

Excluding Stakeholders through Oversight

Sometimes leaders overlook including people in their dialogues because they don't think or realize that some people are involved or have something to contribute to the decision being considered. To avoid problems of this nature ask all known stakeholders who else is involved in the dialogue or decisions under discussion. Consider who will be affected by the decision, who will use the service, who will buy the product, use the products, dispose of the products, and so on.

Stakeholders that are commonly overlooked are sometimes called *unrepresented third parties*. Examples of unrepresented third parties:

- @ work—Customers affected by product selections or workers affected by pay changes.
- @ home—Children affected by their parents' divorce and family members affected when someone decides to emigrate.
- In society—Citizens affected by pollution and public services.

What to Do If Stakeholders Are
Inadvertently Omitted from Dialogue

Reacting to situations where stakeholders are inadvertently omitted from a dialogue will depend at what point you realize your omission:

- Before meeting—Stakeholders can still be consulted before the meeting to ensure that their thoughts and feelings are represented at the meeting.
- At the meeting—Call and try to connect with them through teleconference or videoconference, apologize for the oversight, and welcome their input.
- After the meeting but before release of results—Connect with them to seek their input, apologize for the situation, and keep other stakeholders abreast of matters arising. Apologizing for your omission is important if you wish to motivate their contribution.
- After the release of the results of the meeting—Connect with them, explain the reason for their exclusion, apologize as required, and dialogue on how they can contribute going forward.

The case for tapping the distributed intelligence of the community that needs to change is not advocated as an end in itself or inspired by an ideology of "empowerment," "employee participation," or "workplace democracy." The success in Mexico demonstrates that the rank and file need to be engaged because they often discover ingenious ways to deliver better results. It is also the best way not only of capturing what they know but of enabling them to change what they do.

—Richard T. Pascale, Jerry Sternin,
Monique Sternin[3]

Excluding Stakeholders Intentionally

As satisfying as it might seem to exclude certain stakeholders in the short term, as long as they are affected by your decisions and as long as they are willing to speak up you still risk being affected in several ways:

- Your decision will be suboptimal because you *need* their perspective, experience, or knowledge to get your decision right.
- Your decision will unravel sooner than you think because it will simply be unsustainable without the inclusion of the people who you have excluded intentionally.
- Your leadership will be questioned and your future role in the organization thrown into question regardless of the outcome you achieve in this particular dialogue.

Self-centeredness, the closely held belief that other people are less important than ourselves, directly undermines the happiness of both ourselves and others.

—Alan Wallace[4]

Stakeholders are intentionally omitted from dialogues for a variety of reasons:

- Conflict—Some stakeholders or stakeholder groups hold conflicting views and some dialogue leaders prefer to minimize conflict by excluding people holding opposing views usually because they can't see a way through the conflict or simply don't want to handle the conflict that will arise.

- Representation—Some stakeholder groups don't have a representative to speak on their behalf or have not sufficiently organized themselves to have a common voice.
- Preparedness—Some stakeholders aren't prepared to engage in the dialogue when the dialogue leader wants to proceed and chooses to proceed without them rather than delay the dialogue believing that to wait would be worse than to proceed without the stakeholder in question.
- Availability—Sometimes stakeholders aren't available to attend a meeting and although technology allows for flexibility in terms of on-line connection to meeting participants, for whatever reason the stakeholder involved is knowingly excluded.

Many problems seem intractable precisely because the conventional wisdom surrounding them is reinforced (and compounded) by a closed and limited circle of stakeholders whose minds are already made up.
      —Richard T. Pascale, Jerry Sternin, and Monique Sternin[5]

What to Do If Stakeholders Are Purposefully Omitted from Dialogue

If you are reading this and still considering the value of omitting stakeholders from your dialogues it is either because your goal is short term (e.g., get the bonus and move on) or because you see flexibility in the timing of the inclusion of stakeholders. I address flexible timing later. If however you are thinking of excluding stakeholders because of short-term advantage (e.g., paying bonuses at state-rescued banks, avoiding a fight at the meeting, getting agreement while opposition is away), I encourage you to revisit your intent and ask yourself, "If others knew of your plans would you still proceed?" It takes a lifetime to build your reputation and only minutes for you to lose it.

If you are involved in dialogues led by others who you know to have purposefully omitted stakeholders then you have to make a choice. Either you speak up for the unrepresented or you don't. If you choose to do nothing you are complicit for the quality of the decision and resulting outcomes. If you are a director of a publicly listed company you will be held legally responsible. If you are a member of a professional association, you are liable to your profession. Regardless of your personal or professional affiliation, you still have to look yourself in the mirror, and although you might find your actions acceptable in the short term, ask yourself if you can really live with yourself once all is known. Every situation is different.

Stakeholders Who Exclude Themselves

Sometimes stakeholders omit themselves from meetings and it is important for you as dialogue leader to investigate why they have done so. Common reasons include:

- They don't value the dialogue.
- They aren't available to participate at the scheduled time and place.
- They prefer to read the minutes, send an alternate, or comment separately.
- They don't think they can influence the outcome.
- They wish to avoid conflict with the other stakeholders involved.

What to Do If Stakeholders Purposefully
Omit Themselves from Dialogue

It is important as a dialogue leader that you investigate why key stakeholders are omitting themselves from the dialogue and if appropriate do what you can to encourage their participation. Omission from dialogue includes people who physically show up but remain silent. It is important that you create the space and encourage their contribution even if this means nothing more than to confirm their agreement and acknowledge they have nothing more to add.

When to Include Stakeholders in Your Dialogue

> *Large groups of people are smarter than an elite few, no matter how brilliant.*
>
> —James Surowiecki[6]

Experienced dialogue leaders are like playwrights who choose to insert certain characters into the play at different times to positively influence the outcomes you desire. Likewise having all stakeholders expressing themselves simultaneously doesn't work. So this raises the question of when to include your various stakeholders into the dialogue.

Obviously each situation is unique but here are a few guiding principles:

- **Involve stakeholders early** so they have time to consult with the people they represent and so they can gather their own thoughts and do any research necessary prior to the dialogue.
- **Start your dialogue by focusing on common ground** and then express the existence of disagreements and how this group of stakeholders must "hold the space" of disagreement and dialogue the best way forward.
- **Ensure that people are introduced** sufficiently to each other and understand the process and content before giving them a platform to influence the dialogue.
- **Interrupt the voicing** and expression by stakeholders as required to allow for others to question and challenge the speaker encouraging suspending, respect, and presence throughout your dialogue.
- **Manage confidentiality** and media to ensure the messages going public are the ones you want to go public. Pay particular attention to stakeholders who may feel their voice is being stifled because they will express themselves elsewhere if you don't allow them to do so in the context of your meeting.

Diversity is an absolute necessity for the power of dialogue itself to unfold. Dialogue gains depth and the opportunity for learning from the diversity within it while simultaneously providing a way for that diversity to be honoured.

—Linda Ellinor and Glenna Gerard[7]

Networking

Dialogue [. . .] builds from the premise that the world is an undivided whole, and that the central problem we face is that we do

*not see this. The world is already whole. The challenge lies in coming
to understand the ways in which this is true.*

—William Isaacs[8]

People generally don't enjoy networking, but once connected with others, usually deeply enjoy the dialogue that ensues. Dialogue leaders can enhance their success by extending their networks to include not only the stakeholders with whom you interact, but also people from other groups and sections of society with whom you don't normally interact.

---

*Under the right circumstances, groups are remarkably intelligent, and
are often smarter than the smartest people in them.*

—James Surowiecki[9]

The wider your network the more aware you are of issues and perspectives and the more easily you will be able to manage the people and issues involved in your dialogues. One way to improve your network is to map the key relationships that you currently have and then identify what you know about these people, where you can network with them, and how often you should interact with them.

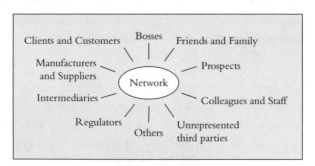

Three useful rules to follow when networking arise out of our training executives to network:

1. **Be proactive** in your networking. As a measure, you should be making 5 contacts per day, 25 contacts/week, 100/month, 1,200 per year. If you constantly network with the people you know, people you have known, and people you have yet to meet you will

be gathering market intelligence and garnering allies to help you in your quest for optimal outcomes.

2. **Identify people's relationship threads**, those things that really excite them—hobbies, passions, and so on—so that you can follow these threads and open nonsales dialogues with them through which you can build friendship, provide mutual support, and exchange referrals and information.

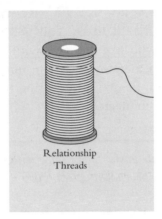

3. **Bring Ma-Ma into your networking**. Ma-Ma is the questioning technique that translates to mirror-ask, mirror-ask. If you are mirroring or reflecting back what people tell you and then asking a question to go deeper you will uncover more of the issues needed and get to know the stakeholders better.

Social Networking

Your networking and connection with stakeholders is enhanced today with social media applications like LinkedIn and Facebook. If you are not proficient at these applications yourself you can appoint someone in your team to manage the communication through these channels. Social networking is negatively affecting dialogue skills and positively affecting networks so the key is to combine your online connections with personal dialogues.

Friends, Enemies, Neutrals—Compassion and Interconnectedness

A discussion of stakeholders and networking would not be complete without addressing the reality that we have more affection for some people than others. Suffice it to say you will get more help in your dialogue from people who like you and with whom you have a relationship. It is important therefore that you minimize your enemies by at least going neutral on them and accepting the world needs all of us and that we are all interconnected.

The smartest groups are made up of people with diverse perspectives who are able to stay independent of each other.

—James Surowiecki[10]

How to manage your emotions with people you don't like or who don't like you? I recommend that you develop your compassion for each of these people by reflecting on the unhappiness they must be suffering through loneliness, frustration, craving, or whatever is afflicting their clear understanding of the situation. It is important that you garner compassion for these people because as a dialogue leader you need to include them to achieve optimal outcomes one way or another.

Today's complex problem solving requires multiple perspectives. The days of Leonardo da Vinci are over.

—Etienne Wenger[11]

In the face of uncertainty, the collective judgment of a group of executives will trump that of even the smartest executive.

—James Surowiecki[12]

Issues

Most decisions involve five to eight categories of issues and each category involves 8 to 12 issues so most negotiations involve 50 to 60 issues. The problem with most decision makers is that they want to simplify things by limiting the number of issues or simply don't have the time or training to handle this level of complexity.

Professional training does a good job preparing professionals to handle the details but not the dialogue that is needed to reach agreement about the issues. What is needed is a way to capture the issues through dialogue and then examine these issues in terms of priority, measure, range, and interconnectedness. The solution of course is in the dialogue but proper analysis and presentation of the issues is needed before the effective dialogue can take place.

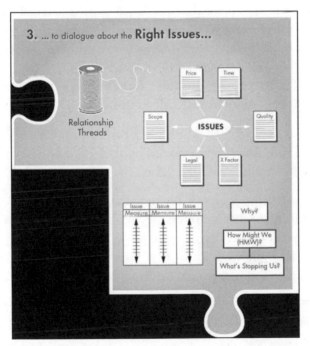

International audit firms employ people trained as chartered accountants who are capable of examining the financial details of a business and report to management, shareholders, and regulators in a standard format that forms the basis of dialogue between stakeholders. Medical doctors do the same with their clinical research and resulting patient dialogues. Lawyers do this with legal clauses and resulting contracts. Engineers do so with their calculations and resulting drawings. Scientists do so with their research and academic papers. Over the years, as the details became ever more complex, our focus on the issues intensified and our ability to dialogue effectively about the issues has not kept up. Dialogue gap is also affecting the success of complex topics involving many detailed and hard to understand issues.

> *To be effective, we must first ask ourselves, How successful am I at listening to and speaking with myself?*
>
> —William Isaacs[13]

Focusing Attention through Challenge Mapping

One of the most useful methodologies that I have been given to facilitate the revealing and prioritization of issues on a particular topic using dialogue is called *challenge mapping*. Challenge mapping was invented by Dr. Min Basadur of Canada and is described in his book on applied creative problem solving.[14]

Challenge mapping invites stakeholders to identify their main problems, challenges, opportunities:

- Neighbors living together in Kashmir are in conflict with each other.
- Tourism in Kashmir is prevented by the conflicts.
- Mining in Kashmir is restricted by the ongoing conflict.

Having listed the topics of interest, stakeholders then select the first problem, challenge, or opportunity they wish to explore further. The topic selected is then converted into a possibility, for example, **How Might We** Resolve the Kashmir Conflict so that the stakeholders can further focus their attention on listing the issues involved.

> *The collective serves as a gateway to access the deeper states of awareness and knowing.*
>
> —C. Otto Scharmer[15]

Listing the Issues

Once the focus of dialogue is agreed, stakeholders then identify all the reasons **why** they want to resolve the topic, for example, why they want to resolve the Kashmir conflict. At the same time (ideas stream out of the dialogue at this point) stakeholders also list all the reasons the topic is not getting resolved independent of their intervention, that is, **what's stopping us** from resolving the Kashmir conflict. Each issue that comes up is then converted into a possible solution and listed with the prefix **How Might We (HMW)**. The following list of issues is just the beginning of a Challenge Map.

Why do we want to resolve the Kashmir conflict?

- HMW stop people killing each other.
- HMW end poverty.
- HMW open the region to tourism.
- HMW open the region to mining.
- HMW better manage water resources.
- HMW better manage the international border.
- HMW allow for religious harmony.

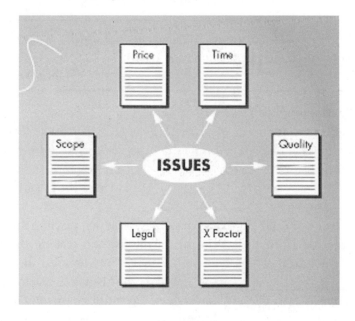

What's stopping us from resolving the Kashmir conflict?

- HMW overcome hatred.
- HMW overcome selfish interests.

- HMW end corruption.
- HMW teach optimal outcomes.
- HMW develop compassion between warring factions.
- HMW stop international interference.
- HMW create local representative responsible government.

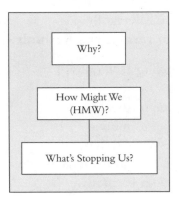

If individuals and teams don't talk about difficult issues . . . they won't reflect on them and nothing will change.

—Chris Argyris[16]

Logically Mapping the Issues

In themselves, differences are neither bad nor good, nor should they necessarily lead to conflict. It is how one deals with those differences that matters.

—His Holiness the Dalai Lama[17]

The issues should be mapped as they arise by placing the reasons why resolution is important on top of the list and placing the reasons stopping resolution on the bottom. Further refinement can be achieved by moving the issues into higher- or lower-level positions thereby logically linking the issues vertically into overarching goals and underlying causes. Further refinement can be achieved by listing the issues horizontally in different categories of issues. A final level of refinement can be achieved by adding lines

---

What we attend to becomes our reality.

—William James[18]

between the boxes to show the logical linkages. Every time you follow a line up on the Challenge Map you are answering the question "Why?" Every time you follow the line down on a Challenge Map you are answering the question "What's Stopping Us?"

Following is a small example of a challenge map using the example "HMW" to resolve the Kashmir conflict. Some challenge maps include hundreds of issues separated vertically into 8 to 10 levels of cause and effect, and categorized horizontally into 5 to 8 categories of issues.

Challenge Map—How Might We (HMW) Resolve the Kashmir Conflict? (Only the Beginning)

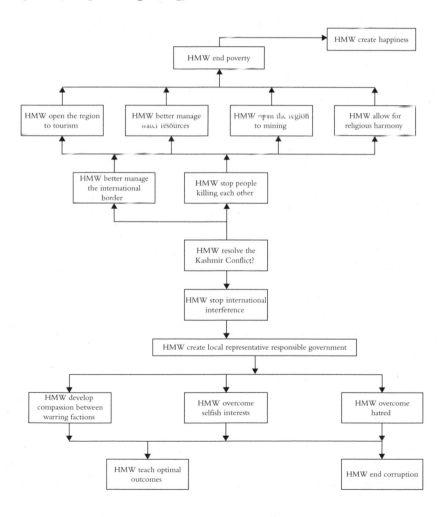

Another challenge mapping example is provided in the appendix of this chapter and relates to project management. It was created together with members of the Association of Project Management, a UK-based group with a good chapter based in Hong Kong. See www.apm.org .uk/news/dialogue-gap-why-project-management-getting-harder.

Prioritize the Issues and Discuss Reasoning

A community of people (whether a group, a company, a town or a nation) is better equipped to be wise than an individual.

—Alan Stewart[19]

Once all the stakeholders have contributed their thinking, the dialogue leader invites the stakeholders to vote for the most important issues identified by the group. To allow for wider thinking it is useful in my experience to give stakeholders two to three votes each allowing them to place all their votes on one issue or spreading their votes over two or more issues. In so doing you develop a prioritized list of issues. It is then useful to ask participants why they voted as they did so as to surface any further issues that might have yet to emerge in the dialogue. For example, two people might vote that opening the region to mining is the number one reason but one might do so to create employment while the other might do so because he or she is a commodity trader wanting to profit from expanded supply.

The most important thing I have learned is that one of the prime elements of human uniqueness is the ability to create and exercise new options and choose from among them.

—Norman Cousins[20]

Once the priority issues have been identified the dialogue leader can move the stakeholders onto the next steps which might include either (a) brainstorming and agreeing actions to address the priority issues agreed on by the group or (b) identifying the measures and range for each issue to prepare for further dialogue and negotiation.

If I can "look out" through your view and you through mine, we will each see something we might not have seen alone.

—Peter M. Senge[21]

Lists, Measures, and Range for Issues

Challenge mapping is useful for surfacing and prioritizing the issues faced by stakeholders but once this is done you may still need to ensure the completeness of your list by categorizing and brainstorming to check if any other issues need to be addressed in your dialogue. For example, continuing our example of resolving the Kashmir conflict, several categories of issues have begun to appear. Once the categories are labeled, stakeholders might think of more issues for consideration:

Natural Resources

- Ownership, oversight, protection of environment

Political Governance

- Representativeness, competence, acceptance, minority rights

Religious Tolerance

- Religious sites, religious education, interfaith dialogue

Health and Education

- Access to health care, access to education, costs, revenues, professional development, professional availability

In dialogue, we begin to reflect on what we have been doing but not noticing. This can be both startling and powerful.

—William Isaacs[22]

Once the dialogue leaders have categorized the issues and identified any further issues of importance that need inclusion to achieve optimal outcomes, then the identification of measures and range for each of the key issues needs to be dialogued and agreed. This is best led by an experienced facilitator knowledgeable about measures and range.

In situations such as negotiation where the dialogue may require concession making and taking it is useful to identify the measure and range for each of the priority issues agreed by the stakeholders. Once this is done the preparation of options can commence in advance of the negotiation, mediation, or trade-related dialogues.

Issue	Issue	Issue
Measure	Measure	Measure

Once you have the key stakeholders included in the dialogue and once you have identified all the key issues to be included in your agenda you are then ready to start the dialogue in earnest.

Dialogue leaders realize that options exist as to the right way to dialogue. Options include behaviors and processes. The next chapter considers behaviors in greater detail and the chapter on sustaining dialogue focuses more on the process options available.

Issue Database

The value of engaging experienced consultants and employees is that they have a good handle on the issues that might be involved in any given situation. This awareness is a defining difference between someone who knows his stuff and someone who gets taken aback when something unexpected arises.

Since most scenarios are repeated over and over with minor changes it is useful to create an issues database and to document dialogues at work in ways that allow new people involved to quickly get up to speed with a particular case.

The Star Negotiator Working Papers© provide an ideal format following on the previous outline to allow for the preparation and recording of important dialogues and negotiations. Readers interested in accessing copies of these working papers are invited to e-mail us at www.potentialdialogue.com.

Right People, Issues, Way

In an age of globalization, we can no longer speak of cultural superiority or inferiority.

Rather, we must focus on cultural dialogue and negotiation.

—Majid Tehranian[23]

Having identified the outcomes we want and the stakeholders and issues involved, the next chapters focus on how to get what we want through dialogue. The next chapter breaks the five attributes of good dialogists (PRESA—presence, respect, expression, suspension, and absorption) into 10 subskills for each attribute.

The Key to Success

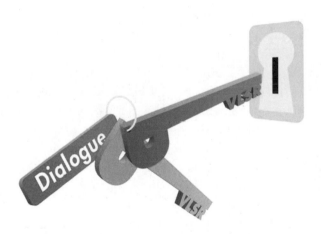

Dialogue Cases for Consideration

The following dialogue cases provide you with a better idea of the breadth and depth of the implications of Dialogue Gap as I see it affecting us at work, home, and in society today.

Political Dialogues

The ongoing **China–Tibet negotiations** are being followed closely by millions of people around the world. I have had the pleasure of sharing some of my ideas with the office of His Holiness the Dalai Lama and I pray for a successful outcome of this terribly long and drawn-out negotiation. The following is an excerpt from a statement made by Lodi Gyari, Special Envoy of His Holiness the Dalai Lama, concerning the dialogue process with China:

> Following the series of demonstrations in Tibetan areas in 2008, we had two rounds of talks and one informal session with the Chinese leadership. During the most recent 8th round held in November 2008 we in fact presented a Memorandum on Genuine Autonomy for the Tibetan People that clearly outlined the basic needs of the Tibetan people that can be fulfilled even under the present Constitutional provisions of the People's Republic of China.
>
> The outright rejection of the Memorandum by the Chinese side, without even looking into many of the points raised therein, did not leave any scope for further contacts. However, His Holiness the Dalai Lama continued to be committed to the dialogue process and impressed upon us the need to take steps to reach out once again to the Chinese leadership. So far, it has been all our initiatives that have been the basis of any perceptible positive side to the dialogue process. It was at our initiative that contact was re-established and continued since 2002. Every time it has been our initiative that has started the process for the rounds of discussions.
>
> The recent statements coming from Beijing, therefore, reminds me of an advice given to me by a Chinese Professor who was involved with the Tibetan issue for many years while serving the Chinese Government. He said that we should not expect the Chinese leadership to have the political courage to remove the hat of

separatism from His Holiness the Dalai Lama even though they clearly are aware that he is not working in that direction. The professor told me that if the Chinese side were to remove such a hat from him, then they would not be able to justify to the Chinese people their current policies in Tibet or on the return of His Holiness the Dalai Lama to Tibet.

Sales and Sourcing Dialogues

I made a visit last year to Lahore and Karachi, Pakistan, to speak with business owners about achieving optimal outcomes through dialogue and negotiation. It was one of the most magical places I have ever been and I can't wait to return despite the obvious dangers inherent today in this nation. One of the most moving dialogues I had was with the owners of a **multigenerational towel producing business** that sells top-quality best price beautiful plush towels for Western markets including hotels and cruise liners. Sadly one of their American clients had contacted them recently to announce that despite their supply record being spotless and despite the absence of equally qualified suppliers to replace them in the short term, the U.S. client has decided to immediately cease purchasing from Pakistan. Obviously the decision taken in the United States was done for political reasons and sadly it was done without dialogue. The owners in Karachi were notified by e-mail. Clearly the optimal outcome has not been achieved. The U.S. buyer is left with lesser quality suppliers at equal or higher prices. The Karachi producer has lost a multigenerational client. What to do? The solution is in the dialogue. If the stakeholders can meet, the next step is to dialogue (I suggest challenge mapping) to clearly define the problem before suggesting ways forward. Solutions like routing product through third countries are already being explored but until the problem is fully understood through dialogue no solution can optimize the outcome.

Performance Management Dialogues—A

Bruce, a high-performing ("hipo") professional met with his boss Martin for his annual performance review. Martin was relatively new on the job but records kept of Bruce's previous work made Martin's job as reviewer easier. Due to the economy, promotions were being cut back and Martin had to tell Bruce that although he had done a great job he was not getting promoted. Bruce, knowing some of his colleagues had been promoted, pushed Martin for reasons but Martin was clearly uncomfortable to discuss this so Bruce thanked Martin and shortly thereafter accepted an international transfer and never returned to work in Martin's office again. Bruce eventually left the company. **Did the performance management system work? No**—mainly because Martin wasn't able to engage in a dialogue with Bruce in a way that met Bruce's needs.

Performance Management Dialogues—B

A new push onto people development had uncovered Linda, a hardworking and dedicated resource who could clearly do more. She was promoted, given direct reports, and provided with training and encouragement to speak up and become the leader she so naturally was. The staff loved Linda and relied on her to look after them. As injustices appeared Linda would step in and point out to senior management in the way she had been trained and encouraged, to speak up diplomatically to make things better. When the economy turned, **senior management decided to ask Linda to leave**. Senior management said at the time that the company had to choose between retaining either Linda or her husband who was also working in the company and that because he earned more, it was in their family interest that she depart so she left. Did the performance management system achieve its objectives? No— because when Linda was asked to leave, all her staff saw it as punishment for her speaking up, and after that, the department head where Linda worked could no longer get people to contribute the way Linda had done.

Performance Management Dialogues—C

Angela was nervous about her annual appraisal. She was expecting a promotion and through a lack of dialogue all year was led to believe that she was doing okay. By the time she met her boss she was really getting worried. Her boss was also seemingly nervous and shortly after inviting Angela into his office he gave her the news—**no promotion and no dialogue**. The result: Angela fainted and to make matters worse as she collapsed she let out a loud burst of air then hit her head on the corner of her boss's desk. When colleagues came running to see what happened, Angela lay on the floor bleeding from the head and her boss looked terribly guilty. Did the system work? No.

Business Development Dialogues

When the recession hit, several professional firms in Asia went almost overnight from being so busy they could fill all the work to being not busy at all. Layoffs were rampant and once the dust had settled the survivors realized that for the first time in many years they would have to learn how to dialogue with clients and generate more work. Business development dialogues were once again the topic for training in Asia and around the world. One large U.S. law firm hired me to work with all their partners and senior associates in Asia. The managing partner's main challenge was simply **convincing his partners that selling was part of the job description of a lawyer**. Using our Dialogic Sales Process and Relationship Sales Principles, which were designed by professionals for professionals, we were able to assure the participants that they didn't need to sell, they needed to reinforce their dialogues with their existing contacts. Network, contact five people per day, and engage in effective dialogue about their needs. The result paid for itself in no time and more importantly all the partners now see how they can contribute to business development even if they don't see themselves as perennial "rain makers."

Notes

1. *Dialogue and the Art of Thinking Together* (New York: Doubleday/Currency, 1999), 279.

2. As quoted in (C. Otto Scharmer) *Theory U* (Cambridge: Society for Organizational Learning, 2007), 168.

3. *The Power of Positive Deviance* (Boston: Harvard Business Press, 2010), 142.

4. *Buddhism with an Attitude: The Tibetan Seven-Point Mind-Training* (New York: Snow Lion, 2001), 218.

5. *The Power of Positive Deviance*, 80.

6. *The Wisdom of Crowds* (New York: Doubleday, 2004), front flap.

7. *Dialogue: Rediscover the Transforming Power of Conversation* (New York: John Wiley & Sons, 1998), 281.

8. *Dialogue and the Art of Thinking Together*, 68.

9. *The Wisdom of Crowds*, xiii.

10. Ibid., 41.

11. As quoted in J. Surowiecki, *The Wisdom of Crowds*, 162.

12. *The Wisdom of Crowds*, 223.

13. *Dialogue and the Art of Thinking Together*, 69.

14. Dr. Min Basadur, *Simplex: A Flight to Creativity* (Creative Education Foundation, 1998).

15. *Theory U*, 375.

16. As quoted in C. Otto Scharmer, *Theory U*, 275.

17. *Toward a True Kinship of Faiths* (New York: Doubleday Religion, 2010), 131.

18. As quoted in B. A. Wallace, *Buddhism with an Attitude*, 27.

19. *The Conversing Company: Its Culture, Power and Potential* 2nd edition. (Adelaide: Multimind Solutions, 2009).

20. As quoted in Daisaku Ikeda and Majid Tehranian, *Global Civilization* (London: British Academic Press, 2004), 175.

21. *The Fifth Discipline* (New York: Currency Doubleday, 2006), 231.

22. *Dialogue and the Art of Thinking Together*, 38.

23. Ikeda and Tehranian, *Global Civilization*, 73.

Chapter 4

Dialogue
Leader Behaviors

D ialogue is the twenty-first century's most important skill and without it I doubt humanity can survive the onslaught of problems that we will face in the coming century. Despite the paramount importance of dialogue it is the only important human skill that we don't teach or train anywhere in the world. Although we train other basic human skills like breathing, eating, walking, running, and sleeping this training only appeared once it became apparent our evolving lifestyles were causing problems in our basic skills. As we learned more about stress, allergies, and venturing into previously inhospitable climates we began training breathing techniques. As we learned more about the dietary effects on health we began teaching people how to eat better. As sport and fitness became a pastime in our otherwise inactive lifestyles we began studying walking and running. And finally as our modern lifestyles overtook our ability to cope we began teaching breathing and meditation techniques.

The advent of the Internet and modern telephony has led to life beyond the digital tipping point and problems of dialogue gap, so it is now essential that we introduce teaching and training in dialogue. Since the start of time people assembled in circles to talk about their survival but since the start of the 1990s we find this happening less and less at home, at work, and in society. The result is that because dialogue happens less and less and because people participate less and less in effective dialogues people, especially young people, are not learning how to dialogue. Employers everywhere are reporting that young people today simply don't have the dialogue skills needed to handle the problems that work and life is throwing at them. It is time therefore that we introduce dialogue courses in schools and corporate training.

Dialogic education is nothing new. Most readers will recognize that Socrates, Plato, Aristotle, and all great teachers at least until the advent of printed books, used dialogue as their principal teaching method. Dialogic education is making a resurgence in some sectors but at the same time digital tools like smart boards, laptops, and online curriculums are forcing education to become more communicative and less dialogic.[1,2] Readers doing online courses will understand exactly what I mean; there is a big difference between learning alone on your computer versus sitting in a circle with your teacher and classmates discussing the subject matter. The more the subject matter involves emerging knowledge the more the dialogic approach is needed.

As former head of learning and development for Coopers & Lybrand in Hong Kong (now part of PricewaterhouseCoopers "PwC") I became well versed in carrying out training needs analysis, designing corporate learning curriculum, and delivering world-class training programs. Skill gaps change and new training is needed to fill these gaps. In the past 20 years it has become apparent that dialogue training is greatly needed because corporate clients everywhere are pointing out that employees of all levels are struggling to create, sustain, and manage dialogue with key stakeholders.

Teaching and training dialogue, be it to teenagers in secondary schools or executives in organizations, needs to incorporate theory, practice, and reflection to be successful. Dialogue practice should focus on the most important topics facing the audience in question (see Chapter 3 on life's big dialogues). Reflection should include time-outs and professional feedback so that participants can identify how to improve their dialogues as they are happening so that optimal outcomes can be achieved before the opportunity is lost.

The theory of dialogue best practice is still evolving although much is already known. I suggest that the best way of understanding dialogue best practice is to consider the skills of good dialogists, the spaces needed for dialogue to take place, and the systems that enable dialogue to take place and that have proven successful over time. This chapter addresses dialogue skills, spaces, and systems in that order and then considers some of the things that block effective dialogue including stress.

Dialogue Skills in Summary

As outlined in Chapter 1, dialogue skills are easily remembered with the acronym PRESA, which stands for: presence, respect, expression (voicing), suspend, and absorb (listen). Each of these five skills can be further subdivided into 10 specific behaviors that good dialogists employ. The behaviors were drawn from the existing literature on dialogue as cited throughout this book. I expand on each of these dialogic behaviors next, but for ease of understanding provide you with the full list before going on.

Presence

1. Balance solitude and social time to maintain your mindfulness.
2. Maintain your calm to calm others.
3. Meditate regularly to develop and strengthen your mindfulness.
4. Interact regularly with different people to open your mind to new perspectives.
5. Control your emotions to enhance your situation rather than hinder it.
6. Be confident, witty, and humorous.
7. Be cheerful, flexible, and without melancholy.
8. Show genuine curiosity in exploring what others have to say.
9. Don't multitask when in dialogue with others.
10. Recognize and listen to your gut feelings (inner-knowing) and those of others.

Respect

1. Be inclusive of others regardless of what diversity separates you.
2. Be diplomatic and don't criticize or use judgmental labels.
3. Demonstrate respect and understanding for others.
4. Be sincere, honest, and dialogue with proper motives.
5. Show that you care and can be trusted.
6. Apologize and take the blame when appropriate.
7. Involve all key stakeholders in the dialogue.
8. Demonstrate that other people's perceptions matter a lot.

9. Accept that you need your opponents' perspectives to make optimal decisions.
10. Recognize that you'll need each other either now or later and explore why.

Expression (e.g., Voicing, Writing, Song, Dance, Art, Body Language)

1. Adjust your tone, speed, vocabulary, and grammar to match the other party.
2. Prime the environment through words and gestures so people respond as you would like.
3. Be polite, courteous, and don't use foul language.
4. Speak from your experience (not that of others) and avoid storytelling.
5. Use "I-messages" to talk about patterns of behavior rather than one-off events.
6. Speak your mind and share your feelings without venting rage or anger or lecturing others.
7. State the mutual purpose and focus on common ground.
8. State what you mean and what you do not mean to leave no doubt in the other's mind.
9. Inquire appreciatively of others by asking engaging questions without causing bad feelings.
10. Don't wait to know it all or get it right before you speak up.

Suspend (Judgments, Beliefs, Ego, etc.)

1. Be equal in mind and not under obligation to others (egalitarian).
2. Invite opposing views and get all the relevant information onto the table.
3. Demonstrate openness to new ideas and interest for subjects not your own.
4. Be flexible—adjust the time, place, and way you dialogue to achieve your outcome.
5. Avoid either/or choices and looking at the world as black and white.
6. Recognize that the solution is found in the dialogue and not in predetermined answers.
7. Investigate and understand your own assumptions.

8. Find compassion for others and accept that everything is interconnected.
9. Help others suspend so they see alternatives.
10. Suspend your opinions about other people's opinions.

Absorb (e.g., Listening, Reading, Watching, Touching, Smelling, Tasting, Gut Feeling)

1. Watch people's body language to check if it validates what they are saying.
2. Balance talking and listening, not every word that comes to you needs to be spoken.
3. Listen to others' feelings to understand their perspective and uncover their intent.
4. Mirror what others say and ask a related question to deepen your understanding (Ma-Ma).
5. Build a ladder of inference connecting the situation to perceptions, conclusions, assumptions, and beliefs.
6. Don't jump to conclusions, invoke your professional skepticism.
7. Think about why they said what they did before you ask them.
8. Recognize effective dialogue results from good questions rather than good answers.
9. Diagnose and explore why they respond with silence.
10. Recognize feedback as a gift regardless of how nicely it is wrapped.

Dialogue Behaviors in Detail

Just as the nozzle of a hose intensifies the force of a current of water, so too does a clear vision channel and focus the purposefulness and energy that arise from presencing.
—Peter Senge, C. Otto Scharmer, Joseph Jaworski, and Betty Sue Flowers[3]

Leaders wanting to know specifically what to do differently to improve their dialogue are welcome to consider the following list of behaviors gleaned from all related texts on the subject and compiled here for the first time in a more comprehensive format. It is hoped that scientific research will be carried out to prove these attributes, but in the meantime, consider them the consolidated wisdom of all the authors quoted throughout this text.

Presence

Presence is a skill that we humans used to have plenty of but as we have become more and more adept at multitasking (e.g., simultaneously talking on the telephone while you check your e-mail and keep an eye on the markets or watching television while you supervise your kids' homework and prepare the evening meal are common examples of multitasking at work and home), we seem to have lost our ability to be 100 percent present when we need to be such as in dialogue. Following are some of the behaviors good dialogists employ to improve their presence.

Balance Solitude and Social Time to Maintain Your Mindfulness

To focus 100 percent on the other party in dialogue (i.e., to be mindful) it is useful to not be constantly talking with others. Obviously as social animals we seek out others and when we balance our time with others with our time alone not only does the time alone allow our brains to synchronize, but our increasing aloneness tends to make us happier to see and engage with others when we are with them.

A simple example is how happy senior citizens are when they receive visitors because much of their time, due to limited physical mobility and the fact they have retired, is typically spent alone or with a small number of people they see daily.

The longest road you will ever walk is the sacred journey from your head to your heart.

—Phil Lane[4]

Maintain Your Calm to Calm Others

When we slow down, when we relate with mindfulness and care, we evoke similar behavior from others. When we are able to be calm, others begin to calm down. When they are calm, their calmness supports us in our efforts, without any explicitly shared practice. Qualities like serenity, wisdom, and kindness are contagious.

—Gregory Kramer[5]

Good dialogists don't repel others through upsetting behavior. People who are stressed, upset, angered, complaining, or negative do not exude calmness attractive to dialogue. If you want to move beyond communication and into dialogue you need to find ways to calm yourself so that you can be open to dialogue with others.

People don't like sitting by the side of a lake in a storm and the same is true in dialogue so when you want to be effective at dialogue you must learn to calm yourself or delay your dialogue until such time as you have calmed down. If you want to engage someone who is upset with your calmness, you can help them calm down. People enraged together don't create dialogue, they create tears.

Meditate Regularly to Develop and Strengthen Your Mindfulness[6]
In Insight Dialogue every meditator participates in listening the others into presence.

—Gregory Kramer

Mindfulness practitioners follow regular practices—daily if not several times per day—to calm their mind. Meditation is the most effective way to calm the mind and develop the ability of being 100 percent present. There are many forms of meditation from the currently popular sitting meditations and yoga to other less obvious forms of meditation such as listening to calming music, gardening, walking in the forest, along the shoreline, or through a park, repetitive low-impact exercise (e.g., swimming lengths of a pool), peaceful hobbies such as knitting, or inspirational reading. Some people even suggest that dialogue itself is a form of meditation.

The key to successful meditation is that it enables you to clear your mind of discursive thoughts until you are able to fully focus on one thing or on nothing at all without the constant chatter of uninvited thoughts entering your mind. We are not normally good at meditation hence the need to practice regularly. The best meditators in the world tend not to be special in any way other than they have dedicated years of practice to developing their mindfulness and presence.[7] It is wonderful to interact with these people because they leave you feeling that they really connected with you and although you may not have been in dialogue for a long time the time together with them is special.

The more I pay attention inward, the more able I am to listen to others. If I am not present with me, I cannot be present for others.
—Unnamed Mediator[8]

The famous U.S. actor Richard Gere, who I had the pleasure of meeting in Washington at the Mind & Life Conference in October 2009, does considerable work with His Holiness the 14th Dalai Lama, a monk who has spent considerable time meditating daily throughout his nearly 80 years. Gere, in discussing what it is like to be in the presence of His Holiness, says, "When you know you are in the presence of a great man, a great mind, a great soul, you can't help but be touched and influenced."[9]

Interact Regularly with Different People to Open Your Mind to New Perspectives

Good dialogists are also good networkers and because they network with different people they are regularly reminded that there are many different perspectives on the same subjects. You cannot get a true picture of something if you don't talk to all the different people involved. By getting out and getting around you begin to realize how limiting your initial views might be.

Listening is more powerful than speaking, asking questions more powerful than knowing.

I had to let go of my fears and trust that others would deliver ideas and actions that were far beyond what I could dream or imagine.
—Richard T. Pascale, Jerry Sternin, and Monique Sternin[10]

A common example today is the great divide between those who started work in the pre-Internet era and those whose careers have always embraced the Internet. The older generation often tells me they don't understand young people today and vice versa. Although this is no different than any previous generational divide I think the differences take on a much greater importance now because of dialogue gap. To overcome the divide, it is important the two groups spend time together in dialogue and in action understanding the views of others.

On a recent trip to Pakistan I was reminded of the importance of meeting with different people so as to see the world through different perspectives. While shopping for a souvenir in Lahore, a beautiful city in Northern Pakistan, I asked the shopkeeper how business was going. Much to my surprise he replied, "9/11 to you meant the crashing down of the Twin Towers in New York but for us it meant the crashing down of the tourism industry. You are my first customer this month. In fact you are my first customer this year. You are bringing me good luck." It has never occurred to me that the small band of terrorists who perpetrated the terrible attack on U.S. soil were at the same time inflicting such damage in their own Muslim world. If only terrorists could learn that solutions come from dialogue, not terrorism.

Control Your Emotions to Enhance Your Situation Rather than Hinder It

I grew up in a family of three boys and as many parents realize, boys, until they learn better, will occasionally defer to fighting instead of dialogue to get what they want. It was perhaps with a view to keeping his sons safe that my father had always told us, "Learn to control your emotions to enhance your situation rather than hinder it." These words always made sense; in fact, at college I had them taped to the mirror in my dormitory beside my desk. The only problem was that it took me another 20 years to figure out how to control my emotions.

Emotional regulation isn't at all that easy but with study, persistence, and some help in seeing the world as it really is people can significantly improve the way they manage their emotions and therefore enhance their situation rather than hinder it.

The secret to succeeding in emotional regulation is to understand the causes of what Buddhists call *afflictive* or *destructive* emotions— eliminate the causes of these afflictive emotions and work to restrain or even eliminate your reactions to the impulses that cause your emotional reaction in the first place.

Research suggests that there are four levels of attainment that you can achieve in learning to regulate your emotions:[11]

1. Normal—You react to the situation without even thinking. In other words, you can become enraged, angry, sad, or depressed relatively easily, none of which necessarily will enhance your situation and more likely will make it worse.

2. Experienced—You adjust your reaction midstream to minimize the negative impact of your reaction on your situation and the people involved. This is obviously better but is still likely to leave you with less than optimal outcomes.

3. Trained and experienced—You don't react negatively. This neutral response to your negative situation begins to liberate you to think your way through and to focus on the other people involved. This is beginning to be a good response but might still leave you with problems under the surface, such as stress that can affect you later and still hurt your situation.

4. Master—The impulse or situation doesn't affect you at all. Practitioners often describe this as being like clouds passing in the sky: things come and go in the natural progression and you are accepting of this as natural.

The core of presence is "a profound opening of the heart, carried into action."

—Joseph Jaworski[12]

Be Confident, Witty, and Humorous

It doesn't perhaps match everyone's personality to be funny and confident, certainly not in any situation or culture (e.g., with friends and with strangers), but good dialogists do demonstrate confidence and wittiness just the same.[13] Some do so because they are nervous and want to connect with people and others do so because they are comfortable and able to see things in a funny way as a result.

In our dialogue workshops we help people practice improving their confidence by learning to stand and speak in more confident ways. In doing so we make reference to *SECS Appeal*, a term I derived by rearranging the attributes of good networkers as described by Malcolm Gladwell in his best-selling book *The Tipping Point*.[14] Gladwell's research suggests that good connectors, people who connect with more people than average, have what he refers to as CESS (curiosity, energy, sociability, and self-confidence). I simply turned around the letters to make this set of behaviors much easier to remember, something Gladwell perhaps recognized but chose not to use out of respect for readers who might be offended by the term.

Be Cheerful, Flexible, and without Melancholy

It is normal to want to be around happy people and avoid unhappy people. It is also well documented that this happy and positive disposition has a positive effect on the people around you.[15] One of the most popular writers on this subject was Norman Vincent Peale, whose 1952 book *The Power of Positive Thinking* sold millions of copies around the world.[16] Since that time an entire science of positive psychology has grown up and spawned all sorts of research and writing.[17] It is perhaps yet another obvious aspect of life that we have chosen to delve deeper into given the availability of time and resource now afforded to us.

Show Genuine Curiosity in Exploring What Others Have to Say

I like to define dialogue graphically as being like a box that, when open, can collect new ideas and insights but when closed is of little use to anyone. To transform simple communication into dialogue requires opening the box and the opening requires close observation and questioning following on what others have said. Showing genuine curiosity is demonstrated in two ways:

1. Your body language is engaged, present, focused, and excited in what the other person is saying.
2. You are asking questions directly arising from what the other person is saying.

A useful tactic that I employ ensures I open the box or open dialogue when in conversation with others is what I call the Ma-Ma technique. The Ma-Ma technique stands for mirror-ask, mirror-ask and is described in greater detail in the systems section of this chapter. First you mirror what the other person has said by reflecting what was said or the emotions with which it was said or both. Then you ask an open-ended question (beginning with what or how) and invite the other parties to tell you more about their thoughts and feelings on the subject at hand.

It is important for readers to note that if you are not genuinely interested in what the other person is saying, your body language will tell the other person you are not interested, so be aware. If you truly want to improve in this area become more compassionate about others and the problems they are living with, whether real or perceived. This compassion will reveal to you many things you might not have otherwise known and things you need to be aware of if you are wanting to achieve optimal outcomes.

Don't Multitask When in Dialogue with Others

Our ability to be 100 percent present has diminished since we became good at multitasking, so it is an obvious reminder that if we want to be present we should not multitask when in dialogue with others. This is equally true for parents (as outlined in Chapter 2), managers, partners, and teachers. If we really want to connect with people effectively we need to give them 100 percent of our attention.

Three common situations that exist today that should be curtailed if dialogue effectiveness is to be improved include:

1. People talking to each other while one of them is working on his or her computer: Stop typing, turn and face the person, and give him or her 100 percent of your attention.
2. People sitting in meetings checking e-mail on their BlackBerrys: Ask for breaks during the meeting when everyone can check their messages so total engagement is possible during the meeting proper.
3. People talking on their cell phones while doing other things noticeable to the listener on the other end of the line: Stop what else you are doing, sit or stand still and complete your conversation.

Recognize and Listen to Your Gut Feelings and Those of Others

Gut feelings are often correct and when not they still tell you something you need to be aware of, but people who lack presence often miss these signs and end up making less than optimal decisions.[18] Gut feelings are often indicated through visual expressions and 100 percent presence will not only make you more aware of your own feelings but allow you to notice the facial signals of the people that you are talking with so as to inquire about how they feel about the issue(s) under discussion.[19]

Often in dialogue with others I will sense that although they are saying that "things are fine" their body language tells me that things are not fine. The cues they give include eyes looking down (indicating possible specifics that cause them doubt that things are fine) or eyes looking up (indicating possibly they have no idea because they aren't really sure if things are fine or not). Another cue I look for is the assuredness of voice. I may be wrong in my assumptions looking at the eyes and listening to the voice and so I follow up with further questioning such as "What makes you think so" or "Why do you say that," and then again I watch their response to see if their body language reinforces the message.

Likewise I have come to listen to my own inner voice, which tends to speak to me in the silence of the night or in the peacefulness of my morning exercise. I should note that the most effective time is often my morning walk, which I take along a nature trail over the hills and along the coast of the South China Sea.[20]

The faraway stick does not kill the snake.

—Mocua tribe of Mozambique[21]

Respect

It goes without saying that dialogue will not generate between people who don't respect each other. What I am getting at here is the subtler aspects of respect that aren't readily apparent but that come through over time. Examples of respect problems can be seen in organizations where "new employees don't know how things really work around here" or where "the CFO only cares about the numbers." Respect is essential between people of differing perspectives but not always easy to create or sustain because the differences of perspective that bring the breakthrough ideas are the same differences that cause people to dislike, discount, or diminish each other's opinions. Good dialogists are able to overcome these problems through the following behaviors.

Be Inclusive of Others Regardless of What Diversity Separates You

Former Pope John Paul II proposed dialogue as "the only way to promote equitable solutions for a society, marked by respect and reciprocal acceptance."[22]

Inclusiveness suggests more than simple tolerance, it suggests actively including people of differing points of view into your dialogues. In my experience the most common reason why people get into conflicts at work is because the early project dialogues did not include all the stakeholders and then, just as new initiatives are being rolled out the user group erupts in disagreement either through surprise, disagreement, or simple disappointment at not having been consulted in the first place.

Examples abound of this sort of problem, but one that arose during the time of writing was in a school where extra work needed to be carried out by the teachers and the senior management team decided to allocate the work to specific individuals without asking the teachers what work they might prefer and how the work might be allocated fairly. By not including the teachers in the dialogue about who was going to be asked to do the extra work the result was predictable: People who had preferred tasks saw them allocated to other people who didn't like them, some tasks allocated were significantly larger than others making the distribution seemingly unfair, and little consideration was given to the ability of people to take on extra tasks given their existing workload. The result was disengagement, disillusionment, even disgust.

If something so straightforward as including teachers up front in the dialogue of extra duties was avoided it begs the question: Why did this happen? It turns out that the senior management team, swamped with work at the start of term, not wanting to handle the resulting conflicts and "waste of time" these conflicts would cause and having other more important matters to deal with, chose instead to simply push things through as they thought best. After all, isn't that what they are paid to do? The answer is yes and no.

Yes it is true that dialogue takes much more time than communication and that including all the stakeholders will take more time, but in doing so the dialogue results in a more optimal and lasting decision because all perspectives are incorporated and all the stakeholders are engaged in the decision. When deciding the extent of your inclusiveness you need to consider the impact on the quality of our decision making and the engagement of the people that will result by excluding stakeholders.

Be Diplomatic and Don't Criticize or
Use Judgmental Labels

A diplomat is someone who is tactful and skillful in personal relations and part of this tact comes from not criticizing people or labeling them as being "ignorant" or "insensitive."[23] Forrest Gump in the movie by the same name portrays a U.S. soldier whose relative lack of education cause some to label him as "stupid" but he learned from his loving mother to respond with the line "stupid is as stupid does." This is good advice for dialogists to remember. The person is not bad but the action that he or she undertakes might be considered bad by some people depending on their perspective. Dialogue allows for understanding different perspectives and results in changing your perspective of behavior.

For example, Americans once considered "unpatriotic" (e.g., liberal thinking citizens hounded during the Cold War for their "communist leanings") are now considered forward thinkers (Communist China is now a major trading partner of the United States).

Demonstrate Respect and Understanding for Others

The point here is that it is not enough to think you respect someone; you have to show them respect and understanding so that they and others around them see the respect that you are demonstrating for them. Dialogue is an interconnected exercise meaning what is in your head only comes alive through the sharing of words and actions with others.

When the Queen of Great Britain welcomed Pope Benedict on a state visit recently it was the first state visit in nearly 500 years ever since the Church of England split from the Catholic Church. By going far beyond anything her predecessors had done the Queen demonstrated respect and understanding to the Pope by welcoming him to make a state visit. The implications for dialogue were set years before and the results are already being seen in the resolution of Catholic versus Protestant problems in Northern Ireland, interfaith dialogue, and so on. It is not enough to simply say you respect or understand someone, you need to show them.

In this country, we deeply appreciate the involvement of the Holy See in the dramatic improvement in the situation in Northern Ireland. . . . Your Holiness, your presence here today reminds us of our common Christian heritage, and of the Christian contribution to the encouragement of world peace, and to the economic and social development of the less prosperous countries of the world. We are all aware of the special contribution of the Roman Catholic Church particularly in its ministry to the poorest and most deprived members of society, its care for the homeless and for the education provided by its extensive network of schools. Religion has always been a crucial element in national identity and historical self-consciousness. This has made the relationship between the different faiths a fundamental factor in the necessary cooperation within and between nation states. It is, therefore, vital to encourage a greater mutual and respectful understanding. We know from experience that through committed dialogue, old suspicions can be transcended and a greater mutual trust established.

—Queen Elizabeth II[24]

Be Sincere, Honest, and Dialogue with Proper Motives

Good dialogue is sincere and sincerity is derived through honesty and proper intent. Failure to be anything less results in suspicion and this can cause backtracking, conflict, and suboptimal outcomes. In my experience it is important that you make your intentions explicit through honest and open discussion because anything less, especially in the really important dialogues will cause the other party to doubt your intent either because "they never said it" or because "they looked distrustful." In our cross-cultural world it is crucial that you make extra efforts to state even what you might consider to be the obvious.

I was invited to assist in resolving a contract dispute that had arisen between a U.S. licensor and an Indonesian licensee. When the Asian currency crisis caused a rapid drop in the value of the Indonesian Rupiah the licensee no longer had the financial ability to pay the license fees. Until it was made explicit that the licensor would carry the licensee through the recession by accepting license payments in Rupiah rather than U.S. dollars, no attempt at dialogue could resolve the dispute caused by stop payment.

Show You Care and Can Be Trusted

Dialogue helps us learn to treat one another with the honor and respect required for helping us all to feel special.

—Linda Ellinor and Glenna Gerard[25]

Care and trust go closely hand in hand. Early in my career I was asked to introduce my chairman, Dr. Robin Stuart-Kotze as a speaker for one of the world's leading consultancies.[26] Robin's reputation preceded him and this led to the local country partner in charge to request the regional head of learning and development to contact me and arrange for Robin to speak at its upcoming regional conference. She called me, we discussed the details, and arrangements were made. In the lead-up to the conference the regional learning and development head received pressure from some of the other country managing partners to provide recorded samples of Robin's sessions so they could endorse his presence at the conference. Knowing that Robin was normally well received and having no recorded sessions available to share I told the learning and development leader that sadly we had no recorded sessions and that she would have to take my word for it that everything would go well. This answer obviously didn't sit well with the other country managing partners who were wanting evidence, so they pressured her to chase me. This caused her to call me repeatedly and in desperation I finally said "Trust me," to which she became quite distrustful (as I now know she should have), and although the session went exceedingly well, the L&D head quit her job shortly after the conference—finding it impossible to deal with her many bosses, making her life intolerable.

So what was the problem? Don't say "trust me." Show people that you can be trusted. She needed assurance and rather than respond with a lack of care I should have been compassionate for the difficult position she found herself in and then dialogued with her and her country-managing partners if needed to explore other possibilities to give them assurance their selected speaker was going to work out. Options included putting them directly in touch with other clients who had engaged Robin or setting up a conference call with Robin directly. In the end the client was happy and became a client of ours for many years, but the road was tortuous and it needn't have been. The more the head of L&D became stressed the less she wanted to dialogue. Showing that you care and can be trusted is infinitely better than saying "trust me," which inevitably causes people to do exactly the opposite. Anything less is simply not respectful.

Apologize and Take the Blame When Appropriate

No one is perfect but customers and clients expect their service providers to do their professional best and then to make arrangements when things go wrong. Failure to address the situation when things go wrong is disrespectful for the people affected. Addressing the situation is, however, very complicated given possible lawsuits if admitting negligence and given cultural biases to preferably not spotlight problems or loss of face.

One publicly reported situation arose when in 2001 a U.S. submarine surfaced rapidly underneath a Japanese fishing trawler causing the death of nearly everyone on board.[27] I happened to be working in Akasaka, a financial district of Tokyo at the time. As the story broke and then protests grew against Americans during the course of the week it became apparent that something very important was needed. It was not until President Clinton called the Japanese Prime Minister to apologize for the incident and suggest that he would help with the investigation that the backlash began to subside. The Japanese were waiting for the apology and its avoidance in the early days of the incident caused a lot of negative reaction.

One thing President Clinton was careful not to do was to assume blame for the incident. Although he apologized that the incident had occurred, he was careful not to give any indication whatsoever as to who was to blame for the incident because claims in any such situations can grow into the millions of dollars. Failure to apologize can be equally damaging in lost relationships and commerce, something we should all be careful to guard against in our dealings.

Involve All Key Stakeholders in the Dialogue

Failure to involve all the key stakeholders in the dialogue is the most common problem (in my experience) to unravel or delay previously agreed on plans. You cannot possibly garner engagement and support or craft an optimal solution if you are not in dialogue with all the key stakeholders.

It is easy to suggest that all key stakeholders should be included in the dialogue, but it is not always obvious how to do this. Many examples come to mind and the most challenging always seem to involve large scores of people who are themselves not well represented so that even if you wanted to include them it would be near impossible to do so.

A well-documented example that I was consulted on is the Samut Prakarn wastewater treatment plant construction that was projected by the Asian Development Bank and financed largely by the Japanese and American governments to significantly clean up the water pollution in the Chao Praya River in Thailand. The goal of the project was to reduce the significant number of deaths and illnesses being caused by the water pollution but the dialogue involved an incredibly large number of stakeholder groups. One of the most difficult groups to involve in the dialogue were the local villagers and fishermen who were not effectively represented (e.g., no "village chief," "mayor," or "senior fisherman" existed). Even if the people were well represented they were still distrustful of the bankers and civil engineers, none of whom came from the same culture as the villagers and fishermen. In the end various dialogue systems had to be used to involve the stakeholders.

In a 2005 paper by the World Bank aimed at encouraging more dialogue inside the World Bank to improve the project outcomes it was financing and managing, the authors identified three problems currently facing the bank's dialogues:[28]

1. Generalized dialogue mechanisms are not well-suited to the current operations of the bank or the state of global civil society.
2. Institutionalized dialogue mechanisms have suffered from weaknesses in transparency, representativeness, and accountability.
3. These mechanisms have been widely perceived as being vulnerable to World Bank manipulation and co-optation.

An excerpt from the same paper included the following assessment of dialogue inside the bank. I include the footnotes provided with this excerpt for readers interested in reading further on this topic. I highlight in **BOLD** what I consider most important.

"We agree with these democratic skeptics that the World Bank will not soon (and may never) be governed under a system that meets the minimum standards of a Madisonian or Continental democracy. *The important point for us, however, is how much more the World Bank could be doing to democratize its decision-making within these structural constraints by opening avenues for meaningful public participation.* Even in the absence of the formal mechanisms of governance that define democratic practice at the national level (such as direct election of representatives), there are substantial opportunities to apply basic democratic and participatory principles to all levels of policy, program, and project bank decision making.[29] Toward this end, we have identified five core participatory principles to inform World Bank decision making. These are:

- Transparency and Access to Information
- **Inclusiveness**
- **Quality of Discourse and Deliberation**
- Fairness under Rule of Law
- Accountability

The consistent application of these principles to all strategic and operational decision-making processes would ameliorate the democratic deficit that is experienced by citizens who seek to influence World Bank decision making. **These principles can help to structure participatory, responsive and predictable decision-making processes that can lead to better, more sustainable development outcomes by reconciling competing interests and visions of the public good through deliberation and negotiation.**[30] To do so, they must be applied with an eye toward redressing the profound inequities of voice, access, and political power between different interests in development debates. If they are applied in this way, they can be powerful tools to enhancing the capacity of poor and marginalized people to influence the decisions that affect their lives. If they are not, they are unlikely to improve outcomes very much."[31]

Demonstrate Other People's Perceptions Matter a Lot

Power that respects no one but includes everyone,
that calls for the best in people,
and that evokes great creativity, is love.
Dialogue can unleash the power of love,
not in a sentimental or moralistic sense
but in the genuine sense of true creativity.

—William Isaacs[32]

Johnny, the head of corporate social responsibility for one of my banking clients in Asia, is also the head of procurement for the bank. He is passionate about the environment and puts a lot of effort into every CSR initiative that he has launched. His passion is infectious and convinces many people to lend their support to his initiatives, all except one, his boss. Johnny's boss is the titular chairman of the environmental committee and is both overstretched in his role as chief financial officer for the bank and significantly more conservative than Johnny who has a background in sales. So what is the problem? Johnny's boss doesn't tell him that his environmental perceptions matter a lot to the Bank and to its image in the community. So in the absence of this lack of saying that his perceptions matter a lot, Johnny now thinks that his perceptions don't matter much to his boss and a divide is arising between them on this topic. The problem is that this is not true, both Johnny and his boss are both passionate about the environment but in their own way—Johnny more vocal and outgoing, his boss more reserved and studious.

Failure to tell others and truly demonstrate that you are interested in their perceptions, views, and opinions causes them to curtail their dialogue with you. In the end you become the loser for not knowing what people really think and at some point this lack of awareness will sting you and you'll ask yourself why they didn't tell you what they thought. People speak when listeners create the right space.

Demonstrating genuine interest in someone's perceptions is a great way to start. What do you think?

Accept that You Need Your Opponents' Perspectives to Make Optimal Decisions

> *To be objective is possible only if we respect the things we observe;*
> *that is, if we are capable of seeing them in their uniqueness and their*
> *interconnectedness.*
>
> —Erich Fromm[33]

Closely linked to the preceding behavior is the reality that you even need to know what your enemies think let alone your opponents. So just when you wanted to put down your opponents for causing you trouble or slowing you down the reality is that you can't possibly develop lasting optimal solutions if your ideas don't incorporate or address the ideas of your opponents. Failure to recognize and engage opposition simply leads to early failure.

Doing this requires strong leadership because in realizing that you might not win all the battles that you want to engage, you are also recognizing the interconnectedness of all things. Some ideas simply come before their time and although your idea might be a good idea it simply doesn't have the support yet of the majority.

I have worked with several situations where great ideas simply aren't getting the airing they should because opponents aren't accepting my client's ideas. In these situations the roles are reversed but the rule is the same—accept your opponent's perspectives to make optimal decisions. When the local newspaper wanted to launch a free supplement in the subway every afternoon, the idea's originator was ridiculed for wanting to give away a newspaper for free. The originator recognized that retail sales of the newspaper were insignificant when compared to the advertising revenue and created a barrier to distribution. When made freely available, readership skyrocketed and so did advertising revenues based on audited circulation numbers. Where did the detractors go? They realized that accepting their opponents' perspectives allowed for a better decision.

Recognize that You'll Need Each Other Either Now or Later and Explore Why

> *Any conversation or dialogue will be as powerful as the intention and skills of those who participate in it.*
>
> —Linda Ellinor and Glenna Gerard[34]

This final respect behavior goes further than simply stating that you should recognize that you need each other. It also suggests that good dialogists talk about why that is so and in so doing they reinforce the bonds that hold people together and through which dialogue can continue.

We all need each other but we seldom accept this and even rarer still do we state it. Some of the less obvious situations that warrant reminding here include:

- Companies need competitors to keep themselves innovating.
- Companies need change to prevent stagnation.
- Unions need management, otherwise they talk only internally.
- Inventors need stale situations to spur their desire to make improvements.

Be nice to people on the way up the ladder because you are going to see them again on your way down.

—Albear (author's father)

Expression (e.g., Voicing, Writing, Song, Dance, Art, Body Language)

> *To change the way we talk is to begin to change the way we think.*
>
> —William Isaacs[35]

Adjust Your Tone, Speed, Vocabulary, and Grammar to Match the Other Party

Good dialogists don't try to outsmart their dialogue partners, rather they upgrade or downgrade their vocabulary to match the other person and therefore remove the issue of education and class from playing a role (implicit or explicit) in the dialogue. Obviously, it is more common to need to simplify language because there exists a greater number of people with limited education, but occasionally it goes the other way and failure to be able to upgrade what you say and how you say it can minimize the conversation.

I have worked with all sorts of people from all sorts of backgrounds, from royalty to street people. One of the best pieces of advice I ever received was to keep my message simple and to compassionately focus on the other party. If you do this in most cases differences will work out for themselves. In those situations where people use language to eliminate people from dialogue (either language complexity or a different language altogether) you can rest assured that optimal outcomes will not be achieved because at least one entire group of stakeholders (those representing the excluded language group) is missed in the dialogue.

Prime the Environment through Words and Gestures so People Respond as You Would Like

> Words count.
> You cannot take back your words.
>
> —William Isaacs[36]

I interact regularly with Dr. Alan Stewart, a writer and practitioner of "conversations that matter." Alan is always priming his groups with lines that build their self-esteem ("Whoever comes are the right people") and puts them at ease among strangers ("When you are nice to people great things happen"). Dr. Stewart (who contributes to this chapter's section on dialogue systems) is a master of priming. He also understands the importance of asking people how they are doing and making personal links before diving into his business conversations. He recognizes the importance that food plays in priming people for dialogue as well.

Other people I have worked with like to prime for dialogue through making use of background music, simple kindness, showing respect, and so on. Of course you can also prime people by forewarning less happy emotions by wearing black, announcing sadness, muted tones, and so on. What good dialogists do is recognize that priming has a role to play and they do so consciously. Priming in negotiation has a long history with tactics ranging from general service complaints as a way to kick off a meeting with your service supplier, to loud rebukes at pricing offers when negotiating price. One client I know arrived for a technical service contract renewal only to find that his client had decorated the vendor-installed machinery with lemons to send a visible and scented impression that the machinery was no good.

Be Polite, Courteous, and Don't Use Foul Language

Not every word that comes to us needs to be spoken.

—William Isaacs[37]

Diplomacy generally refers to being tactful and respectful because good dialogists recognize that anything less can be misconstrued by the other party *especially* when the other party comes from another culture, which today is most of the time.

I attended a conference recently where the speakers managed to insult every group in the audience by the end of the day. Cutting jokes about weight, ethnic origin, intelligence, national origin, hairstyles, and accents were all used to ensure that everyone was laughed at. The conference organizers' intent was to encourage people to feel at ease, but I know some who were left feeling a lack of respect and thus unwillingness to indulge in extensive dialogue with the organizers, exactly the opposite of what the organizers had intended when planning the conference and selecting the speakers.

Speak from Your Experience (Not That of Others) and Avoid Storytelling

Communication inevitably arises in the moment of emergent interpersonal contact.

With or without the use of words, seeing and being seen yield an emotional interchange. Mere bodily proximity generates a flow of energy between people.

It is uniquely powerful, however, to meet each other through the power of language.

When we speak, some bit of the heart-mind is revealed.

Every day, through the mystery of language, we touch each other: mind to mind, heart to heart.

—Gregory Kramer[38]

Part of the success of good dialogists is that they aren't telling some-one else's story, they are telling their own and as a result their experience sharing is genuine, sincere, and convincing. If you find yourself telling other people's stories because you are limited in experiences yourself then you are singing from the wrong song sheet. Be yourself, don't make up stories, tell the truth because in sharing your actual experience you are helping the person(s) that you are in dialogue with to learn from different perspectives. Your actual life story, the good and the bad and how you responded to the ups and downs, is unique and worthy of telling. Let the other party do with it as they wish knowing that it is the only story they will ever believe of you anyway.[39]

It is worth mentioning here that in dialogue when two people speak from their experience an important new combined experience emerges that can lead to the jewels of wisdom, insight, and value that I spoke of earlier and that can fill the dialogue box. Anything short of honest and sincere expression risks degrading the dialogue back to simple two-way communication where little is learned or gained other than possibly awareness of each other.

Use "I-Messages" to Talk about Patterns of Behavior Rather Than One-Off Events

To speak the truth we must know the truth.

Because we are referring to the subjective truth, the truth of our experience, we must listen internally in order to discern this truth.

Thus, speaking enters meditative practice through the door of mindfulness.

—Gregory Kramer[40]

When sharing your personal experience it is useful to use "I-messages" to ensure that your observations are grounded in your experience and not mere opinions. Furthermore it is best that your observations reflect patterns of behavior rather than one-off events. Let's consider some examples.

- Ineffective message that can be construed as opinion and countered: "You always interrupt our dialogue to tell the kids to stop interrupting you." "You aren't role-modeling very well. If you did the right thing the kids would learn."

- I-Message: "I am frustrated when you repeatedly interrupt your dialogue with me to tell the children not to interrupt you. I think you are demonstrating exactly the opposite behavior of what you are asking them. I think if you ignored them they'd see they can't interrupt you effectively and they'd stop doing it."

The two preceding styles are both expressive and get the message out to the other party, but in dialogue the I-message is better received and defended than are messages not ground in personal observations. Although the other parties might disagree with your idea they cannot deny your perspective as expressed in your I-message. The most common responses are:

- Response to ineffective message: "I don't interrupt anything, it's the kids and if you were to tell them to behave it would be much easier to talk to you at night when you get home from work."
- Response to I-message: "I'm sorry I frustrate you but the kids frustrate me. Since I find it hard to ignore them what if we reinstate our Friday nights out so we have a time and place when we can regularly dialogue about family matters of importance without the kids being around?"

In needing to acknowledge the observations arising from personal experience and expressed through I-messages, the back and forth communication opened up into dialogue with a proposed idea to find a different space for dialogue and an admittance of their difficulty to avoid the children's interruptions in the evening after work. In this case, the I-messages generated two additional pieces of information whereas the traditional opinionated messages led to objection and rebuttal and not toward an optimal outcome.

Speak Your Mind and Share Your Feelings without Venting Rage or Anger or Lecturing Others

What we talk about matters. What we talk about, we think about, and what we think about forms the root of our actions and sets the tone of our lives.

—Gregory Kramer[41]

Dialogue by its very nature takes place after the storm of rage and anger. Even if emotions are under control sometimes people have a need to lecture others or to highlight the mistakes they have made by saying things like, "I told you to stay in touch with your clients. Now they are upset and say you never call. I told you so." Whether this piece of feedback is given with an angry tone or not it sounds more like parenting and less like leadership. Whereas children need to learn lessons as they grown up and experience life for the first time, adults don't respond well to being reminded of their mistakes and being put down by their superiors.

In situations where rage, anger, and lecturing occur, it is usually the needs of people expressing themselves that are being addressed rather than the need of the subject to, for example, learn strategies to prevent the problems they have caused from recurring. Expressing yourself and saying, "You are disappointed," "You thought they could handle it," "You are unhappy, you have to pick up the pieces," and so on, are all effective forms of dialogue, but losing your head, getting angry, and venting rage only serve to shut down dialogue and delay solutions from being found.

State the Mutual Purpose and Focus on Common Ground

The various religions are different languages through which God speaks to the human heart.

—His Holiness the Dalai Lama[42]

In a difficult dialogue I was helping resolve in Malaysia, my client needed data from a group company in order to complete its analysis and report to the regulators. Initially there were problems obtaining the data, ensuring that what was given was correct and ensuring it was complete. After repeated conflicts between the group companies and complaints from the regulators for late submission, the stakeholders involved agreed to focus on the common ground up front in the process and agree together on timelines they all could meet. By focusing on the common ground (satisfy regulators so we keep our trading license) and agreeing to mutually acceptable timelines the stakeholders evolved from blaming each other for why reports were late to actually working together to ensure that the regulator was kept happy. If the people involved did not switch and focus on their shared purpose and common timelines, no solution would have been reached and optimal outcomes would have remained elusive.

State What You Mean and What You Do Not Mean to Leave No Doubt in Other's Mind

Speech itself is just the tip of the tornado where mind touches down on the interpersonal terrain.

— Gregory Kramer[43]

Many people select this behavior as being more important than some of the others on this list, not because it is more important but because having overlooked it in the past, people are reminded of the problems they have incurred by only stating what they wanted without stating what they don't want. Making your instructions clear to someone is always difficult, so use dialogue to ensure that through your two-way communication what you want and don't want is in fact what they understand and state to be their understanding.

In preparing a consulting report on data collected from senior hotel marketing executives from around the world it became obvious that the junior consultant needed to do more than simply compile the data—she needed to make sense of the data. Making sense of the data required grouping like data, providing headings, eliminating duplication but weighting the data in a way that identified the most common responses. Finally the format of the data must also reinforce the key messages for which the data was collected in the first place.

The first version of the report resulted from simple instructions (communicated only) to compile the results. The second version resulted from more instructions and an attempt at dialogue but the junior consultants did not express their understanding and proceeded to make amendments that required further amendments. How could the formatting of the data been better communicated the first time? It should not have been communicated at all, it should have been dialogued with both parties expressing their perceived needs of the readers, their experience compiling such data, and their understanding of what the final product should look like.[44]

Inquire Appreciatively of Others by Asking Engaging Questions without Causing Bad Feelings

The first opportunity to shift the quality of conversation in a working group often arises when people are confronted with an opinion with which they disagree and find they must choose whether or not to defend their views.

—William Isaacs[45]

Appreciative inquiry has become a buzzword for an approach to organization development that through effective dialogue encourages finding out what is working well now, what processes would look like if they were working well in the future, and then designing and implementing change to achieve this better future. At its heart is the questioning of the stakeholders in a way that demonstrates appreciation for their first-hand knowledge and experience (good or bad), and most importantly not leaving people feeling bad through your questioning. For example, "Why did you do that?" is sure to cause ill feelings in situations where negative outcomes have resulted from someone's poor judgment. A more appreciative question might include "What conditions caused things to turn out differently than you had predicted?"[46]

Knowledge is developed from questions that arise in conversing.
—Alan Stewart[47]

When you inquire appreciatively or mindfully you aim to access what people know inside rather than what they have learned on the outside. Quoting Bentz and Shapiro:

"Learning involves taking things in from the outside whereas knowing is what happens inside. I may know because I've learned or simply because I find what was inside all along."[48]

My concept of dialogue aims to reveal the jewels of insight and wisdom, the breakthrough ideas that are always there but simply awaiting stakeholders in effective dialogue to reveal them.

Don't Wait to Know It All or Get It Right
before You Speak Up

> *Creating a positive future begins in human conversation. The simplest*
> *and most powerful investment any member of a community or an*
> *organization may make in renewal is to begin talking with other*
> *people as though the answers mattered.*

> —Alan Stewart[49]

When people communicate they work hard to polish their delivery. They rehearse their speech, get their PowerPoint slides in just the right order and wording, edit their texts to ensure that everything is just perfect. In dialogue we can't achieve optimal outcomes if we wait for things to be expressed in their final form because the very nature of dialogue suggests that ideas emerge and are given voice by the stakeholders.

Suspend (Judgments, Beliefs, Ego, etc.)

> *Getting to the "different place" that allows presencing to occur*
> *begins as we develop a capacity to let go and surrender our perceived*
> *need to control.*

> —Peter Senge, C. Otto Scharmer,
> Joseph Jaworski, and Betty Sue Flowers[50]

Good dialogists are able to put aside their own convictions long enough to ensure that they don't cloud their connection with people who present different views than their own. Put aside your beliefs, which doesn't mean dropping them or changing them but rather suspending them as you would suspend laundry to dry in the sun before taking them down and putting them on once again to wear in your daily life. It is difficult to suspend your judgment, beliefs, and self-interests because they have been well honed through upbringing, personal life experience, education, and culture. Despite the fact that it is difficult to suspend it is still the ability of people to do so, which allows for the opening needed where learning and compassion creeps in and, in doing so, the meeting of the minds often results in a new way of seeing things, a new insight or a jewel of dialogue that—without the coming together of differing views—it would have been impossible to see the breakthrough idea that was awaiting discovery.

So what behaviors am I actually referring to when I say that good dialogists are able to suspend their thoughts, beliefs, convictions, and egos long enough to connect with and understand the other stakeholders in a dialogue?

We don't know what is going to arise in the mind of our dialogue partner; we don't even know what is in his or her mind right now. How can we possibly know what will arise from our complex interactions? Humans are remarkably subtle, unpredictable, capricious, mysterious, and endlessly varied. Each of us arrives at the interpersonal moment deeply conditioned, with our bodies in certain states, our emotions and thoughts already careening down the mountain of the moment.

To think we can understand, let alone predict, what will emerge in any given conversation is a folly with a price. Prediction fills us with assumptions rather than truth. Rather than experience others, we experience our own projections, and the subtlety of emergence is lost.

—Gregory Kramer[51]

Sometimes it is easier to understand suspending when considering those people who don't. A current example is Pastor Terry Jones, the Protestant minister in the United States who threatened to burn the Koran on the anniversary of the attacks on the World Trade Center in New York (9/11) to make the point that Islam was a violent religion.[52] When asked to explain himself on a BBC Radio interview he admitted that he had never read the Koran but that because the only way to salvation was through Jesus Christ then all non-Christians, while possibly being good people, were not possibly going to experience salvation unless they converted. Pastor Jones could not suspend his belief that anyone other than Christians could possibly reach salvation regardless of how one defines salvation. His inability to suspend his opinion even for the short time of the interview, prevented any effective dialogue related to salvation, interreligious conflict, and so on.

Be Equal in Mind and Not Under Obligation to Others (Egalitarian)

Genuine dialogue requires an ultimate trust in the goodness people are endowed with and an effort to strike the right chord in their minds.

—Daisaku Ikeda[53]

The dawn of the twenty-first century is witness to the largest wealth and knowledge gaps in the history of mankind. These gaps cause people to think of themselves as having or not having wealth and knowledge more than ever before. This sentiment likewise leads to craving for more (for those with less) or a sense of being better off (for those with more). To compound the problems caused by the wealth and knowledge gaps, the hierarchical nature of organizations today, especially global multinationals, has caused the ladder from local to head office to have grown out of all proportion further leading to a mind-set of have and have not.

Successful leaders can, despite their position in life, dialogue with people in situations different than their own. This ability does not result from being equal but rather from being egalitarian, believing that we all have an important role to play and that our contributions are of equal importance because we must all give our best and realize our potential in doing so. Being equal in mind involves compassion on behalf of those more fortunate and respect by those less fortunate. Successful dialogue, however, is seriously broken when the less fortunate see their leaders taking advantage to enrich themselves at the expense of others either through corruption or privilege of office.

Obligations toward others, which result from the lack of an egalitarian culture, causes problems for achieving optimal outcomes because dialogue can often be affected by people "telling the boss what he wants to hear" or "not telling people the whole story because they can't do anything about it." Effective dialogue requires a voluntary exchange in an egalitarian context so that issues can be exposed and dealt with knowing the impact they have on the people involved.

Invite Opposing Views and Get All the Relevant Information onto the Table

> *We feel that when someone attacks our idea, they are attacking us. So to give up our idea is almost like committing a kind of suicide. But non-negotiable positions are like rocks in the stream of dialogue: They dam it up. One of the central processes for enabling us to enter into dialogue is the practice of suspension, the art of loosening our grip and gaining perspective.*

—William Isaacs[54]

Good dialogists know that there are always opposing views and seek out these views to enable the crafting of optimal solutions. Failure to incorporate opposing or differing views leads people to think that everyone thinks the same and that the decision they take will be the best decision.

A simple example of this behavior arises from the local municipal administration where I live in Hong Kong. In order to minimize the risk of accidents between bicycles and vehicles at intersections the local administration decided to install posts on the bicycle path, forcing cyclists to disembark before crossing the intersection. Their solution was taken without any input from cyclists who obviously have opposing views and believe that the line of sight at the intersections is sufficient to prevent accidents provided cyclists and vehicle drivers are looking out for oncoming traffic at the intersection, something they should be doing anyway. At first the posts were installed at a distance that allowed for the cyclists to drive through them without slowing down. This angered the local administration so the posts were pulled up and moved closer together making it virtually impossible to drive through the posts without stopping. In a classic suboptimal outcome the cyclists simply stopped using the bike path and now drive their bicycles on the road where their presence is not only a threat to the drivers but also slows down the road traffic. Rather than attempt to dialogue toward an optimal solution the local administration chose not to listen to opposing views and ended up spending money on an outcome that was worse than the situation they started with.

Thinking we know, costs us all we don't know—which is nearly everything.

—Gregory Kramer[55]

Demonstrate Openness to New Ideas and Interest for Subjects Not Your Own

Suspension is "the first basic gesture in enhancing our awareness."

—Francisco Varela[56]

Good dialogists are open to new ideas and welcome learning about subjects they know little about. This genuine interest motivates others to share with them what they know, allowing the dialogist to learn faster and more effectively about the issues at hand. As readers know from experience this behavior can be more or less positive but both ends of the spectrum are obvious and full of implications. We can all think of times when we wanted to discuss subjects of importance with people who showed little or no interest. Dialogue cannot proceed. Although it takes time to engage and show interest, failure to do so will limit the value of your decision making, so find the time for dialogue and show interest. It might make all the difference in the world. In scientific research today it is often the interdisciplinary researchers that are making the groundbreaking discoveries simply because they started with an interest for subjects different from their own.

When I became emotional, I could not even hear what was being said because I was swept away by my own mental tide of thoughts.

—Gail[57]

Be Flexible—Adjust the Time, Place, and Way You Dialogue to Achieve Your Outcome

In the presence of genuine understanding, goodwill and collaboration displace judging and blaming.

—Deborah L. Flick[58]

We are all creatures of habit and tend to fall into patterns talking about the same things in the same way and with the same people in familiar surroundings. You need only think of discussions with your family to realize that even as you age and return "home" the roles you plan in discussions with family members and their views seldom change. But when you take the same people and drop them into a new environment or change your morning discussions to lunch-hour discussions or adopt some new way of discussing issues, the quality of the dialogue can change significantly. The key here is that you should be flexible to change and hopefully the people with whom you are in dialogue are willing to change things around a bit, too.

People in offices over the past 20 years will know what I mean by changing the place when you think how much time you spend in dialogue in coffee shops today compared to 20 years ago when coffee shops were not nearly as present as they are today. Starbucks and similarly popular coffee shop outlets have become the staging areas for sales calls, appraisal meetings, job interviews, relationship building, and so on. Facilities management professionals and office designer architects are fully aware of the importance of providing a variety of places where people can dialogue today. Don't arrange to meet at the same time and place as you always do, ask yourself where should we go to stimulate the best possible outcome, for example, boardroom, art gallery, restaurant, golf course. Be flexible and you'll be surprised at how the outcome can change.

Avoid Either/Or Choices and Looking at the World as Black and White

> By observing my thought processes I transform them. This is one of the central transformational vehicles of dialogue.
>
> —William Isaacs[59]

The most typical signpost of people who fail to suspend are those who insist on things being right or wrong, black or white, yes or no. The tender process is an example of this mind-set. I was involved in a selection process recently to assist a not-for-profit organization plan and implement corporate governance changes. Several consultancies were selected to bid for the work and in the end there were two left—myself and the largest firm in the world. The choice facing the executive committee was which to choose. In my experience the best solution would have involved asking both vendors to collaborate together and address the solutions the organization was asking for. Many procurement situations today lead to forced collaboration between competitors, sometimes to good effect and sometimes not. At any rate in this particular situation, with a board famous for its lack of dialogue, the decision was always going to be an either/or decision and the majority went with the large well-established brand as opposed to the independent consultant. I subsequently met with the large firm and we agreed that the best outcome for the client in question would have been one of collaboration.

Readers are strongly advised to look out for either/or situations because they often lead to suboptimal outcomes and are based on an inability to dialogue through the conflicting gray area that inevitably exists between the two positions.

Another example is my dialogue work in environmental sustainability. Whereas eco-warriors want to put an end to, for example, oil extraction, they also fail to encompass into the dialogue how we can begin living without all the oil-based products that we all use on a daily basis. I don't pretend to have solutions to our present overreliance on oil but I know for certain that effective dialogue requires us to stop seeing oil production as a yes or no question and that the solution falls in the gray area, which suggests a declining reliance on petroleum-based products over a period of time to be agreed through dialogue.

Recognize That the Solution Is Found in the Dialogue and Not in Predetermined Answers

> *Suspension asks us to put on hold the temptation to fix, correct, or problem-solve what we see so that we can begin to inquire into what we observe. For those of us addicted to problem solving, this can be a challenging skill to develop.*
>
> —William Isaacs[60]

The main thesis of this book is that the solution is found in dialogue and that we need to rebuild dialogue into our lives if we are to have a hope at achieving optimal solutions. One of the impediments to finding the solution through dialogue arises when people believe the solution exists and needs simply to be researched or calculated and then followed.

In my conflict work with engineers it is common that the conflicting parties will agree to end the negotiation and create a working party that will study the variations (for example) and then conclude based on the scientific evidence who is responsible for what and they apply the compensation or liability accordingly. Readers with experience will know, however, that many situations lead to inconclusive evidence after which professional judgment, senior or negotiation takes over.

The power of dialogue emerges in the cultivation (in ourselves, as well as in others) of questions for which we do not have answers. Identifying one good question can be vastly more significant than offering many partial answers. To mine for questions is to cultivate the suspension of answers and to open the way for the dialogic way of being.

—William Isaacs[61]

Before wasting considerable amounts of time resolving conflicts by sending teams of experts away to study the situation, ask yourself if it is reasonable to think a scientific answer can be found and if not then pick a dialogue system and dialogue your way through. The more important the decision the more important it is that you suspend the thought you can avoid dialogue and simply do a study to find the solution. In most cases where the stakes are high you need research and dialogue to achieve an optimal solution.

Google + DIALOGUE = Optimal Outcome

The following reminders will help ensure your dialogues lead to better outcomes than might currently be the case.

Investigate and Understand Your Own Assumptions

As the noted physicist David Bohm used to say,

Normally, our thoughts have us rather than we have them.

—*David Bohm*[62]

Good dialogists investigate and understand their assumptions. By assumptions I refer to the common assumptions that seem so obvious we don't normally even question them. **Examples include:**

- Is it necessary?
- Can we help?
- Will it make a difference?
- Is it our fault?
- Is it their fault?
- Is it impossible?

And so on.

Investigating assumptions simply means that you ask questions of the stakeholders involved to check their perceptions and see if they have evidence your assumptions are right or wrong. Failure to test your assumptions makes an ass-u-me.

When you listen to somebody else, whether you like it or not, what they say becomes a part of you . . . the common pool is created, where people begin suspending their own opinions and listening to other peoples'. . . . At some point people begin recognizing that the common pool is more important than their separate pools.

—David Bohm[63]

Prior to the 2008 recession I was helping a large financial institution grow its organization in the Asia Pacific region. Asia was its fastest-growing market and everyone assumed that the U.S. head office wanted to strengthen its presence in Asia to sustain its global and local growth. This all made sense until the recession started and our assumption was found to be wrong. When cutbacks were deemed necessary and the board had to decide where in the world to make cut-backs in headcount, the majority of the board members happened to be from the United

States and Europe. As a result, in the board dialogue about cutbacks Asia's minority view meant that Asia was outvoted and the largest number of job cuts were applied to Asia. This decision, still considered by many as suboptimal, significantly hindered the presence and sustainability of the organization in their fastest-growing marketplace. Our initial assumption was wrong.

Find Compassion for Others and Accept That Everything Is Interconnected

Suspension of judgment is fundamental to dialogue. Without a strong intention to focus on its practice, conversations remain superficial or turn into battlegrounds. It is vital that we learn to suspend our judgments both internally and with others if we are to create conversations where the information we need is available to help us learn about and move beyond our current thinking into new territories.
                                        —Linda Ellinor and Glenna Gerard[64]

If you travel extensively and have the good fortune to step into many different organizations and cultures, you begin to realize how everything is interconnected and how everyone is simply trying to do their best to improve their own situations. Accepting that everything is interconnected and having compassion for others is part of what makes people good dialogists because they know that they have to understand others and uncover how the interconnections affect what it is they want to accomplish.

Dialogue is at the heart of our work as leaders.
                                        —Phil Carroll[65]

Continuing with my previous example, after the financial institution decided to significantly reduce headcount in Asia to survive the recession its main competitor saw this as an opportunity to pick up talented people with market knowledge in the market most strategic to their growth. The company losing the staff simply said it was getting rid of its least-productive staff. The competitor picking up the staff said it was delighted to acquire such talented people to grow

the market. The acquiring organization is now two years later significantly stronger and the people it recruited from the competitor are
performing better than ever because they are valued and given the
resources to do so.

---

*The method is mindfulness, the expression is compassion, and the
essence is wisdom.*

—Joseph Goldstein[66]

Readers are reminded that everything is interconnected as is the
compassion that you demonstrate to others because when you care for
your people they tend to put in the extra effort that makes you successful as a leader and makes your organization successful under your
tutelage. Give and thou shalt receive.

Help Others Suspend So They See Alternatives

*The Voice of Judgment can stifle creativity for groups as surely as for
individuals. It is what we typically call "groupthink," the continual,
albeit often subtle, censoring of honesty and authenticity in a team.*

—Peter Senge, C. Otto Scharmer,
Joseph Jaworski, and Betty Sue Flowers[67]

Many readers find themselves working in situations where they
are able to suspend their thoughts and emotions but are working or
living with people who find it difficult to suspend their thoughts and
emotions thereby causing problems for the organization or community
involved. How do good dialogists help others suspend their judgments
and beliefs long enough to open to dialogue? This requires care, compassion, and handholding.

Think for a moment of what it was like when you were a child
and the combination of your colorful imagination combined with
your lack of knowledge caused you to worry about things that should
not normally cause problems. Just such a situation occurred yesterday
when I hiked with my family over the mountain to the beach and
came across a neighbor with her son playing in the waves. Someone

nearby had captured a small fish and ask my neighbor's four-year-old son if he wanted to see it. Afraid, the boy said no so the man with the fish in his hands released it back into the waves. The fish, disoriented after being returned to the water, swam directly at the boy. In reaction to what was perceived as a shark attack the boy ran from the water. Only soothing words and a confident hand from his mother allowed the boy to return to the water and suspend his view of the small fish being a maneater.

In organizations we need to share our calming experience and sometimes hold the hands of people as we walk them into new territory where they can see how we suspend our judgments and learn to understand new perspectives. Being a role model is one of the strongest ways to encourage others so when you find yourself suspending your opinions explain to others what you think and what you are doing and then after-ward it is useful to explain how your perspective has changed. Your perspective always changes and although you might not change your beliefs you at least have gained a better understanding of the people with whom you disagree or diverge in opinion thereby making it easier to move forward into another round of negotiations.

> *You cannot do great things. You can only do small things with great love.*
> —Mother Teresa

> *If we can simply observe without forming conclusions as to what our observations mean and allow ourselves to sit with all the seemingly unrelated bits and pieces of information we see, fresh ways to understand a situation can eventually emerge.*
> —Peter Senge, C. Otto Scharmer,
> Joseph Jaworski, and Betty Sue Flowers[68]

Suspend Your Opinions about Other People's Opinions

This play on words is in fact something we often see in ourselves if we are looking and in others who express their opinions around us. People who are firm and vocal in their opinions often express disagreement with the opinions of others without realizing that in doing so they create similar reactions in others.

A client asked me recently to examine the financial statements and company situation for a business it was considering acquiring in Canada. The business in its mind was not worth what the seller was asking for it and yet it believed it could make a lot of money if it bought the business and turned it around. Inherent in the buyers thinking was the opinion that the seller thought its business was worth the asking price and was destined to grow at a rate greater than GDP in the coming five years. The buyer's opinion about the seller was narrowing the dialogue to the selling price and causing the buyer to overlook some of the underlying conditions that were affecting the industry and would almost certainly take effect in the coming five years. The dialogue had to widen to include these underlying issues if an optimal outcome was to be achieved but getting these other issues onto the agenda was only possible once the buyer was able to suspend (at least temporarily) his opinions of the seller.

Individuals and groups not aware of their assumptions are like planes on autopilot with no pilot in attendance.
                                          —Linda Ellinor and Glenna Gerard[69]

Absorb (e.g., Listening, Reading, Watching, Touching, Smelling, Tasting, Gut Feeling)

When the "theys" go away and the "we" shows up, people's awareness and capabilities change.
                              —Peter Senge, C. Otto Scharmer, Joseph Jaworski,
                                                  and Betty Sue Flowers[70]

Most books on communication will cover speaking and listening. In writing on dialogue I not only add respect, suspend, and presence to speaking and listening but I also find it important that we extend our concept to listening to cover all the ways that we absorb messages from others be it through our seeing, smelling, tasting, touching, or intuition. For this reason I like to call this set of behaviors absorbing. In cross-cultural and conflictual situations it is often these other forms of knowing that allow us to achieve optimal outcomes through effective dialogue with the stakeholders involved.

Watch People's Body Language to Check If It Validates What They Are Saying

The science of watching others is best summarized in the work by Dr. Paul Ekman who has spent more than four decades understanding the meaning of facial expressions.[71] People who want to excel at dialogue, especially dialogue across cultures, are suggested to learn more about this skill by reading one of his books, taking one of his tests, or watching one of his videos. I was drawn to the work of Dr. Ekman through his association with the Mind and Life Institute and its examination of how to regulate and minimize negative emotions. The ability to read body language also correlates with someone's emotional intelligence, what Daniel Goleman became famous for and which has come to be known as EQ (emotional quotient rather than IQ intelligence quotient).[72]

Listening to others requires quieting some of the voices that already exist within us.

—Deborah L. Flick[73]

It is not the role of this book to go into details on EQ and body language, but if you are in dialogue and you are hearing affirmative words but seeing doubt and concern in the face and body movements of the person in front of you then you need to ask questions and investigate why you are absorbing conflicting messages. For example: "I hear you agree with our proposition but when I look at you I don't see you smiling, I don't see light in your eyes; instead I see what looks to me as a feeling of resignation and surrender as if you cannot win so you are going to learn to live with the decision. What is causing this mixed signal?"

Often the mixed signals that you detect in dialogue are subtle, come from a deep place, and are not even recognized by the person sending the messages. By being observant and putting words to what you are noticing you can help others recognize their own emotions. To engage in dialogue in these situations it is often good to come back to the topic later in an informal time and place to see what more you can learn.

Balance Talking and Listening, Not Every Word That Comes to You Needs to Be Spoken

People do not listen, they reload.

—Tara Poseley[74]

Good dialogists manage to limit how much they talk to others so that they can listen carefully and absorb the full message being delivered in the dialogue by the other stakeholders involved. The analogy that comes to mind is that of the wild deer I often see on my early-morning walks in Canada. In that special time between when the deer sees me and when it runs off deeper into the forest it exhibits a heightened sense of focus as if it can absorb every noise and movement between and around us so as to understand and assess the situation. It does not make a noise. Good dialogists also demonstrate this same presence, assessing continuously if expression is needed or if expressing their thoughts at all would get in the way of absorbing the expressions of others. Good dialogists ask themselves whose needs are being met when you express yourself. If it is better for the outcome to shut up and listen, they have no difficulty doing so. If you find it difficult to remain silent like the deer then I encourage you to give it a try and you'll be amazed at what you learn in the silence.

Listen to Others' Feelings to Understand Their Perspective and Uncover Their Intent

A mind that listens with complete attention, will never look for a result, because it is constantly unfolding; like a river, it is always in movement. Such a mind is totally unconscious of its own activity, in the sense that there is no perpetuation of a self, of a "me" that is seeking to achieve an end.

—J. Krishnamurti[75]

Peter Senge provides us with a practical approach to listening for feelings. In his *Fifth Discipline Fieldbook* Senge suggests listening to dialogues with a two-column blank sheet of paper in front of you.[76] In the right-hand column jot down notes of what is said and in the left-hand column write in what you are thinking and feeling about what is said. This practice heightens your awareness of emotions underlying words in dialogue. It is based on the research method of Chris Argyris and Donald Schon.[77]

The heart of dialogue is a simple but profound capacity to listen.

—William Isaacs[78]

A variation of the preceding practice has you write down what is said in the left-hand column and what you think the speaker is feeling in the right-hand column. Regardless of how you handle this reflection, hone your understanding that what we say and why we say it need not be the same and that both need to be understood if you are to absorb the full message being sent from the other parties in your dialogue. Following is an example of several interpretations of the same message and a reminder of how important it is to continue the dialogue after absorbing these incomplete messages:

What Is Said	Perceived Emotions of Speaker
I'm okay with your suggestions.	I don't like your suggestions but I'm not going to fight them.
I'm okay with your suggestions.	I like your ideas and only have a small enhancement to recommend.
I'm okay with your suggestions.	I disagree with your suggestions but I'm not going to tell you. I'm just going to quit so I don't get blamed after things go wrong.
I'm okay with your suggestions.	I don't understand what you are talking about but won't say so in case you think less of me.
I'm okay with your suggestions.	What I understand is completely different from what you are thinking.

Mirror What Others Say and Ask a Related Question to Deepen Your Understanding (Ma–Ma)

The greatest compliment that was ever paid me was when one asked me what I thought, and attended to my answer.

—Thoreau[79]

Possibly my favorite tactic after nearly two decades of international negotiation and dialogue consulting is what I call the Ma–Ma tactic (mirror-ask, mirror-ask), exemplified by the Russian doll that has several layers and after opening one layer it reveals another then another and so on. The Ma–Ma tactic does the same thing by revealing increasing levels of awareness by asking questions of the other party based on what you have absorbed to date. Following is an example of the Ma–Ma tactic.

Speaker	Listener Absorbing Message and Using Ma-Ma Tactic to Open Up the Other Party to Gain Greater Understanding
I'm okay with your suggestions.	Mirror—So you are comfortable with my suggestions?
No, not comfortable but okay.	Ask—What would it take to move you from okay to comfortable?
I don't think we have the working capital to afford the purchase in this quarter.	Mirror—So you are concerned about cash flow?
Yes, exactly.	Ask—How can we improve the impact on the cash flow?
We can tell the vendor, we prefer to wait for delivery, or we can take delivery but defer payment.	Mirror—So you think the vendor might be flexible?
Yes, in this recession they'll do anything for a sale even if it means financing sales through deferred payment terms.	Ask—How long do you think we can defer payment?
Don't know but I can ask.	Great.

In the previous dialogue, if the listener had accepted okay to mean yes and had moved on to another topic the opportunity of deferred payment might have been lost forever; however, booking the sale in the current quarter with payment only next year might well define an optimal outcome to the vendor and the client, and yet it might never have been achieved if the dialogue was not pursued inside the acquiring company.

Build a Ladder of Inference Connecting the Situation to Perceptions, Conclusions, Assumptions, and Beliefs

> For it is a listener's experience, yes the listener—the hearer—who
> determines the meaning of an utterance. . . . The listener hears
> whatever he or she hears, and we never know what that is.
>
> —Pille Bunnell[80]

Ladder of inference is another idea strengthened by the valuable work of Peter Senge and his team and documented in the *Fifth Discipline Fieldbook* referred to previously. A ladder of inference, descending from the top, suggests that our **actions** are based on our **beliefs**, which are based on our **conclusions** about the world, which are based on the **assumptions** drawn from the **meanings** we add to the **data** that we **observe**. One of the great values of dialogue is that by building on the observations of all the stakeholders, the basis for our actions will be much more robust. Let's consider the role of dialogue at each rung of the ladder of inference:

Rung of Ladder of Inference	Where We Can Go Wrong	How Dialogue Can Help
Actions based on beliefs	We take the wrong decision and do the wrong thing.	Dialogue among people will ensure common ground despite differing perceptions about how to achieve the same objectives.
Beliefs based on conclusions	Our beliefs could be wrong simply because our conclusions are wrong.	Beliefs are influenced by culture, so effective dialogue up to this point can begin to expose how different cultures can derive different beliefs from the same situations.
Conclusions drawn from assumptions	The same set of assumptions can lead to different conclusions, ours could be wrong.	Dialogue about meaning can mislead but if done well will more often lead to the right conclusion.
Assumptions drawn from meanings	Without testing, our assumptions can be wrong.	

(Continued)

Rung of Ladder of Inference	Where We Can Go Wrong	How Dialogue Can Help
Meanings derived	We can err in what we think it means.	
Data selected	We can select biased data from our observations.	Dialogue about data selection tends to ensure the most accurate selection.
Observations	We can't see everything.	Dialogue among stakeholders gives us the most complete view possible at any given time.

Understanding the value of dialogue in Senge's Ladder of Inference reminds good dialogists of what James Surowiecki described in his book *The Wisdom of Crowds*—if you ask enough people you will reveal the right answer.[81]

Don't Jump to Conclusions, Invoke Your Professional Skepticism

When we listen deeply for the collective meaning moving through a conversation and speak from this place, our contributions will prove to enhance the shared meaning.

—Linda Ellinor and Glenna Gerard[82]

As an auditor with one of the world's leading external audit firms I had an intense apprenticeship in professional skepticism. Never will a highly trained auditor look at a set of unaudited financial statements and assume they are correct. Likewise, professionals of all shades are trained to use their professional training and experience to substantiate their belief of what is correct and true and not to assume or jump to conclusions. Likewise in dialogue it is important to absorb the various messages that are being emitted from the situation (what is being said, done, written, etc.) and then assess if these messages are one of consistency or if something seems amiss. If you begin with a skeptical mind you will tend to find problems or opportunities for improvement more often than if you blindly accept what is said, done, or put in front of you for signature.

A common situation where mistakes are made in this regard is when decision makers are presented with a single option, a need to take a black or white decision and some external pressure, for example, a deadline, to make a decision. In my experience, in these situations people are often left renting the wrong flat, buying the wrong asset, hiring the wrong person, engaging the wrong supplier. So what to do? Test your assumption about the deadline, examine the gray area of the decision and invoke your professional skepticism.

Think about *Why They Said What They Did before You Ask Them*

In dialogue we draw something forth from the unknown together,
but taking turns.

— Gregory Kramer[83]

This is similar to the previous suggestion that you reflect on the emotions behind what you hear said; however, this step takes it one step further and asks the question "Why?" so that you can build your own assumptions before asking the other parties to explain themselves. This heightened awareness will prevent surprises, allow you to alter how you might ask follow-up questions, and so on. Here is an example:

What Is Said	Why You Think They Said It	How You Might Follow Up
I'm okay with your suggestions.	They want to signal their willingness to proceed.	"How would you like to help?"
I'm okay with your suggestions.	They are reluctant to give 100 percent endorsement.	"How can I get your 100 percent commitment?"
I'm okay with your suggestions.	They disagree but don't want to tell you so as to avoid conflict.	"I'm glad you see some merit in my suggestions but I'm a bit concerned others might oppose me. What can we do to make these proposals air tight?"

Recognize *Effective Dialogue Results from Good Questions Rather than Good Answers*

You know, I have always prepared myself to speak. But I have never prepared myself to listen.

— Jiddu Krishnamurti[84]

This point is exemplified by the preceding sample of questions that will obviously lead to different outcomes. I am reminded of something I heard years ago when training as an auditor. Someone told us, "You can tell how experienced someone is by the questions they ask you."

All these years later I realize this to be dramatically true. Some dialogue systems are focused on getting the question just right. I'm less concerned about getting one question just right and am more interested in surfacing the various questions that need to be resolved in organizational contexts so that optimal outcomes can be achieved. Yes, some questions are more important to answer than others but importance changes with the situation and questions come and go because when one gets answered another appears. Good dialogists recognize that asking questions is what takes a conversation from being two-way communication and opens the box into which jewels of insight can emerge.

Opportunities are often missed because we are broadcasting when we should be listening.
> NB: The author of this quote is unknown, but his or her thought-provoking words provide an interesting perspective on what is taking place in business today, where more and more discussions center around the "voice of the customer" (VOC).[85]

Diagnose and Explore Why They Respond with Silence

The awareness and understanding that we need to resolve difficult conflicts, to align disparate cultures, and to integrate the dissociated forces prevalent in our wider society are already present within us.
> —William Isaacs[86]

Some questions lead to silence and it is importance to diagnose and explore what causes their silent response. Silence is very telling and while nothing is being said it is important you continue to absorb the body language because body language never stops talking.

All listening starts in silence.
> —Jiddu Krishnamurti[87]

Some of the more common reasons people respond with silence include:

- They are thinking about the question.
- They are offended by the question.

- They don't know the answer.
- Their culture tells them to let others answer first.
- Their culture suggests this is a conflictual issue and better left unaddressed.
- They don't know how you will respond to what they want to say.
- They are pausing for effect.

The clearest truths are spoken from silence.

—Gregory Kramer[88]

Recognize feedback as a gift regardless of how nicely it is wrapped.

Dialogue is not just talking with one another.
    More than speaking, it is a special way of listening to one another . . . listening without resistance . . . it is listening from a stand of being willing to be influenced.

—Sarita Chawla[89]

Some cultures wrap feedback in the most beautiful packing and others give it to you on the edge of a knife in the stomach. Regardless of how you receive your feedback it is important that you see it as a gift because in so doing you will respond positively. For example: "Thank you for letting me know this is obviously important and you clearly feel strongly about it."

Living and working in Hong Kong allows me to observe many forms of delivered feedback from the veiled feedback common to conflict-averse Confucian cultures to cynical British culture that points out what's wrong with something before focusing on what is right to sometimes overly optimistic American culture, which tends to believe everything is possible. Of course, optimal outcomes need a proper dose of positive thinking to see the light of day, a bit of cynical conservatism to moderate the risks involved, and sensitivity to how the ideas fit culturally into the Asian context because missing feedback on any of these fronts can lead to failure or suboptimal outcomes.

Not providing the answer, when it was so evident, was described by one infection control officer as "more difficult than trying to stifle an oncoming sneeze. To take the extra few minutes to pose questions," he continued, "rather than provide the answer, took a lot of self-control and practice on my part. Only after did I begin to realize that the extra time I thought was being wasted in getting the staff to come up with the solution, actually translated into immediate uptake of their solution once they were discovered or created. Far from time wasted, it was saved. With positive deviance you go fast by going slow."
—Richard T. Pascale, Jerry Sternin, and Monique Sternin[90]

Dialogue Skills in Summary

The preceding discussion of basic dialogue skills (PRESA—presence, respect, expression, suspension, absorbing) is meant to remind us of our human gift of dialogue and your role as dialogue leaders. None of these skills are alien to us but as we superimpose ethnic culture and life beyond the digital tipping point we are losing touch with these important skills. Practice will allow you to rebuild and hone these skills. You can practice anywhere and anytime with the people around you.

The dialogue leadership skills I refer to as PRESA overlap and reinforce the conversing skills I listed at the start of this book. Take a moment to compare PRESA with the following list of conditions needed for successful conversing:

What we do when conversing in dialogue:

- We welcome and introduce people to each other as we would friends in our home.
- We introduce the purpose or question.
- We collaborate in an open, friendly format.
- We build ideas together with enthusiasm.
- We develop ideas rather than try to score points or persuade others.
- We harness the collective intelligence of the group.
- We enlarge each other's vision.
- We express our mind and heart (thoughts and feelings).
- We listen to understand and to identify deeper questions that further our dialogue.

How we converse in dialogue:

- We interact with curiosity rather than telling.
- We notice and honor the emotional underpinnings of others and our own responses.
- We recognize that right and wrong, winning and losing are irrelevant.
- We welcome diversity of opinion as the wellspring of creativity.
- We sustain openness to creativity.
- We appreciate the value of interdependency.
- We recognize and acknowledge blind spots in our own perspectives without losing face.
- Whenever we treat each other well good things happen.
- We assemble stakeholders to stimulate each other in an interactive live setting.
- We invite people into the dialogue to share their perspectives at key junctures and whenever they feel moved to do so.
- We link ideas and disparate perspectives.

Rebuilding dialogue skill is not the only thing needed to reduce dialogue gaps. We also need to pay attention to rebuilding dialogue spaces where dialogues take place. We need to put in place dialogue systems to ensure that dialogue continues once our focus diverts back to the content of our problems and away from how we might solve them. The next part of this book looks at the foundational elements of dialogue space and how to rebuild dialogue spaces back into our lives at work, at home, and in society.

Dialogue Cases for Consideration

Business Development Dialogues—A

One of the world's largest accounting firms worked with me to design a **three-pronged approach to improving their engagement management.** The basis of our international intervention was dialogue and after training an internal team of senior leaders to help drive the message, training was rolled out to various groups through one-day workshops. A day on dialogue helped everyone understand the quality of the dialogues differentiated everything from risk management to client engagement and service excellence. A day on engagement negotiation dialogues helped improve recoveries and a day on business development dialogues helped win new business both with existing clients and with new clients.

Business Development Dialogues—B

The president of a significant **asset management company in the Caribbean** hired me to work with his teams in Cayman, Bahamas, and London to introduce dialogue and set them on course for rapid growth. Their previous leadership had been conservative and the corporate culture was introverted and not client-focused with little exception. Due to legal and regulatory changes it became imperative that the organization learn to dialogue effectively and quickly for three reasons: (1) to improve operations, (2) to improve business development, and (3) to improve customer service. We provided training to all staff, top to bottom, something that had never been done, and the result was a significant transformation. The result was that this firm survived the industry changes while many of their competitors did not. One small example was the readiness that account executives showed when clients flew in on their private jets or sailed in on their private yachts and demanded, as one would expect, six-star service from their bankers. Part of the problem here resulted from the service providers living a dramatically different lifestyle than their clients. Once dialogue helped identify the differences and the impact on expectations, dialogue also derived workable and reasonable solutions.

Service Dialogues—A

A few years back I got to **"hot jack" with a girl called Su** in the Philippines. Before your imagination gets the better of you let me explain that "hot jacking" is the term used for people who listen in live to call center dialogues. Su was the operator and I was invited to listen in and learn about the operations in the call center so that I could suggest some ways to improve the quality of the dialogues. Su and the overall operations left me very impressed with the level of training, supervision, and automation. In only a few minutes Su was fielding calls from five different countries, committed the organization to financial commitments (within her allowed limits), handled customer inquiries and complaints, and kept on top of a technically challenging environment knowing that I was watching and listening to everything she said and did. She was being recorded by the system for subsequent review. How can call centers improve their dialogues? Ask the people. Su felt she definitely could use training especially around de-escalating angry callers and handling her own emotions while in dialogue with the callers. Do call center employees really dialogue or do they mainly communicate? Obviously following my definitions most of what call centers offer today is communication but occasionally—to great positive or negative effect—the opportunity for dialogue arises and is either seized or missed. This is where training can assist.

Service Dialogues—B

When asked to help improve **customer service dialogues in the Bahamas** I realized I had a tall challenge ahead. All cultures have their strengths and weaknesses and my time in Nassau had shown me both—a real willingness to take all the money the cruise-line passengers could disperse and say your prayers at church for times to improve. Indeed the combination of incoming storms and outgoing capital has left much of the Caribbean challenged economically. The typical U.S. tourist was now returning home having been delighted by top Thai service in Asia only to make a dash down to Nassau at Spring Break and wondered why the same could not be achieved closer to home.

To help get my message across I looked to two local heroes: one was the local basketball coach who graciously received me (peering down from seven feet) at his church Sunday morning; the other was the doorman, Eric, at the Hilton. Eric had a razor memory and a presence that filled the entire lobby of the big Colonial Hilton. What was it that these two people had that others were lacking and how could it be replicated? Presence—the feeling you get when someone is 100 percent focused on you, remembers you, your name, and in Eric's case, the time you left the hotel, where you went, a genuine desire to know how your visit went, where you are going for dinner, when's the best time to arrive there, and so on. Some think this behavior is reserved for paying guests but the same impression was had by local bank staff who knew him for years and frequented the hotel for lunch. The basketball coach was busy but Eric accepted my invitation to speak to my group. I wanted him to try and tell the audience what made him the best service ambassador for the hotel and possibly the best in all the Bahamas. What did Eric say? He'd never been to school, he grew up "over the hill" (which in Nassau meant a very poor part of town complete with crime, malnutrition, and disease), and he wasn't good with words, but when he looked someone in the eye he remembered them forever and he genuinely cared about them because it was people like that who got him to where he was today, greeting some of the most important visitors to his country. Presence and compassion. Do some have this executive presence while others don't? I think we all have it and we simply misplace it sometimes when we aren't thinking straight. Next time you want to win a client's trust and admiration, just think of Eric at the big door to the Colonial Hilton and talk to your client like she is the most special person in the world at this moment. Your presence will enable you to recognize and remember things about that person that you'd otherwise overlook and if you overlook these things so, too, will your client easily forget you.

Service Dialogues—C

At their global conference in Cebu I had the chance to share some of my dialogue ideas with members of the **Worldwide Airlines Customer Relations Association** (WACRA). These are the people—typically the directors of customer service or communication—who have to deal with the inevitable glitches in service that range from lost bags to loss of life, not an easy role for anyone. The more years these people had been in the industry the more stories they could share, good and bad. They were particularly interested in the following dialogue ideas I shared with them:

- The Ma-Ma technique (mirror-ask, mirror-ask) as a simple reminder for their staff not to overlook the emotional state the passengers are in when they address the ground staff looking for help.
- Challenge mapping as a technique to quickly understand a problem from many different stakeholder perspectives.
- Motivational dialects and how to change what you say and how you say it to better connect and influence people.
- Conflict sequence to understand that some people who seem to be handling the stress in fact are near breaking point and useful de-escalation techniques should be used.

Organization Development Dialogues

I was invited to work with one of the world's leading six-star hotel groups in connection with the opening of their new property in Shanghai ahead of the Shanghai EXPO in 2010. A conference had been arranged for all the leading directors of marketing and communication from around the world and I was to be a speaker cum seminar leader for a half day. Obviously I focused on dialogue and together with the organizers we looked at the need, quality, and **ways to improve dialogue internally with colleagues and externally with customers.** It was a great session and plenty of valuable ideas were shared and recorded. Following the event we surveyed all the participants asking them what they were doing to implement the ideas they committed to at the conference. That's when we began to see signs of the digital tipping point and dialogue gap slipping in because even though we had a great dialogue together, once the participants were dispersed again around the world into their local hotels working with colleagues who weren't equally inspired to improve dialogue the initiative fizzled. To sustain interest we analyzed the ideas and separated them into actionable items and other ideas that needed work. Again these were sent out, but there was little or no response. What's the problem? Here is a glimpse of the world today in a six-star hotel in China. How do you manage the dialogue with your most important customers? Internet. Don't you have drinks with the hotel manager anymore? No, those were discontinued because everyone was uncomfortable in the setting. Is there any coordination between group communications personnel and local hotel personnel? Yes, but it is focused on the communication campaigns more than on dialogue with customers. But people choose to spend more of their money where they feel appreciated so shouldn't any campaign start with this? Yes, but . . . the dialogue continues.

Notes

1. Smart boards are interactive screens, like large tablet computers, which teachers can use to lead classroom learning. Their use is relatively new (invented in the early 1990s) but quickly becoming widespread because research (http://partners.becta.org.uk/page_documents/research/wtrs_whiteboards.pdf) suggests positive results. Although I am sure they improve teaching and learning, I encourage teachers to ensure that they don't replace simple dialogue, especially in kindergarten and early primary where sitting in a circle on the floor still results in some of the most valuable learning and could usefully be imitated in families and offices if only people were willing to give it a go.

2. Readers interested in learning more about dialogic education are directed to www.robinalexander.org.uk/downloads.htm. Robin Alexander has written two commonly cited books on the subject: *Towards Dialogic Teaching: Rethinking Classroom Talk* (Dialogos, 2008) and *Education as Dialogue: Moral and Pedagogical Choices for a Runaway World* (Dialogos in conjunction with Hong Kong Institute of Education, 2006). Alexander's five principles of dialogic education (2006) include:

   Collective: Teachers and children address learning tasks together, whether as a group or as a class, rather than in isolation.
   Reciprocal: Teachers and children listen to each other, share ideas, and consider alternative viewpoints.
   Supportive: Children articulate their ideas freely, without fear of embarrassment over "wrong" answers; and they help each other to reach common understandings.
   Cumulative: Teachers and children build on their own and each other's ideas and chain them into coherent lines of thinking and inquiry.
   Purposeful: Teachers plan and facilitate dialogic teaching with particular educational goals in view.

3. *Presence* (New York: Doubleday/Currency, 2005), 140.

4. As quoted in P. Senge, C. O. Scharmer, J. Jaworski, and B. S. Flowers, *Presence* (New York: Doubleday/Currency, 2005), 234.

5. *Insight Dialogue* (Boston: Shambhala Publications, 2007), 229.

6. John Kabat-Zinn, *Full Catastrophe Living* (New York: Random House, 2009).

7. Readers looking to improve their mindfulness are suggested to consider books related to Buddhist philosophy such as those by the famous Vietnamese Buddhist Monk Thich Nhat Hanh whose bestsellers include *Anger, Living Buddha-Living Christ, No death-No fear* (Riverhead Books) or books on Christian-centering prayer such as *Call to the Center*, Basil Pennington, First Image Books, 1990.

8. As quoted in Gregory Kramer, *Insight Dialogue* (Boston: Shambhala Publications, Inc., 2007), 161.

9. Mayank Chhaya, *Dalai Lama, Man, Monk, Mystic,* (New York: Doubleday, 2005).

10. *The Power of Positive Deviance* (Boston: Harvard Business Press, 2010), 77.

11. Readers wanting to learn more about this important topic are directed to the following books: *Destructive Emotions*, Daniel Goleman, Bloomsbury, 2003; *Happiness*, Mathieu Ricard, Little Brown, 2003; *Anger*, Robert Thurman, Oxford University Press, 2005; *Anger*, Thich Nhat Hanh, Riverhead Books, 2001.

12. As quoted in Senge, Scharmer, Jaworski, and Flowers, *Presence*, 234.

13. Many of the attributes of good dialogists were uncovered reading between the lines of the following books: *Conversation, A History of a Declining Art,* Stephen Miller, Yale University Press, 2006; *Dialogue, Rediscovering the Transforming Power of Conversation,* Linda Ellinor and Glenna Gerard, John Wiley & Sons, 1998.

14. *The Tipping Point, How Little Things Can Make a Big Difference,* Abacus, 2000.

15. Alan Loy McGinnis, *The Power of Optimism* (New York: Harper & Rowe, 1987).

16. Norman Vincent Peale, *The Power of Positive Thinking,* Foundation for Christian Living, 1952.

17. Dr. Martin Seligman, working out of the University of Pennsylvania, Positive Psychology Center is perhaps the best-known researcher in the subject of positive psychology. According to the center's website: "Positive Psychology is founded on the belief that people want more than an end to suffering. People want to lead meaningful and fulfilling lives, to cultivate what is best within themselves, to enhance their experiences of love, work, and play. We have the opportunity to create a science and a profession that not only heals psychological damage but also builds strengths to enable people to achieve the best things in life." Further details available at: www.ppc.sas.upenn.edu/index.html.

18. Malcolm Gladwell, *Blink: The Power of Thinking without Thinking* (New York: Penguin Books, 2005).

19. Paul Ekman, *Emotions Revealed* (New York: Henry Holt, 2003).

20. In his book *Awake in the Wild, Mindfulness in Nature as a Path of Self-Discovery* (New World Library, 2006), Mark Coleman suggests that putting yourself into nature is an effective way to build mindfulness and presence. Coleman quotes William Blake "Great things are done when men and mountains meet."

21. As quoted in Richard T. Pascale, Jerry Sternin, and Monique Sternin, *The Power of Positive Deviance* (Boston: Harvard Business Press, 2010), 7.

22. As quoted in W. Isaacs, *Dialogue and the Art of Thinking Together* (New York: Doubleday/Currency, 1999), 360.

23. *The Concise Oxford Dictionary,* Clarendon Press, 1992.

24. Excerpt from the speech given by Queen Elizabeth II to Pope Benedict on occasion of the Pope's historic state visit to Great Britain, September 2010.

25. *Dialogue: Rediscover the Transforming Power of Conversation* (New York: John Wiley & Sons, 1998), xlix.

26. Dr. Robin Stuart-Kotze is chairman of Behavioural Science Systems and author of several books including *Performance*, Prentice Hall, 2006. Readers interested in learning more can visit www.momentumcpi.com/html/ aboutbss.html.

27. www.independent.co.uk/news/world/americas/nine-remain-missing-after-us-sub-hits-japanese-fishing-boat-691244.html.

28. *A Call for Participatory Decision Making: Discussion Paper on World Bank – Civil Society Engagement,* April 2005, commissioned and presented by Civil Society Members of World Bank – Civil Society Joint Facilitation Committee.

29. Daniel D. Bradlow, "The World Commission on Dams' Contribution to the Broader Debate on Development Decision-making," 16 Am. U. Int'l L. Rev. 1531, 1551 (2001c); William D. Coleman and Tony Porter, "International Institutions, Globalisation and Democracy: Assessing the Challenges," Global Society, vol. 14, no. 3 (2000): 388.

30. *World Commission on Dams* (2000), xxxiv; Michael Edwards, *Civil Society*, Polity Press (2004), 60; Woods (2003).

31. *A Call for Participatory Decision Making.*

32. *Dialogue and the Art of Thinking Together* (New York: Doubleday/Currency, 1999), 395.

33. *Man for Himself* (New York: Henry Holt, 1990), 104.

34. *Dialogue: Rediscover the Transforming Power of Conversation* (New York: John Wiley & Sons, 1998), 62.

35. *Dialogue and the Art of Thinking Together,* 308.

36. Ibid., 309.

37. Ibid., 163.

38. *Insight Dialogue* (Boston: Shambhala Publications, 2007), 163.

39. Parker Palmer, author of *To Know as You Are Known* (New York: HarperCollins, 1993), is a firm believer of the fact that long after your expertise fades it is you and your persona that people remember.

40. *Insight Dialogue,* 165.

41. Ibid., 186.

42. *Toward a True Kinship of Faiths* (New York: Doubleday Religion, 2010), 49.

43. *Insight Dialogue,* 168.

44. Readers might recognize valuable management theories underlying this case such as *Situational Leadership* by Hersey and Blanchard or "Begin with the End in Mind," Steven Covey, *7 Habits of Highly Effective People,* Simon & Schuster.

45. *Dialogue and the Art of Thinking Together,* 41.

46. Readers interested in learning more about this area are recommended to read *Mindful Inquiry in Social Research,* Valerie M. Bentz and Jeremy J. Shapiro, Sage, 1998. This book was co-authored by my professor (Bentz) from the Fielding Graduate Institute and widens the subject of inquiry by looking at various traditions and cultures of inquiry that affect dialogue and the achievement of optimal outcomes.

47. *The Conversing Company: Its Culture, Power and Potential,* 2nd edition (Adelaide: Multimind Solutions, 2009).

48. Bentz and Shapiro, *Mindful Inquiry in Social Research.*

49. Ibid.

50. *Presence,* 96.

51. *Insight Dialogue,* 143.

52. www.theaustralian.com.au/news/world/terry-joness-koran-fire-protest-plan-burns-out/story-e6frg6so-1225918479142.

53. Daisaku Ikeda and Majid Tehranian, *Global Civilization* (London: British Academic Press, 2004), 9.

54. *Dialogue and the Art of Thinking Together,* 135.

55. *Insight Dialogue,* 144.

56. Francisco Varela, http://en.wikipedia.org/wiki/Francisco_Varela; as quoted in Senge, Scharmer, Jaworski, and Flowers, *Presence,* 29.

57. As quoted in Gregory Kramer, *Insight Dialogue,* 121.

58. *From Debate to Dialogue* (Boulder: Orchid, 1998), 40.

59. *Dialogue and the Art of Thinking Together,* 144.

60. Ibid., 147.

61. Ibid., 148.

62. *Thought as a System* (London: Routledge, 1994); D. Bohm, *On Dialogue* (London: Routledge, 1996).

63. As quoted in (Alan Stewart) 2nd edition. *The Conversing Company: Its Culture, Power and Potential* (Adelaide: Multimind Solutions, 2009).

64. *Dialogue: Rediscover the Transforming Power of Conversation,* 77.

65. As quoted in Isaacs, *Dialogue and the Art of Thinking Together,* 22.

66. As quoted in (Melvin McLeod) *Mindful Politics* (Boston: Wisdom, 2006), 126.

67. *Presence,* 31.

68. Ibid.

69. *Dialogue: Rediscover the Transforming Power of Conversation,* 79.

70. *Presence,* 45.

71. *Emotions Revealed,* Paul Ekman, Henry Holt, 2003. www.paulekman.com/.

72. Readers will find several books by Daniel Goleman but my favorite is *Destructive Emotions,* Bloomsbury, 2003.

73. *From Debate to Dialogue,* 71.

74. As quoted in Isaacs, *Dialogue and the Art of Thinking Together,* 18.

75. *Can Humanity Change?* (Boston: Shambhala, 2003), 168.

76. Peter Senge, Art Kleiner, Charlotte Roberts, Richard Ross, and Bryan Smith, *The Fifth Discipline Fieldbook* (New York: Doubleday, 1994).

77. Chris Argyris and Donald Schon, *Theory in Practice* (San Francisco, Jossey-Bass, 1974).

78. *Dialogue and the Art of Thinking Together,* 83.

79. As quoted in Kramer, *Insight Dialogue,* 151.

80. As quoted in Alan Stewart, *The Conversing Company.*

81. James Surowiecki, *The Wisdom of Crowds* (New York: Doubleday, 2004).

82. *Dialogue: Rediscover the Transforming Power of Conversation,* 289.

83. *Insight Dialogue,* 159.

84. As quoted in Isaacs, *Dialogue and the Art of Thinking Together,* 83.

85. www.telusinternational.com/_ pdf/Voice_of_Customer_TELUS_0609.pdf.

86. *Dialogue and the Art of Thinking Together,* 385.

87. As quoted in L. Ellinor and G. Gerard, *Dialogue: Rediscover the Transforming Power of Conversation* (New York: John Wiley & Sons, 1998), xxxviii.

88. *Insight Dialogue,* 178.

89. William N. Isaacs, "Taking Flight: Dialogue, Collective Thinking and Organizational Learning," *Organizational Dynamics* 22 (Autumn 1993).

90. *The Power of Positive Deviance* (Boston: Harvard Business Press, 2010), 117–118.

Chapter 5

Dialogue Time and Space

Your work as a leader is to create environments where it is safe and highly valued to speak up and contribute different views.

—*Linda Ellinor and Glenna Gerard*[1]

D ialogues take place in time and space and good dialogue lead-ers manage these factors knowing that they are both of great importance. In this chapter we explore the elements of both time and space and share experiences where these factors made a differ-ence in outcomes achieved.

Dialogue time refers to the fact it is time to dialogue versus com-municate. Dialogue timing refers to the actual timing of the dialogue (e.g., start time, duration, finish time, and pace). In this chapter we cover both dialogue time and dialogue timing as well as other aspects related to time.

Dialogue Time

At our summer home in Lac Des Iles the boys around my age seemed to outnumber the girls 11 to zero. It wasn't surprising therefore that my father used to impose a "quiet time" during which kids were meant to be quiet and parents could enjoy their happy hour watching the sunset over the lake. This quiet time reminded us of the importance of being quiet and proved to be a positive reminder later in life of taking time for silence. Somehow this silence also created space later on for more positive dialogue.

In addition to the importance of having quiet times, it is important that we reinstate dialogue times into our daily lives. Dialogue times are purposeful intervals amid the noise and haste and communication of our daily lives when we slow down to think together in dialogue. These times are needed to synchronize our understanding and prepare our response to the increasingly dynamic world in which we live.

We need to reinstate dialogue times at work, at home, and in society. Here are a few examples of what is suggested.

Dialogue Times @ Work

Team meetings should include an agenda item called *Dialogue* in which important issues are thought through with a view to achieving optimal outcomes. It is useful when these discussions are not cut short to agree on conclusions, actions, or decisions because it is often better to "sleep on it," connect with others informally, meditate personally, do research, and resume the dialogue later with a view to reaching conclusions.

Dialogue time is needed to allow people to think together and address the issues facing the organization. In work places today these important moments are few and far between but differentiate successful from unsuccessful organizations.

Some of the common dialogue times used by organizations are listed in the following table. Consider which of these opportunities your organization uses and which, if any, you can adopt to create more dialogue time for yourself.

Dialogue Times @ Work	Advantages	Disadvantages
Employee focus groups	To get input from employees when you know they won't otherwise express themselves. To allow employees to generate ideas together.	Can be dominated by expressive employees. Can be perceived as being directed from the top.
Skip level meetings	Good for situations where staff are motivated to tell the boss directly. Useful where you know middle managers are arresting the flow of ideas.	Can cause middle managers to feel stepped on. Can create opportunity for politicking.
Town hall meetings	Efficient way to dialogue with large groups. High-profile demonstration of dialogue.	Can unravel into conflict. Need to be professionally facilitated.

(Continued)

Dialogue Times @ Work	Advantages	Disadvantages
Financial results announcements	Simple communication of results gives opportunity for dialogue on related topics.	Speakers need to know how to handle prying questions.
Lunch with the boss	Informal environment gives staff chance for mentoring. Useful for introverted bosses who don't like formal settings.	Information might be misconstrued. Opportunity might be highjacked for personal agendas.
Employee appraisal meetings	Great chance to motivate. Align personal and corporate goals.	Nervousness prevents dialogue. Solely interested in rating.
Employee development plans	Focus on training and experience opportunities. Clarification of career aspirations.	Development plan nonexistent. Employee has no idea of what they want.
Career development path-sharing days	Employees learn how people made it to the top.	Requires preparation. Not all career paths are worthy of sharing.
Women's interest network	Helps retention and development of women.	Can't be assumed men don't need the same, too.
Brown bag lunch talks	Low cost and easy to organize.	Informality sometimes leads to low-quality dialogue.
Customer appreciation days	Great chance to hear from your key accounts.	Biased sample because those who participate are already converts.
Staff appreciation days	Great chance to generate discussion.	Need facilitation as these tend to be more related to saying thanks than for dialogue.
Birthdays and anniversaries	Pure celebration leads to learning about things informally.	Don't want to weigh down celebrations with heavy topics of dialogue.
React to news release sessions	Staff often have questions and emotions they want to share about company news releases. Allows you to gauge reactions. Allows you to better manage leaks after announcements.	Can turn into gripe sessions. Routine announcements not always seen as worth meeting to discuss.

Dialogue Times @ Work	Advantages	Disadvantages
Periodic departmental meetings	Useful for standing agenda items. People save items for the meeting.	Leaders not always prepared for unexpected topics.
Quarterly and annual dinner	Celebrations and useful times when most people are together in person.	Bosses aren't always well prepared to speak to large crowds. Needs facilitation.
Annual strategy sessions and updates	Very useful since things change and people need alignment.	Needs professional facilitation. Some people think they are a waste of time.
Leadership development workshops	Leadership development should include training and dialogue. Allows time for reflection and sharing.	Trainers aren't always prepared to handle off-agenda topics of importance to participants.
Regular training workshops	Nonthreatening opportunity for organization development.	Participants want to get the skills and leave. Requires proper facilitation and follow-up.
Local project team meetings	Improve efficiency and effectiveness. Improve relationships.	Hard to find time to stop doing work long enough to discuss how you do the work.
Appraisal sessions	Good to put appraisal into larger context of career and organization development.	Hard feelings can shut down dialogue and allow only for communication of the ratings.
Award presentations and celebrations	People are assembled and motivated.	Must be careful of who is not in the room.
One to one with direct reports	Good old management discussions are still the best.	Managers need training as today few experience proper feedback sessions.
Others		

Dialogue Times @ Home

Families and couples should turn off the television and other digital gadgets in the evening when they are home from work so they can connect with each other in full presence on a daily basis. Although life today naturally prevents us from achieving ideal connections on a daily basis, it is important that couples and families attempt to connect every few days if possible.

Common dialogue opportunities:

- Meals
- Birthdays, anniversaries
- Weekends
- Festivals
- Special achievements

Something I encourage couples and families *not* to do is to replace dialogue times with communication times and think they are still connecting because they aren't. Examples of this include sitting around watching TV or movies or playing PC games together. Although some connection is made, the problems associated with the digital tipping point prevent full presence and inevitably important thoughts and feelings will be brushed aside in favor of the diversion at hand.

Dialogue Time in Society

Community leaders should ensure that their meetings include periods of dialogue where people can dialogue on matters of importance to them. It is recommended that trained facilitators lead these dialogues because the topics are often full of conflicting views and personal agendas and the number of people involved is often quite large.

Examples of dialogue opportunities in society:

- Town hall meetings
- Committee meetings, for example, school, club, church
- City council meetings
- Charity events
- Sports and recreation groups and events

- Environmental and social concern groups
- Commercial groups
- Spiritual gatherings
- Births, deaths, marriages, anniversaries
- Festivals
- And so on

Starting Time

Human knowledge is limited by time and space.
  Only through dialogue can we expand that time and space.

—Kant[2]

Too early—Dialogue leaders know that if they start a dialogue too early people won't be interested for a variety of reasons:

- It isn't urgent.
- We don't yet understand the importance.
- We aren't prepared.
- Something else has to get done first.
- Other stakeholders aren't ready yet.

Climate change is one example of the challenge faced by dialogue leaders who want to engage people into the topic but find that people are asleep to the urgency of the conversation. This has led to one nongovernmental organization (NGO) called Pachamama Alliance to launch what has become a globally popular seminar entitled www .awakenthedreamer.org.

Too late—Dialogue leaders also know that if they commence the dialogue too late people won't be interested, for example, teenagers aren't generally interested in sex education at school if they have previously learned everything they want to know from other sources.

Not enough time—Dialogue leaders also know that if they cut off dialogue on key topics before issues have been fully aired then the topic is likely to move to another space and time and not really come to an end.

If, for example, the boss is talking to his or her direct reports about changes at work and asks for people's input but then after a while says, "Okay, that's all the time we have, everyone back to work," if the changes aren't fully talked through the employees will continue the topic at lunch, over coffee, through instant messaging, at the next meeting or elsewhere.

Too much time—Dialogue leaders don't like overdoing a topic because people lose interest and it can waste time and resources but achieve little additional benefit. Good dialogue leaders know when to start a dialogue and when to bring it to a close.

Duration—Dialogues tend to follow regular timing and provided the number of meeting participants is say 10 to 30 people, then in my experience the following rules apply:

- Each issue takes roughly 20 minutes.
- Issues where conflict exists, time can easily double to 40 minutes.
- Issues take longer after lunch when people have low energy after eating.
- Issues are resolved faster when people want to depart, for example, end of the day.
- The speed of dialogue is altered depending on use of a facilitator, moderator.
- Process moves can speed dialogue and reduce conflict, for example, following the three-step rule for questioners:
  - First ask them why they ask this question.
  - Then ask others what they think.
  - Finally you can address whatever issues remain, not otherwise addressed by the questioner themselves or the other stakeholders involved.
- Experience teaches you what topics/issues will lead to conflict but if you lack insight just ask the stakeholders to get a handle on the key issues

Pace

> *Speed is the source of all suffering.*
>
> —Unknown[3]

The pace of a dialogue is related to several things:

- The number of stakeholders.
- Stakeholder willingness to express themselves.
- Knowledge of the topic.
- Inherent conflict.

Dialogue leaders need to be adept at ensuring that people are okay to move on without cutting off important input. They do this in a few simple ways and become better at it the more they work with groups:

- Watch body language of stakeholders to see if they are impatient and want to move on or hesitant and have something to add.
- Ask stakeholders, especially the silent ones, if they have anything more to add and, if yes, great, if not, thanks and move on.
- Ask overexpressive stakeholders to not repeat anything already covered so as to keep things moving along.
- Change the style of the meeting to address mood and energy changes, for example, bio breaks, stretch breaks, BlackBerry breaks are all commonly used by experienced dialogue leaders.

Frequency

One aspect of time that is important to address is the frequency of dialogues. In situations where change happens fast, more occasions for dialogue are recommended; for example, daily, weekly, monthly, but in situations where operations are fairly stable then dialogues can be timed around natural evolution such as quarterly, semi-annual, annual (at least), or when there is a new account manager, service representative, and so on.

The Present Moment

One of the powers of dialogue is that it can teach us to develop a membrane or a muscle so that we can be big enough to receive someone else's pain deeply enough to learn from it.

—Linda Ellinor and Glenna Gerard[4]

The dialogue puzzle also includes several icons of time. The candle, stress meter, and the word presence remind us that focusing on the present moment is important if we are going to successfully achieve optimal outcomes. If we are focused on the past we will be stressed about what was and if we are focused on the future we will be stressed about what might be, but if we focus on the present we will be able to dialogue better and achieve the outcomes we aim to achieve effectively.

Time Management

The stopwatch, urgent/important table, and 960 months are all reminders of the importance of managing our time effectively. Nine hundred and sixty months is simply an average lifespan. Our time is finite and for many of us, myself included, we have much less than 960 months of life left in us. As a result of our limited time on this earth we must be vigilant of how we spend our time, choosing to focus on what is important and not necessarily only on what is urgent. Some of our most important dialogues revolve around what is important but not urgent. Examples of these sorts of topics include the following.

Important not urgent—often pushed away by current concerns:

- Self-development, nutrition, and fitness.
- Organization development, including evolving products, services, and talent.
- Societal development.
- Environmental development and protection.
- Spiritual development.

Dialogue Space

Just as the cauldron contains the energies of molten steel, dialogue involves creating a container that can hold human energy, so that it can be transformative rather than destructive.

—John Cottrell[5]

Dialogue time is hard to consider without considering space, and the dialogue puzzle purposefully fits them side by side for this reason. The easiest way to understand dialogue space is to consider the word PATH. In business school, students are taught about the importance of the carrot and stick when discussing motivation and getting people to do things. The carrot is the incentive like compensation and benefits and the stick is a bad appraisal or lack of bonus. Having spent time with animals who are directly literal with carrots and sticks I also noticed that the path on which they travel is also important. If a mule doesn't like the path you are trying to motivate them to take in the mountains both your carrots and your sticks will come up short and they will sit or lie down not wanting to proceed.

We are reminded that the path or the environment that you create is also an important factor in creating effective dialogue leading to optimal outcomes. PATH in this case refers to the place, the agenda, the trust, and the healthiness of the environment. I address each of these factors next.

Place

The place you choose for your dialogues should be effective, efficient, and culturally in tune with the audience and objectives of the dialogue. It is important that you take the time to consider your options available and not limit yourself to the places you have always met. You can dialogue anywhere in the world, so ask yourself where would be the best place for this dialogue given the outcomes the stakeholders want to achieve. The place you choose should take into account the following:

- **Effective:** For example, modern office furniture and fittings allow for comfort while being connected with each other face-to-face and via video conference.
- **Efficient:** For example, well-chaired meetings all for the best route from a to b.
- **Culturally in tune:** For example, no inappropriate words and actions—everyone is comfortable along the way.

Agenda

People will participate in dialogues if they believe that the agenda will address their needs. If not, they might attend in person but never show up mentally and the meeting is likely to be a communication session rather than a dialogue. To get the agenda just right you should address the following issues:

- **Complete with contradictions:** For example, most challenging dialogues hold inherent contradictions like "cut down the trees to build the park" or "spend to save." Your agenda has to include these inherent contradictions if you want people to believe you. You need to visit all the issues en route to achieving optimal outcomes.
- **Prioritized:** Dialogue participants will be focused on what is important for them so your agenda should reflect this and if you don't know what is important then the best way to start your meeting is to ask them what they consider to be priority.
- **Goal-oriented:** People are committed to the path because they know it will get them to their goal no matter how hard it is along the way. If your path doesn't take them to their goal they won't be joining you for long.

Trusting

Communication takes place everywhere whether people are engaged or not but dialogue needs trust if it is to take place. A trusting space needs at least three elements to be present:

- **Safe** to voice out: For example, pointing out mistakes or areas for improvement is okay because doing so will lead to corrections and improvements but if constructive feedback leads to a backlash then the safety is lost and it will be impossible to continue the dialogue.
- **Open** to new, wild, even conflicting ideas: for example, you only arrive at breakthrough ideas when starting out with what might appear to be wild ideas in their first instance. Dialogue participants who discount or disregard different ideas (because people are not suspending their beliefs and assumptions) will quickly fall short of achieving optimal outcomes.
- **Fun:** For example, we can sing and dance together, we will rejoice along the way. Optimal outcomes often come out of a fun space and not out of an environment of dislike or conflict or boredom. If you want to create valuable dialogues you need to consider what you can do to make it fun.

Building Trust

> *Dialogue is the weapon of peace.*
>
> —Daisaku Ikeda[6]

Trust creates a sharing that goes a long way to creating the dialogue space you require. Parker Palmer reports from a lifetime developing *Circles of Trust* around the globe, which we must trust in four areas:[7]

- Trust that the soul will help us listen and respond.
- Trust that each stakeholder has goodwill and intent sufficient to hold the dialogue space.
- Trust that our methods will safeguard our relationships.
- Trust that the solution is in the dialogue.[8]

Trust is really PRESA in practice because if stakeholders are in fact present, respectful, expressive, suspending, and absorbing then trust will exist. When some or all of PRESA is absent so, too, will be trust.

One important element to build trust is inviting, welcoming, listening to, and respecting the input of others. People should react positively (even if you disagree you can say it is a valid point or acknowledge their feelings) and transparently (don't say one thing and do another).

After dialogue it is important that stakeholders close the loop or tell each other what was done as a result of the dialogue. Absence of closing the loop simply leaves people wondering what happened, if anything, doubting the trustworthiness of the other stakeholders and reluctant to invest their time in future dialogues.

We believe that there is a greater need than ever for leaders to meet and genuinely "think together"—the real meaning of dialogue.

Only through creating such opportunities can there be any hope of building the shared understanding and coordinated innovative action that the world desperately needs.

The Marblehead Letter[9]

Healthy

Dialogues also need to be healthy for the mind, body, and soul. Although dialogue itself has been shown in earlier chapters to be conducive to health, the topic of the dialogue also needs to be healthy if it is to lead to optimal outcomes. Healthy dialogues should be good for the mind, body, and soul.

- **Head**—The main consideration here is the **purpose** and **intent** of the dialogue, what will it really address, for example, speaking out will help rather than hinder your career, our awareness will grow, we will win, achieve peace, and so on; for example, being a part of the dialogue will help rather than hinder, we will tire but grow stronger.
- **Heart**—Two aspects that affect the heart in any dialogue are whether the dialogue is inviting and validating. Absence of either of these things will lead to a shutting down of the dialogue and non-attainment of optimal outcomes.
  1. **Inviting**—It is important that people feel comfortable in your space so pay particular attention to cultural-, gender-, and age-related needs.
  2. **Validating**—It is important that stakeholders feel that their thoughts and emotions are validated by the dialogue participants

so they feel empowered to continue to contribute. Once validation is lost, dialogue will diminish and soon all you will have between the stakeholders is communication (sadly).

- **Soul**—There are a number of things that link dialogue and soul and for me the most important of these include:
  - **Inspiring**—For example, tackling the real challenges inspires people to higher performance. Effective dialogue should inspire and energize by helping stakeholders see beyond what individually people might not think possible. Dialogue is sometimes described as a form of meditation, helping you get centered and connected with others. Some dialogues even result in what some people describe as a spiritual calling resulting in transformational change. Dialogue space can inspire because of who is involved, the timing, and the history, architecture, decoration, scent, lighting, and so on of the location selected.
  - **Truthful**—People have to be honest with each other and with themselves if optimal outcomes are going to be achieved. Although it is not always easy for us to be honest with ourselves it is important that we are honest with others and when they observe things about us we must honestly take on board their perspectives because others can often see things about ourselves that we can't see well ourselves. Anything less than full honesty leads to a separation of role and soul, which can only lead to unhappiness.[10]
  - **Contradictory**—A leader's ability to "hold the space" in difficult dialogues is defined by his or her ability to continue dialogue despite:
    - Knowing the history of conflict between the parties involved.
    - Understanding and acknowledging currently conflicting issues.
    - Handling the strong emotions inherent in the dialogue with compassion and care.
    - Having faith that the solution is in the dialogue.
    - Having conviction to persist despite the cynicism, resistance, and negative behaviors that would cause lesser people to give up.

Place Options

There are several icons on the puzzle and these are to remind you of the options that present themselves to you when you dialogue. Traditional communication places like the Internet and cell phone are not recommended for dialogue. Instead I recommend face-to-face locations like a meeting table, a recreation location (golf course), over drinks (martini glass, but I am not suggesting that alcohol is needed, indeed usually it is better without), and my personal favorite is nature (among the trees).

Sustaining Dialogue

The next chapter addresses the challenge of sustaining dialogue over the course of time in an organization regardless of whether leaders are dialogic. In my experience it becomes important to inculcate processes to ensure that dialogue is sustained because as people change so does the willingness and ability to dialogue effectively.

Dialogue Cases for Consideration

Relationship Dialogues

Annie saw me on the local bus from the pier to my home and asked me what I had been up to lately. I explained my writing about dialogue gap and then Annie became all serious and the remaining five minutes until our stop was filled with complaining about her husband Alan who spent all his time now on his computer but the couple never talked anymore. They were married before the dawn of the Internet and Annie longed for the times she and Alan used to sit around just chatting. Annie still enjoyed chatting regularly with friends and you seldom see her on her cell phone either for voice or text calls. Annie fears that Alan has been lost to life beyond the digital tipping point where relationships get shortchanged and communication continues but genuine dialogue and presence seem to recede into nothing but a memory. What can Annie do to regain dialogue with her husband? She has to schedule time, agree that all digital gadgets will be turned off (phones, TVs, BlackBerrys), and they can focus time for each other for a while in dialogue on subjects that matter to them and their family.

Sourcing Dialogues

I was invited to facilitate and train technology procurement experts on the finer points of negotiation and dialogue. As part of this exercise we completed a challenge map to understand what was stopping them from achieving optimal outcomes. It turned out that the main challenges did not lie with the vendors from whom they purchased hundreds of millions of dollars of hardware and software every year; it was the internal dialogues with the technology experts who work with the kit purchased by procurement. Although this wasn't a surprise to me because I know that most people have their hardest dialogues and negotiations internally, the revelation did come as a surprise to the procurement group. An obvious next step is to widen the dialogue to include these stakeholders, but why is it not happening? It is back to the question of dialogue gap. If there is a gap between the quality of the dialogue we need and the dialogue we have, can the one or two people responsible for the dialogue gap recognize a need to fix it? Not normally. So in this case time is needed to garner more support to help identify opportunities for more optimal outcomes.

Education Dialogues

Universities used to be ivory towers that sat on the top of the hill and all the privileged and smartest kids from the area would go there to acquire knowledge and earn a degree before finding their way in the world. Then came globalization and the Internet and suddenly some universities expanded their "hill" to cover the world while others stayed put on their original hill where they had been for hundreds of years. Suddenly the global universities were earning fees from hundreds of thousands of students from around the world and moving in the jet stream of knowledge creation and dissemination while the local ossifying universities were battling growing costs and declining profits. I was approached by one university interested in expanding their hill into Asia. When I explained what might be needed to expand the university's footprint, the university representatives explained their professors declined invitations to travel overseas and preferred to stay home given their busy schedules. So how to change people and engage in dialogues of this sort? It is important that everyone become more aware of how the world has changed and that ways be found to comfortably (and quickly) get the professors expanding the university footprint. And as one client loves to tell me "If you can't change the people, change the people."

Societal Development Dialogues—A

I was invited to meet Talat at the poolside of the Taj Mahal Palace in Mumbai. Being from Istanbul, the meeting point between Europe and Asia, Talat felt it necessary to share his thoughts on dialogue with me because as he said, "Even taking these few days leave to be on vacation here in India makes me nervous because while I am away adults with terrorist intents might well talk to my students and convince them to join their terrorist groups which are recruiting students in Istanbul. Learning to dialogue is essential and is the only way forward in these turbulent times but doing so with proper intent is very important."

Societal Development Dialogues—B

In May 2009, through a referral from Malaysia I was contacted by a quasi-government organization in Iran to explore visiting Tehran and speaking on the importance of dialogue. Recognizing the security issues faced related to Westerners visiting Iran and especially speaking on the topic of dialogue in a highly authoritarian regime I commenced a dialogue with friends, clients, and government officials who confirmed the legitimacy of the host organization and the fact that I should normally be safe in the country given it was receiving record amounts of visitors at the time I was requested to visit. The more I investigated what a visit to Iran could offer both personally and professionally the more I wanted to go. After roughly a month had passed and I was due to confirm my travel and speaking arrangements, reformist protests began to boil over in the political confrontation between reformist leader Mir Hossein Mousavi (http://en .wikipedia.org/wiki/Mir-Hossein_Mousavi) and current president Mahmoud Amadinejad (http://en.wikipedia.org/wiki/ Mahmoud_Ahmadinejad). On June 27 a public protest went horribly wrong and a beautiful girl called Neda Soltani (www .guardian.co.uk/world/2009/jun/22/neda-soltani-death-iran) was killed. The ensuring crackdown put a brutal end to any hope of dialogue for the next couple of years and I patiently await my invitation to Iran to be reactivated. As the recent revolutionary changes in Tunisia, Egypt, Yemen, and Jordan have shown, people want dialogic leaders, people who will engage with and respond to the people. Effective dialogic leadership rather than the right to vote leaders out of office is what people really want. Too many examples can be found where elections simply replaced ineffective (nondialogic) leaders with other ineffective leaders. I remain hopeful for Iran's future.

Performance Management Dialogues

A friend recounted how she returned from work after the holidays only to be asked to meet with a representative from human resources (HR) who handed them a letter, which stated they had been terminated due to restructuring. No further explanation or warning and certainly no dialogue. The representative of HR suggested the person should leave immediately. "Can I finish the work open on my computer?" No, you should leave immediately was the reply. As a senior executive in this highly visible customer-facing organization it was important that the departure was swift and as trouble-free as possible. My friend left, her computer account and access cards were terminated immediately, and she sent movers to collect her things from her office. Her secretary was so shocked she took the rest of the day off and many others in the company have pointed to this example as yet further proof the company is being badly managed. Is it being badly managed? I think that the main thing missing is dialogue. Everyone recognizes the need to contain costs. Everyone recognizes the pyramid narrows as you move to the top. But few people understand why organizations get rid of good loyal employees so awkwardly. The real reason is lack of experience and training on how to handle the moment notice is given and far more importantly a lack of dialogue in the days and months leading up to the point where such a decision needs to be made. There are few surprises when dialogue is present and difficult times can be much better managed when handled in more of a dialogic way.

Notes

1. *Dialogue: Rediscover the Transforming Power of Conversation* (New York: John Wiley & Sons, 1998), 188.
2. As quoted in Daisaku Ikeda and Majid Tehranian, *Global Civilization* (London: British Academic Press, 2004), 105.
3. As quoted in L. Ellinor and G. Gerard, *Dialogue: Rediscover the Transforming Power of Conversation* (New York: John Wiley & Sons, 1998), 286.
4. *Dialogue: Rediscover the Transforming Power of Conversation*, xxvii.
5. W. Isaacs, *Dialogue and the Art of Thinking Together* (New York: Doubleday/Currency, 1999).
6. Ikeda and Tehranian, *Global Civilization*, 9.
7. Parker J. Palmer, *A Hidden Wholeness* (San Francisco: Jossey-Bass, 2004).
8. Parker Palmer did not say that trusting the solution is in the dialogue but rather trust that welcoming the soul into dialogue with no particular agenda in mind can have a transforming effect for individuals and institutions.
9. www.solonline.org.
10. Parker Palmer is particularly famous for helping teachers reconnect their soul and role and much of his work is reported in *The Courage to Teach Guide for Reflection and Renewal*, John Wiley & Sons, 1999.

Part III

DIALOGUE LEADERSHIP

Chapter 6

The Cost
of Failed Dialogue

U.S.-based research carried out on 1,000 executives from 40 companies comprising 2,200 projects ranging in value from US$10,000 to US$1 billion per project uncovered what I call the Big Five Dialogue Failures:[1]

1. Projects are set up with unrealistic timelines and a shortage of resources.
2. Project sponsors fail to lead or give the political clout, time, and energy to see a project through to completion.
3. Unrealistic priorities are established and followed.
4. Team leaders and members don't admit problems exist and wait for others to act.
5. Team members are either unable or unwilling to support the project.

Up to 85 percent of those surveyed failed in one of the previous dialogue areas affecting as many as 39 percent of their projects. As many as 91 percent of those surveyed said it was hard to confront and resolve one or more of these issues. Of the 50 percent who tried to dialogue, as few as 11 percent did so skillfully while 20 percent were able to solve the problem. Of those projects that failed or ran over budget the amounting loss was approximately US$64 billion.

The research just quoted has one piece of good news. Where dialogue was improved, performance improved by 50 to 70 percent.

Dialogue Leader Behavior Rating

As we know from the previous chapters dialogue fails for several reasons, including the advent of digital communication, the retreat of traditional occasions for dialogue from our lives, a lowering of importance placed on dialogue, and as a result of all of these our diminishing dialogue skills. In order to focus on and enhance dialogue skills we developed two assessments. Our *Dialogue Leader Behavior Rating*© identifies how often the respondent demonstrates good dialogue behaviors.

Individual Dialogue Behavior Blockers

Once you have identified your least common dialogue behaviors you can proceed on to the list of dialogue blockers that have been identified by thousands of respondents to be the main reasons preventing good dialogue leadership behavior.

Organizational Dialogue Assessment

Our Organization Dialogue Assessment identifies organizational blockers to effective dialogue at the group level. All the assessments are included here to help you identify what is blocking effective dialogue in your situations @ work, @ home, and @ large in society.

Individual Dialogue Assessment

On the basis that optimal outcomes simply needed people to talk and listen (i.e., communicate) I began asking people why they didn't talk and listen to others. This began the current version of this assessment some 20 years ago while I was still employed at Coopers & Lybrand in Hong Kong. It became clear through this assessment that it was more than just speaking and listening that was missing and this led to my differentiation of communication and dialogue. This led to further reading and research and suspending, respect, and presence were added. Then as the dialogue assessment was used internationally it was further enhanced by the widening of listening and speaking to absorbing and expressing. The current version is the basis for the online version that we hope to launch with this book so that we can report back on the main dialogue behaviors that need help and what to do about them.

Our research has already identified that people don't speak mainly because people aren't listening, not because they lack the ability to express themselves. And what is the biggest problem? Most people say suspending their beliefs is the biggest challenge. Where do I think we can gain the greatest return on investment if we make improvements? Presence. If we improve our presence the other attributes of a good dialogist will also improve and optimal outcomes, represented by jewels of insight, wisdom, and opportunity will befall us.

I encourage you to take a few minutes to identify what is blocking your own dialogues and what you might do to make improvements. Once you have completed this assessment yourself it is useful to share the results with your team at work, your family at home, and to consider the dialogue skills of others in the wider circles of your community.

Dialogue Leader Behavior Rating© v1.8

- **P** – Be 100% Present
- **R** – Respect Others
- **E** – Express Yourself
- **S** – Suspend Your Beliefs
- **A** – Absorb All Messages
- Your Name
- Today's Date
- Who are you rating? Self? Other? Name
- Organization/Department of Person Being Rated

Are you a dialogic leader? Do you regularly achieve optimal outcomes? Can you get the right people talking about the right issues in the right way, at the right time and in the right space?

Dialogic leaders have been found to have good presence, to demonstrate respect for others, to have an above average ability to express their views, are able to suspend their assumptions and beliefs, and are particularly good at absorbing messages.

Leaders today need to be dialogic leaders to succeed in the complex, dynamic cross-cultural environments typical of most organizations in the twenty-first century.

Take 5 to 10 minutes to read through the behaviors of dialogic leaders listed here and assess how often you think you demonstrate these behaviors: 0 = never, 1 = rarely, 2 = occasionally, 3 = half the time, 4 = most of the time, 5 = all the time.

Presence	Rating 0 = Never 5 = All the time	Flag Low Scores ☑
Balance solitude and social time to maintain your mindfulness.		
Maintain your calm to calm others.		
Meditate regularly to develop and strengthen your mindfulness.		
Interact regularly with different people to open your mind to new perspectives.		
Control your emotions to enhance your situation rather than hinder it.		
Confident, witty, and humorous.		
Cheerful, flexible, and without melancholy.		
Show genuine curiosity in exploring what others have to say.		
Don't multitask when in dialogue with others.		
Recognize and listen to your gut feelings (inner-knowing) and those of others.		
Total Behavior Rating for Presence		

Respect	Rating 0 = Never 5 = All the time	Flag Low Scores ☑
Inclusive of others regardless of what diversity separates you.		
Diplomatic and don't criticize or use judgmental labels.		
Demonstrate respect and understanding for others.		
Sincere, honest, and dialogue with proper motives.		
Show you care and can be trusted.		
Apologize and take the blame when appropriate.		
Involve all key stakeholders in the dialogue.		
Demonstrate other people's perceptions matter a lot.		
Accept that you need your opponents' perspectives to make optimal decisions.		
Recognize that you'll need each other either now or later and explore why.		
Total Behavior Rating for Respect		

Expression	Rating 0 = Never 5 = All the time	Flag Low Scores ☑
Adjust your tone, speed, vocabulary, and grammar to match other party.		
Prime the environment through words and gestures so people respond as you would like.		
Polite, courteous, and don't use foul language.		
Speak from your experience (not that of others) and avoid storytelling.		
Use "I messages" to talk about patterns of behavior rather than one-off events.		

(Continued)

Expression	Rating 0 = Never 5 = All the time	Flag Low Scores ☑
Speak your mind and share your feelings without venting rage or anger or lecturing others.		
State the mutual purpose and focus on common ground.		
State what you mean and what you do not mean to leave no doubt in the other's mind.		
Inquire appreciatively of others by asking engaging questions without causing bad feelings.		
Don't wait to know it all or get it right before you speak up.		
Total Behavior Rating for Expression		

Suspend	Rating 0 = Never 5 = All the time	Flag Low Scores ☑
Equal in mind and not under obligation to others (egalitarian).		
Invite opposing views and get all the relevant information onto the table.		
Demonstrate openness to new ideas and interest for subjects not your own.		
Flexible—adjust the time, the place, and the way you dialogue to achieve your outcome		
Avoid either/or choices and looking at the world as black and white.		
Recognize that the solution is found in the dialogue and not in predetermined answers.		
Investigate and understand your own assumptions.		
Find compassion for others and accept everything is interconnected.		
Help others suspend so they see alternatives.		
Suspend your opinions about other people's opinions		
Total Behavior Rating for Suspend		

Absorb	Rating 0 = Never 5 = All the time	Flag Low Scores ☑
Watch people's body language to check if it validates what they are saying.		
Balance talking and listening, not every word that comes to you needs to be spoken.		
Listen to others' feelings to understand their perspective and uncover their intent.		
Mirror what others say and ask a related question to deepen your understanding (Ma–Ma).		
Build a ladder of inference connecting the situation to perceptions, conclusions, assumptions, and beliefs.		
Don't jump to conclusions, invoke your professional skepticism.		
Think about why they said what they did before you ask them.		
Recognize effective dialogue results from good questions rather than good answers.		
Diagnose and explore why they respond with silence.		
Recognize feedback as a gift regardless of how nicely it is wrapped.		
Total Behavior Rating for Absorb		

Dialogic Leadership Behavior Rating

Raters can summarize the previous findings into the following table in order to focus attention on the areas needing attention—both behaviors done well and behaviors needing improvement.

Category	Total Rating	Strength (Highest Rating)	Weakness (Lowest Rating)	Behaviors to Leverage (Strengths) and to Improve (Weaknesses)
Presence	/50			
Respect	/50			
Expression	/50			
Suspending	/50			
Absorbing	/50			
Total Score	/250			

As Humberto Maturana puts it, you cannot see the place on which you stand; it is too close, too connected to you. Once you see it, you realize you have moved, and your field is enlarged. For this reason, seeing our limits clearly—perhaps for the first time—is actually evidence of progress, not falling back, though the experience can at first be depressing or disturbing.[2,3]

How to Improve Dialogue Leadership Behavior

The common reasons identified by leaders preventing them from effective dialogue with others are listed in our accompanying list "What Prevents Effective Dialogue" v1.8 in Appendix A.

The *organizational dialogue assessment* was designed to create dialogue around how the various pieces of the dialogue puzzle play out inside the organization at work. By addressing common problems identified inside organizations this assessment stimulates dialogue on differing perceptions of how good or bad things really are and then ways to make improvements. See Appendix B.

Stress Management

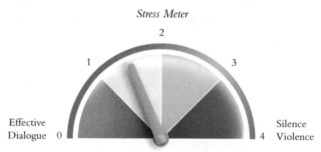

Conflict is a tough part of life, and we long for ways of working with it that are more creative and profound than our habitual extremes of avoidance or aggression.

—James Gimian[4]

Our reaction to stress is a principle contributor to dialogue success or failure. As the stress meter shows, we naturally move from effective dialogue up to silence and violence, but the speed and frequency that our dial moves is a factor of both nature and nurture. Even people with a "short fuse" who react quickly and negatively can learn to regulate their reaction.

The most valuable instruction that I have found for emotional regulation exists within the Buddhist literature where scholars have paid attention to its importance for thousands of years.

What Is Conflict?

A person's definition of conflict depends largely on his or her personality (motives and types) and cultural background but also on his or her life experience, education, upbringing, and so on. Some situations you find perfectly tame will cause conflict for others. Despite these differences people around the world tend to link the following factors together with conflict of some degree:

- Lack of response from the other party; that is, blank stare and silence.
- Lack of cooperation.
- Threats to self-worth, rights, freedoms, material, or spiritual position.
- Unnaturally aggressive response from the other party, for example, yelling
- Mean and hurtful behavior.
- Hostility.

Warranted versus Unwarranted Conflict

Dr Elias Porter, originator of the *Strength Deployment Inventory* differentiated warranted conflict from unwarranted conflict.[5] Warranted conflict arises when two or more people want two different things. Unwarranted conflict arises when two or more people want the same thing but wish to achieve it in a different way. In both cases conflict exists. Warranted conflict needs to be resolved with negotiation, but unwarranted conflict requires dialogue so that both parties understand each other's differing perspectives before resolution can be achieved. Some conflicts combine both warranted and unwarranted conflict.

Preparing for war and fighting a war means allowing our human nature to die.

—Thich Nhat Hanh[6]

Culture and Conflict

Culture has a significant impact on how people react to conflict situations. Some cultures have been found to be more willing to accept and even promote conflict (e.g., U.S. culture) whereas some cultures have for centuries believed it is best to avoid conflict (e.g., Confucian cultures).

My work with organizations, teams, and individuals facing conflict has taught me that conflict occurs naturally everywhere. The main difference, however, is how people react to it. Some, like author Dean Tysvold, believe *Conflict is Good.*[7] Others believe that conflict is to be avoided. The answer, like so many things, depends on the situation. Some believe that no conflict = no new ideas and that a healthy level of conflict indicates an active creative environment in which people challenge each other for the collective good. At the other extreme, situations exist that contain too much conflict. These situations inevitably cause a lack of sharing, stifle learning, and cause individuals to "retire on the job."

The only way societies, organizations, and individuals can improve is if we find ways to see things from other people's perspectives and in so doing improve on what we have already achieved either by altering what we have to something new, convincing them our way is better, or accepting their way is superior. All possible outcomes necessitate traveling through some form of conflict and to do so, the solution is in the dialogue.

Conflict Models

There are numerous conflict models available, for example, Thomas-Kilmann (Kenneth W. Thomas and Ralph H. Kilmann: Thomas-Kilmann Conflict Mode Instrument, 1974). The two instruments that I have found most useful are those developed by the master trainers using the Strength Deployment Inventory.[8] These are portrayed here as:

- *Conflict Sequence*, which shows how individuals predictably change the behaviors they choose to employ as conflict escalates.
- *Narrowing Focus,* which helps us understand the narrowing interests of people in conflict.

In conflict sequence the underlying behaviors one uses at the different levels of conflict depends on their results on the Strength Deployment Inventory (SDI). The SDI identifies whether someone is primarily motivated by results, relationships, or rationale. This primary motivation predicts their choice of behaviors at Stage 0, which is when things are going well and the subject is not feeling any stress.

If someone was asked what had changed as a result of the dialogue, the answer was "everything"—a sea of change in the ways people saw one another and worked together.

—William Isaacs[9]

Conflict Gauge and Stages of Conflict

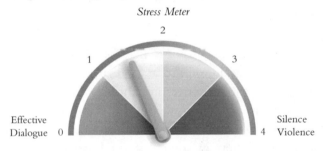

It is useful to consider stress increasing in a way similar to temperature—it has been found that as stress increases, it changes behaviors and focus.

1. The beginning of stress.

   As things begin to go wrong and the subject begins to feel stressed (e.g., when you go to work or even as you battle traffic on the way to work) then people move into Stage 1. At this stage, depending on a person's conflict sequence, people may adopt different motives than in Stage 0. Even if people maintain the same motives at this stage they may already appear to be less patient and more on edge than they are normally.

2. The escalation of stress.

   The movement from Stage 1 to Stage 2 of conflict occurs only if the tactics employed at Stage 1 failed to resolve the situation. As the tension mounts and previous tactics have failed, research has identified that individuals choose new tactics to resolve the situation. It is this choice of new tactics that can be predicted, not when they will be employed but rather which ones.

3. When things move out of control.

People continue to adopt new behaviors when those they have selected previously fail to reverse the escalation of conflict. While the timing of the change is difficult to predict, the choice of behaviors is easier to predict, which means if we are watching carefully we can see the conflict escalation taking place. Research has also identified the "triggers" that cause people to move into the next higher stage of conflict. A person's comfort level and experience working in conflict situations will determine how much control they can exercise both on themselves and the situation when in these higher stages.

4. Destructiveness.

Although Stage 3 behaviors may be destructive for relationships and projects and even the individual self if the behaviors chosen at this stage still do not resolve the situation for the individual, in rare occasions we are now finding that some people go one step too far—that is to Stage 4 where they become destructive to themselves and others in some last ditch attempt to regain their self-worth.

Team Conflict Sequence

It is useful to assess team conflict sequences because team members who individually might react effectively in certain situations may as a team become ineffective together. One example of this was a project team I worked with, which was in extreme conflict with its client. Although the previous project had won the team awards, the two sides of this conflict were opposites of each other in conflict and this was the source of most of their problems. As stress escalated, the project team retreated to study the problem but the client team jumped up to act. The stark contrast between the two teams was too much for the client team to handle, causing them to get more upset and causing the project team to become even more reflective.

At What Stage Are Conflicts Resolved?

Our experience tells us that most conflicts are resolved in Stage 1 after both parties recognize that differences exist and that dialogue is required to resolve those differences. In our consulting work we find that parties in negotiation tend more often than not to be already in conflict Stage 2. This typically means that they have tried and failed to resolve the conflict; that narrowed focus still is failing to surface a solution; that the problem has not gone away (and in fact may have actually got ten worse) and that they have decided the problem at hand was worth going outside for professional help to resolve the situation.

Understanding how behaviors predictably sequence in conflict situations is not enough to fully understand the situation. We must also understand how the tension caused by conflict causes the focus of parties in conflict to become narrowed.

Narrowed Focus

As stress increases and behaviors change predictably, it has also been found that the focus we place on things also changes or, more specifically, narrows.

Stage 0 and 1   Life in general

As the following table shows, research conducted by Dr. Porter indicated that as tensions mount the focus of people in conflict narrows. Normally (at Stage 0) people are concerned about themselves (self), the situation they are working on (situation), the other party they are working with to address the situation at hand (other party), as well as peripheral matters of lesser importance (other matters). As tensions mount, the person moves into Stage 1 and tends to lose focus on all other matters and focuses exclusively (at least for a time) on themselves, the situation, and the other party.

Stage 2 and 3   Tension, negotiation, and conflict situations

At Stage 2 the focus narrows further and people no longer pay attention to the other party in a conflict. This is one of the principal reasons why it is so difficult for them to diagnose what the other party wants at this stage. At Stage 3 the focus has narrowed still further and the person in conflict is only now interested in themselves. It is at this stage that we notice people doing things that make no sense to others around them (e.g., asset stripping in companies) because the parties' actions can best be described as self-preservation (we do what we do to maintain our perceived self-worth).

Stage 4   Destructiveness

Stage 4 is thought to be typical of people who are prepared even to hurt themselves (e.g., suicide bombers) if they think that by acting as they do they will redeem themselves in some way (e.g., in the eyes of their God, their family, their friends).

Focus Narrows as Stress Increases

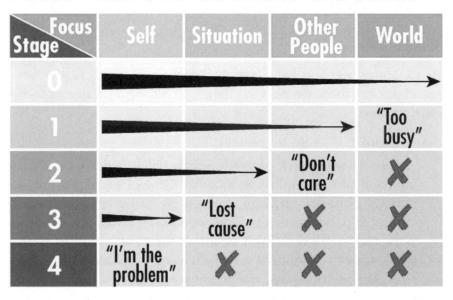

Stage / Focus	Self	Situation	Other People	World
0				
1				"Too busy"
2			"Don't care"	X
3		"Lost cause"	X	X
4	"I'm the problem"	X	X	X

How to De-Escalate Conflict

The following tactics, if employed effectively, will significantly help you cause the other party to become less tense and more reasonable to work with (i.e., widen focus and de-escalate conflict). In so doing you are paving the way forward for the parties in conflict to resolve their differences and either find a way forward or agree to disagree and move on.

Reduce Stress to Improve Dialogue

De-escalate YOUR stress

1. Do nothing and allow time to better define your reaction

2. Recognize and manage your emotions

3. Meditate: Breath in reflecting on suffering and breath out reflecting on compassion

4. Prepare your concessions: "If I do this... then will you do that?"

5. Remember we are all one

6. Take a time out to calm down

7. Accept accusations and write them down without reacting

8. Practice non-attachment

9. Recognize the impermanence of both the problem and the solution

10. Recognize others suffer and hurt like you

11. Address their motivational style

12. Be polite, your rudeness and anger returns to you intensified

13. Stop seeing the situation as black or white, right or wrong, look for a middle way

14. Ask "Whose needs are being addressed"

15. Stop thinking me vs. you and think us

16. Stop, wait, shut up, and listen

17. Ask other party what you don't know

18. Replace your assumptions, accusations, and assertions about others with questions to test the correctness of your views

19. Stop your revenge and ask "how can I help this person overcome their strong emotions?"

20. Apologize and admit mistakes

De-escalate THEIR stress

21. Show patience to others

22. Demonstrate love for others

23. Be compassionate about their situation

24. Smile at anger and don't let it affect you

25. Work together to define the problem

26. Propose solutions hypothetically ("What if we....?")

27. Encourage polite behavior and reward it when shown by others

28. Replace your anger with diplomacy

29. Share your thinking about the situation

30. Share why you think the way you do

31. Encourage them to talk

32. Don't react, explain you are listening and considering next steps

33. Validate their feelings (e.g., "It's okay that you feel this way about me/the situation")

34. Brainstorm alternative solutions

35. Forgive others genuinely

36. Encourage dialogue among stakeholders to explore different perspectives before deciding how best to proceed

37. Ask others about themselves, their thoughts, and feelings

38. Spend informal time together

39. Ask others if they are intentionally accusing you and if so to provide examples

40. Use a mediator or facilitator to assist difficult dialogues and those involving a lot of stakeholders

The Top Five De-Escalation Tactics

In my book *Negotiation*, I outline in detail five useful tactics for de-escalating conflict.[10] These include:

1. Bring Ma-Ma to the table (Mirror-Ask, Mirror-Ask), a questioning technique whereby you mirror what the other says and ask follow-up questions to probe deeper, usually starting with What or How?

2. Change your dialect to match that of the other party (Relationship, Rationale, Results). This refers to changing your motivational focus, what you say, and how you say it, to match the motivational focus of the other party.

3. Talk about them (from wide to narrow focus, people are self-interested). People, especially when upset, want to talk about themselves and their own problems.

4. Talk about the common ground (rather than the differences). It is useful to remind the other party of your common needs and interests, which in stressful situations can become overlooked.

5. Propose reciprocal solutions hypothetically (If we . . . then will you). Venturing solutions is a great way to move the dialogue forward into a joint problem-solving mode.

Four Levels of Ability in Regulating Emotion

1. Normal—You react without thinking.
2. Experienced—You adjust your reaction midstream to minimize negative impact.
3. Trained and experienced—You don't react negatively.
4. Master—The impulse doesn't even affect you.

How to achieve the Master Level 4 of anger management? **Study and practice Mindfulness.**[11]

Getting better at dialogue requires practice and fortunately it is easy to find opportunities to do so. The list of practice activities in Appendix C gives you additional ideas on how to go about improving dialogue yourself or for your organization.

Changing behavior requires practice. The activities will enhance your knowledge, role-playing will allow you to practice, and employing these skills in your daily dialogues will cement the new behaviors into place. If you find yourself needing coaching—just ask. See Appendix C for dialogue skill practice activities.

We are what we repeatedly do.

—Aristotle

Dialogue represents a new frontier for human beings—perhaps the true final frontier. In it we can come to know ourselves and our relatedness to the whole of life.

—William Isaacs[12]

To open yourself to begin to understand the theory behind dialogue is to open yourself up to the forces that make human endeavours effective or not. Once you are aware of these forces, you can no longer simply blame people for situations that don't work out. And you can begin to set up conversations that will engender better results.

—William Isaacs[13]

Conclusion

Assuming that you are successful in identifying and removing the blocks to effective dialogue, your next challenge is sustaining dialogue over the long haul. This is important personally, organizationally, and at a community level. Sadly, organizations tend to go through waves alternating from good to bad dialogue dependent largely on the dialogue skills of the leaders. Smart organizations create a culture of dialogue and put in place systems to sustain dialogue so that positive practices can be sustained even if less dialogic leaders step in the way for a time at the top. The next chapter explores the systems available to sustain dialogue over the long haul.

Notes

1. *Silence Fails* (Vital Smarts, 2007).
2. http://en.wikipedia.org/wiki/Humberto_Maturana.
3. As quoted in W. Isaacs, *Dialogue and the Art of Thinking Together* (New York: Doubleday/Currency, 1999), 340.
4. As quoted in Melvin McLeod, *Mindful Politics* (Boston: Wisdom Publications, 2006), 241.

5. *The Strength Deployment Inventory ("SDI")*® is owned and published by Personal Strengths Publishing. Readers interested in learning more about this valuable instrument can contact the author or Personal Strengths directly at www.personalstrengths.com.

6. As quoted in McLeod, *Mindful Politics*, 274.

7. Kwok Leung and Dean Tjosvold, *Conflict Management in the Asia Pacific* (John Wiley & Sons, Asia, 1998).

8. See SDI above.

9. *Dialogue and the Art of Thinking Together*, 23.

10. Peter Nixon, *Negotiation: Mastering Business in Asia* (John Wiley & Sons, 2005), 89–98.

11. Readers interested in learning more about this are encouraged to learn about the work and resulting publications of the Mind & Life Institute to which I have been a donor over the years. For further details visit: www.mindandlife.org.

12. *Dialogue and the Art of Thinking Together*, 48.

13. Ibid., 71.

Chapter 7

Sustaining Dialogue

I have worked with many organizations over the years. Dialogic leaders come and go and for this reason the quality of dialogue in organizations fluctuates over time from good to bad or bad to good. Successful organizations sustain effective dialogue over time by leveraging approaches, methods, and processes into their operating systems in order to sustain dialogue even when current leaders don't demonstrate a skill or favor for dialogue.

Dialogue Approaches, Methods, Processes, and Systems

I list next some of the most common and robust dialogue systems, methods, and processes that I know to exist and/or have personal experience with myself and that I recommend to dialogue leaders. Before proceeding it is useful to clarify terminology as I tend to hear many different terms used for the list that follows. **My Oxford dictionary provides the following useful definitions:**[1]

- Approach—A way of dealing with a person or thing.
- Method—The orderly arrangement of ideas.
- Methodology—A body of methods used in a particular activity.
- Process—A course of action or proceeding as in the stages of manufacture.
- Procedure—A series of actions conducted in a certain order or manner.
- System—A complex whole, an organized body of material or immaterial things, or a method of choosing one's procedure.
- Theory—A supposition or system of ideas explaining something.

Although I allow the reader to decide if the following list is best described as approaches, methodologies, processes, or systems, I think my depiction of the dialogue puzzle (right outcomes = right people + right issues + right way, time, space) is a system and that the various approaches, methods, and processes listed can be useful when selected by dialogue leaders to achieve optimal outcomes. Which method is selected depends on the situation you face and the theories you subscribe to. Theories help to inform our selection of approach, method, and process so I wish to highlight two theories of importance to me with respect to dialogue.

Theories Influencing Selection

Constructionism is a theory of learning where humans construct meaning from current knowledge structures. All knowledge, including the most basic, taken-for-granted commonsense knowledge of everyday reality, is derived from and maintained by social interactions.

- When people interact, they do so with the understanding that their respective perceptions of reality are related, and as they act on this understanding their common knowledge of reality becomes reinforced.
- Since this commonsense knowledge is negotiated by people, human typifications, significations, and institutions come to be presented

as part of an objective reality. It is in this sense that it can be said that reality is socially constructed (Wikipedia).

Systems Theory and Systems Thinking

- Systems theory describes the interdependence of relationships in organizations composed of regularly interacting or interrelating groups of activities. For example, in noting the influence in organizational psychology as the field evolved from "an individually oriented industrial psychology to a systems and developmentally oriented organizational psychology," it was recognized that organizations are complex social systems—reducing the parts from the whole reduces the overall effectiveness of organizations.
- Systems theory is different from conventional models that center on individuals, structures, departments, and units separate in part from the whole instead of recognizing the interdependence between groups of individuals, structures, and processes that enable an organization to function. The relationship between organizations and their environments became recognized as the foremost source of complexity and interdependence.
- Systems thinking is the process of understanding how things influence one another within a whole. In nature, systems thinking examples include ecosystems in which various elements such as air, water, movement, plants, and animals work together to survive or perish. In organizations, systems consist of people, structures, and processes that work together to make an organization healthy or unhealthy.
- Systems thinking has been defined as an approach to problem solving, by viewing "problems" as parts of an overall system, rather than reacting to specific parts, outcomes, or events and potentially contributing to further development of unintended consequences.

Systems thinking, as described in Wikipedia, is not one thing but a set of habits or practices within a framework that is based on the belief that the component parts of a system can best be understood in the context of relationships with each other and with other systems, rather than in isolation. Systems thinking focuses on cyclical rather than linear cause and effect. The following list of approaches, methods, and processes includes some generic things like happy hours and some copyrighted approaches that have become widely known and used. To maintain my neutrality in describing the following choices available to dialogue leaders I have relied on Wikipedia for general descriptions and on related websites for more specific information as needed. Where appropriate I have also provided my personal experience with these choices and in each case I have attempted to leave you the reader with greater insight to the choices you have available and, as appropriate, links to uncover more information should you so choose.

The Ways to Dialogue—List

Action Learning and Play	Force Field Analysis	Positive Deviance
Alcoholics Anonymous	Future Search	Quiet Time
Appreciative Inquiry	Gestalt Therapy	Robert's Rules of Order
Après Ski	Group Coaching	Scenario Planning
Art of Hosting	Happy Hours	Six Thinking Hats
Audits	Indaba	Sunday Brunch
Brainstorming	Inquiry-Based Learning	Technology of
Budgeting	Insight Dialogue	Participation
Celebrity Roast	Interfaith Dialogue	Theatrical Skits
Challenge Mapping	Learning Organizations	Theory U
Circles of Trust	Lego Serious Play	Town Halls
Conversare	Mind Mapping	Truth and Reconciliation
Cybernetics	Occupy Wall Street	Commissions
Dialogue Cafés	People's Assemblies	United Nations
Dialogue Education	Open Space Technology	Videos (e.g., *Change the*
Drawing Pictures	Parliamentary Systems	*Dream*)
Facilitation	Performance Appraisals	World Café
Festivals		

The Ways to Dialogue—Detail

Action Learning and Play

- Action learning and play are educational processes whereby participants study and dialogue about their own actions and experience in order to improve performance. Action learning is done in dialogue with others, in small groups called *action learning sets.*

- It is proposed as particularly suitable for adults, as it enables each person to reflect on and dialogue on the action they have taken and the learning points arising. This should then guide future action and improve performance (Wikipedia).
- Facilitators spend considerable time helping reflective practitioners dialogue to tease out the improvements possible and as such it is a valuable dialogic process worthy of note.
- From experience the most important part of this process is the reflection and resulting dialogue, which then transforms into learning and improvement. Without the pause, reflection, and dialogue, improvements will seldom arise.

Alcoholics Anonymous (AA)

- www.aa.org/lang/en/subpage.cfm?page=1.
- The AA program, a dialogic process, sets forth in the Twelve Steps a way to develop a satisfying life without alcohol. This program is the basis of dialogue at AA group meetings. There are several different types of dialogues at AA meetings including:
  - Open speaker meetings—Open to alcoholics and nonalcoholics where AA members describe their experiences with alcohol, how they came to AA, and how their lives have changed as a result of Alcoholics Anonymous.
  - Open discussion meetings, where one member speaks briefly about his or her drinking experience, and then leads a dialogue on AA recovery or any drinking-related problem anyone brings up.
  - Closed meetings for AAs or anyone who may have a drinking problem, are conducted just as open discussions are, but for alcoholics or prospective AAs only.
  - Step meetings (usually closed)—Discussion of one of the Twelve Steps.

Appreciative Inquiry (AI)

- http://appreciativeinquiry.case.edu/default.cfm.
- AI involves, in a central way, the art and practice of asking questions that strengthen a system's capacity to apprehend, anticipate, and

heighten positive potential. It centrally involves the mobilization of inquiry through the crafting of the "unconditional positive question," often involving hundreds or sometimes thousands of people.

- AI was created by David Cooperrider.
- In AI the arduous task of intervention gives way to the speed of imagination and innovation; instead of negation, criticism, and spiraling diagnosis, there is discovery, dream, and design.
- AI seeks, fundamentally, to build a constructive union between a whole people and the massive entirety of what people talk about as past and present capacities: achievements, assets, unexplored potentials, innovations, strengths, elevated thoughts, opportunities, benchmarks, high-point moments, lived values, traditions, strategic competencies, stories, expressions of wisdom, insights into the deeper corporate spirit or soul—and visions of valued and possible futures.
- Taking all of these together as a gestalt, AI deliberately, in everything it does, seeks to work from accounts of this "positive change core"—and it assumes that every living system has many untapped and rich and inspiring accounts of the positive.
- Link the energy of this core directly to any change agenda and changes never thought possible are suddenly and democratically mobilized.

Après Ski

- Après Ski is listed here because in my experience some of the best dialogues are after a satisfying day of sport enjoyed in the outdoors. In this case I use the term Après Ski to include not just sitting around with friends after a day of skiing but also hiking, walking, skating, swimming, or other fine outdoor activities when the mind is fresh and clear and the body tired and relaxed.

Art of Hosting

- www.artofhosting.org.
- The Art of Hosting and Convening Meaningful Conversations explores hosting as an individual and collective leadership practice. The challenges of these times call for collective intelligence. We must co-create the solutions we seek.

- The Art of Hosting pattern and practice is based on our assumptions that it is common sense to bring stakeholders together in conversation when you seek new solutions for the common good.
- We believe that when human beings are invited to work together on what truly matters to them, they will take ownership and responsibility for moving their issues and ideas into wiser actions that last.

Audits

- Effective auditing leads from investigation to dialogue but most auditing leads from investigation to communication of findings. Sometimes the communication of audit findings results in understanding and changes and sometimes it doesn't. When auditing leads to dialogue then real value is created because the auditors gain the insights they need to develop more effective controls and the auditee gains the insights they need to understand the implications and full cost impact of their work. There are many kinds of auditing and they differ based on what the auditor is looking for.
- External auditors look for compliance to generally accepted accounting principles (GAAP) and the internal controls, which lead to accurate, complete, and timely financial reporting. Internal auditors look for compliance to management controls to ensure effective and efficient use of the organization's resources. International Standard Organization (ISO) auditors look for compliance to ISO standards on such things as quality (ISO 9,000), environment (ISO 14,000), and social responsibility (ISO 26,000). Compliance officers check for compliance to regulations related to tax, pollution, stock exchange, and other requirements.
- Auditors struggle because the communication of their findings commonly leads to conflict with auditees who disagree with their findings, prefer the findings be dismissed, or both. Auditors need to leverage the skills outlined in this book to handle the conflict and extend the communication of their findings into a dialogue with the auditees focused on realizing sustainable operations, which are legal, profitable, effective, and efficient.

- Two particularly valuable tools that can improve the value of audit dialogues are challenge mapping and change of dialect based on the motivational style of the auditee.

Brainstorming
- Most readers will have experienced brainstorming, which is a technique designed to generate a large number of ideas for the solution of a problem. In 1953 the method was popularized by Alex Osborn in a book called *Applied Imagination*.[2] Osborn proposed that groups could double their creative output with brainstorming.
- Although brainstorming has become a popular group technique, when applied in a traditional group setting, researchers have not found evidence of its effectiveness for enhancing either quantity or quality of ideas generated. Because of such problems as distraction, social loafing, evaluation apprehension, and production blocking, conventional brainstorming groups are little more effective than other types of groups, and they are actually less effective than individuals working independently. Although traditional brainstorming does not increase the productivity of groups (as measured by the number of ideas generated), it may still provide benefits, such as boosting morale, enhancing work enjoyment, and improving teamwork. Thus, numerous attempts have been made to improve brainstorming or use more effective variations of the basic technique (Wikipedia).
- In my experience brainstorming can be improved if properly facilitated and led to be a dialogue more than simple communication (i.e., blurting out) of ideas. A definite improvement on basic brainstorming is challenge mapping listed further on.

Budgeting
- The annual budgeting process creates one of the rare times for organizations to come together and dialogue. Sadly most budgeting processes tend to be accounting exercises done in isolation of the key stakeholders and the opportunity is missed to genuinely create dialogue about optimizing use of resources. The most common reason for restricting the dialogue on budget is its inherent conflictual nature—if my department gets more money your department will

inevitably get less. This is the zero-sum nature of the budgeting mind-set, which is compounded by the fact that it is hard to keep things confidential, which is especially important in listed companies and entities in highly competitive situations.

- I encourage organizations to employ the tools put forth in this book to improve their budgeting outcomes. I also encourage readers to consider the success of their budgeting not exclusively by considering the variance between budget and actual but also by quantifying and sharing the valuable ideas arising from the budgeting process.

- One form of budgeting that is particularly useful is called *zero-based budgeting* and it assumes each year that your budget is zero and that you need to justify your request for capital from the bottom up. The most useful aspect of this form of budgeting is the fact it tests the common assumption that you will have at least as much money as last year and that you might even get more based on inflation. The solution is in the dialogue.

- One tool that readers will find particularly useful for improved budgeting is the Ma-Ma technique with which you can invite budget holders to explain in detail what they will do with their budget, what they expect to achieve, what they hope this will lead to, what they will do if their predictions are wrong, and so on. When your questioning opens dialogue you are bound to uncover more ways of achieving similar objectives. It is important that the people you choose to manage the budgeting process are themselves effective at dialogue.

Celebrity Roast

- A roast is an event in which an individual is subjected to a public presentation of comedic insults, praise, outlandish true and untrue stories, and heartwarming tributes, the implication being that the roastee is able to take the jokes in good humor and not as serious criticism or insult, and therefore, show their good nature.

- It is seen by some as a great honor to be roasted, as the individual is surrounded by friends, fans, and well-wishers, who can receive some of the same treatment as well during the course of the evening.

- The party and presentation itself are both referred to as a roast. The host of the event is called the *roastmaster*. Anyone who is honored in such a way is said to have been "roasted" (Wikipedia).
- In my experience roasts create a terrific opportunity for dialogue focused on the life of the person being roasted. The jewels of the dialogue include amusing stories, and sometimes information little known about the person surfaces to the bemusement of the participants and the person roasted.

Challenge Mapping

- www.basadur.com/research/recentpubs029.htm.
- It is often difficult for groups of people to think together innovatively, especially in situations that are ill-defined and involve complex issues. Challenge mapping is a unique conceptual thinking method for reducing complexity and identifying strategic and tactical challenges (goals) and relating them to one another.
- The dialogic method can be deliberately applied to help individuals, groups and whole organizations think through, clarify, and conceptualize complex, ambiguous, and strategic issues and increase understanding of fuzzy situations both from big picture and specific standpoints.
- Challenge mapping is a special tool of the *Simplex system of applied creativity* that synergizes analytical and imaginative thinking through four stages, emphasizing problem generation and conceptualization prior to solution development and implementation. Such emphasis is not taught in formal education. On the contrary, most students leave school totally immersed in the solutions they have learned then find that in everyday work these solutions don't often match the ill-structured problems they encounter. The most important skill needed seems to be finding and defining the right problems to work on.
- Challenge mapping is one of my favorite dialogue systems because it generates dialogue and allows for clearly evidenced "jewels" of insight, wisdom, and opportunity to fall into the hands of the participants, usually things they would never have discovered otherwise.

Circles of Trust

- www.couragerenewal.org/about/foundations.
- The Circle of Trust Approach was created by Parker J Palmer and is described in his book *A Hidden Wholeness*.[3] Palmer has devoted his life's work to creating spaces that are open and hospitable, but resource-rich and charged with expectancy: In a circle of trust, people are invited to slow down, listen, and reflect in a quiet and focused space. At the same time, they engage in dialogue with others in the circle—a dialogue about things that matter. As this "sorting and sifting" goes on, and people are able to clarify and affirm their truth in the presence of others, a truth that is more likely to overflow into their work and lives. Circles of trust are based on a number of practices including:
  - Committing to no fixing, advising, "saving," or setting each other straight.
  - Asking honest, open questions to "hear each other into speech."
  - Exploring the intersection of the universal stories of human experience with the personal stories of our lives.
  - Using multiple modes of reflection so everyone can find his or her place and pace.
  - Honoring confidentiality.
- I was first introduced to the writings of Parker Palmer as part of my doctoral studies at the Fielding Graduate Institute in Santa Barbara because Palmer has had considerable success renewing the value of teachers. I then came to know about his Circles of Trust from Mardi Tindal, moderator of the United Church of Canada, who is a facilitator herself who speaks highly of the process for encouraging dialogic solutions.[4]

Conversare

- http://conversare.net/.
- Dr. Alan Stewart has created Conversare, a facilitated or hosted meal where people, some strangers to each other prior to the session, gather for no other reason than to get to know each other and rejoice in conversation.

- The purpose is to enable participants to experience conversing with a person with whom they have little common history and possibly no personal future. This happens through the guidance of a host or facilitator who ensures that all present feel welcome and included. The host encourages everyone to engage with their conversing partner in a spirit of curiosity, careful listening and speaking, and no judgment. Participants invariably report great satisfaction and enjoyment from this.

- Proven to be a wonderful system to get people together and overcome their natural shyness, Conversare has already grown international and is being considered by social groups needing to do more to connect their members, customers, and guests to overcome the dialogue gap brought on by the Internet age and life beyond the digital tipping point.

Cybernetics

Cybernetics is defined by Louis Kauffman, a past president of the American Society for Cybernetics, as "the study of systems and processes that interact with themselves and produce themselves from themselves."

- Dialogic approaches, methods, and processes can't be considered without understanding their link to cybernetics and systems theory.

- A self-dialogue process, which I came to know in Canada many years ago, is **psycho-cybernetics** based on a book of the same name written by Maxwell Maltz in 1960 and published by the nonprofit Psycho-Cybernetics Foundation.

- Motivational and self-help experts in personal development, including Zig Ziglar, Tony Robbins, and Brian Tracy, have based their techniques on Maxwell Maltz. Many of the psychological methods of training elite athletes are based on the concepts in Psycho-Cybernetics, which combines the cognitive behavioral technique of teaching an individual how to regulate self-concept and defines the mind-body connection as the core in succeeding in attaining personal goals.

- Maltz found that his plastic surgery patients often had expectations that were not satisfied by the surgery, so he pursued a means of helping them set the goal of a positive outcome through visualization of that positive outcome.

- Maltz became interested in why setting goals works. He learned that the power of self-affirmation and mental visualization techniques used the connection between the mind and the body. He specified techniques to develop a positive inner goal as a means of developing a positive outer goal. This concentration on inner attitudes is essential to his approach, as a person's outer success can never rise above the one visualized internally (Wikipedia).

Dialogue Cafés

- This popular name is used to represent several different methodologies. One solution that has become recently publicized leverages new tele-presence solutions from Cisco to bring together like-minded groups around the world to share experiences, learn from each other, and work together to make the world a better place. Readers interested in learning more about this group are encouraged to visit www.dialoguecafe.org/.
- I also use the name Dialogue Cafés for a methodology I use with groups of people who (a) have a common thread (e.g., university alumni), (b) don't necessarily know each other well (e.g., employees in a big company), and (c) are likely to be of use to each other.
- In my Dialogue Cafés we commence with all participants introducing themselves and stating one thing they would like help with from anyone in the group. Following introductions people network and dialogue and solutions emerge from the contacts made. In these situations people are welcome to ask for anything at all provided it is reasonable and specific. This methodology works well with diverse groups because people of all ages and backgrounds bring with them an endless diversity of interests and connections, which only dialogue can uncover.

Dialogue Education

- www.globalearning.com/approach.htm.
- In the Dialogue Education approach, the idea of dialogue is used in contrast to the monologue approach often seen in traditional

adult education, whereby teachers present information to learners who receive information without engaging with it.

- According to Paulo Freire, the traditional monologue approach to adult education views learners as empty vessels ready for teachers to deposit information into.[5] Freire and others recognized a need for reform in adult education practices, particularly with respect to equity in the relationship between adult learners and teachers.

- Influenced by these theorists, Jane Vella began to develop a structured set of principles and practices to translate the theory into action and results. She began using dialogue education practices in her teaching in the 1970s and these were further developed into a systematic approach while completing her doctoral dissertation at the University of Massachusetts.

- Dialogue education positions dialogue as the means to the end result of learning, rather than as an end in itself. The principle assumes that any adult has enough life experience to converse with any teacher on any subject and that learners learn best when content relates to their experience. Thus, two-way open dialogue needs to be a part of all learning activities (Wikipedia).

Drawing Pictures

- A popular and simple activity to create dialogue is asking people to draw pictures describing the topic of dialogue under consideration. Once created the drawing then becomes the basis for dialogue with observers questioning and the artist explaining.

- Drawing as a form of artistic expression is just one of many options available to generate dialogue in a fun way. Others include drama, music, and so on. A related dialogue process is described later in this list using Lego building blocks.

Facilitation

- Assigning someone to manage the process of your dialogue while you and the other stakeholders focus on the content is in my mind a system in itself. Although facilitators might use dialogue systems themselves to improve the quality of the dialogue, they are also personally part of the solution.

- Provided facilitators have established themselves and gained the respect of the stakeholders, they will empower the facilitators to help guide their dialogue by keeping time, ensuring the equipment is working, helping them through conflict, ensuring everyone is contributing, and so on.

- I follow a simple formula: outcome desired + input acquired = process required. This means that the facilitator must work with the dialogue sponsor to determine the outcome desired and then determine the input the stakeholders get to work with and then based on this information the facilitator uses his or her experience to determine process steps to achieve the outcome.

- Less experienced facilitators sometimes err by sticking to the process rather than allowing for flexibility in the process to achieve the outcome desired. As stated in earlier chapters it is important the outcome desired be optimal, otherwise the facilitator is helping achieve biased or suboptimal outcomes. Although this might be commercially attractive to the dialogue sponsor and facilitator, it seldom achieves optimal outcomes and satisfies all the stakeholders. The following list highlights questions facilitators should ask in planning process steps to achieve the desired outcome.

Output Questions
- What is the purpose of the meeting?
- Who should contribute to the output of the meeting?
- When do the results of the meeting need to be available?
- How should people feel after the meeting?
- What is the best place for this meeting?

Input Questions
- What do they know now?
- What should they learn before the meeting?
- Who is invited/coming?
- What hidden agendas are people bringing to the meeting?
- What time should we start?
- How long should we meet?
- How do people feel about the subject now?
- Where does the conflict reside?
- Where do people typically meet?
- What is the typical room setup?

Festivals

- Since the beginning of time cultures around the world have interrupted their working lives to assemble and dialogue during festivals lasting from hours to weeks at a time. The Haji remains today the largest annual migration of people in the world and the quality and quantity of dialogues during the Haji is part of what motivates people to return or encourage family and friends to participate at least once in their lives. Festivals historically were related to season changes highlighted by changes in solar, lunar, or climactic conditions. These evolved into religious festivals and today the large regular congregations of people tend to be commercial; for example, trade fairs, recreational, sporting events, traditional New Year parties, educational alumni parties, or simply fun music festivals.

- Whatever the excuse, people love to assemble and dialogue and the more you can harness these natural coming-together events to improve the quality of the dialogue, the better you will achieve your outcomes.

- One example of taking traditional events and making them better for dialogue include VIP tents and lodges for corporate entertainment at major sporting events, client-focused sessions at major trade fairs, and congregational assemblies as part of religious gatherings. In all these examples there are opportunities for making these dialogue opportunities top quality or leaving them unmanaged and squandering the opportunity, thinking entertainment is all that is needed to develop business.

Force Field Analysis

- Force field analysis provides a framework for looking at the factors (*forces*) that influence social situations. It looks at forces that are either driving movement toward a goal (helping forces) or blocking movement toward a goal (hindering forces). The principle was developed by Kurt Lewin, a social psychologist, who believed the "field" to be a gestalt psychological environment existing in an individual's (or in the collective group) mind at a certain point in time that can be mathematically described in a topological constellation of constructs. The "field" is dynamic, changing with time and experience. When fully constructed, an individual's field (Lewin used the term *life space*) describes that person's motives, values, needs, moods, goals, anxieties, and ideals.

- Lewin believed that changes of an individual's life space depend on that individual's internalization of external stimuli (from the physical and social world) into the life space. For Lewin, development (or regression) of individuals occurs when their life space has a "boundary zone" experience with external stimuli. Note, it is not merely the experience that causes change in the life space, but the acceptance (internalization) of external stimuli.

- Lewin took these same principles and applied them to the analysis of group conflict, learning, and so on, allowing him to break down common misconceptions of these social phenomena, and to determine their basic elemental constructs. He used theory, mathematics, and common sense to define a force field, and hence to determine the causes of human and group behavior (Wikipedia).

- I first came to learn about force field analysis through my work with Drs. Stuart-Kotze and West of Behavioural Science Systems of the UK. Dr Stuart-Kotze builds on the work of Lewin and others in his analysis of leadership behaviors, which accelerate, sustain, or block momentum in an organization.[6]

- As a method of stimulating dialogue among stakeholders I have found force field analysis to be a useful process for surfacing issues of importance and conceptualizing them as conflicting forces.

Future Search

- www.futuresearch.net/method/whatis/index.cfm.

- Future search is the name for a three-day planning meeting that enables people to cooperate in complex situations, including those of high conflict and uncertainty. The method typically involves groups of 40 to 80 people in one room and as many as 300 in parallel conferences. People from diverse backgrounds use future searches to make systemic improvements in their communities and organizations, working entirely from their own experience. It has been employed with most social, technological, and economic issues in North and South America, Africa, Australia, Europe, India, and South Asia. People achieve four outputs from one meeting—*shared values, a plan for the future, concrete goals,* and *an implementation strategy.*

- Started by Marvin Weisbord and Sandra Janoff, future search functions to help people collaborate despite differences of culture, class, gender, age, race, ethnicity, language, and education. The method has been employed in communities, schools, hospitals, churches, government agencies, foundations, and NGOs.
- Future search methods have been used to help: organize the demobilization of child soldiers in Southern Sudan, develop an integrated economic development plan in Northern Ireland, work with a Hawaiian community to reconnect with traditional values, and determine the future of urban mobility in Salt Lake City, Utah, among many other examples.

  Four principles underlie a successful future search:

  1. Getting the "whole system in the room."

  2. Exploring all aspects of a system before trying to fix any part.

  3. Putting common ground and future action front and center, treating problems and conflicts as information, not action items.

  4. Having people accept responsibility for their own work, conclusions, and action plans.

- People follow a generic agenda, regardless of topic. It consists of four or five half-day sessions on the Past, the Present, the Future, Common Ground, and Action Planning. The techniques used—timelines, a mind map, creative future scenarios, common ground dialogue—are all managed to support the principles. People need no special training, orientation, vocabulary, or background to participate. They work in small groups, make reports to the whole, and join in whole group dialogues on what they are learning.
- Future search managers practice a "hands-off" approach to facilitation, encouraging people to share information and draw their own conclusions. They rarely become involved except to help people clarify goals or to head off situations that might result in conflict or flight from their task.
- There is a vast literature documenting successful future searches. There also have been notable failures that people need to be aware of. The commonest causes of failure are:
  - Noninterdependent groups (people who do not need each other).
  - Issues on which most participants do not wish to act.
  - Key actors missing.

- Allowing too little time for the size of the task.
- Overactive/controlling facilitation.
- The preceding description is drawn from both Wikipedia and the Future Search website. Clearly a successful dialogue system and integrating many of the aspects of successful dialogue outlined in these pages.

Gestalt Therapy

- www.gestaltcleveland.org/about.php.
- Gestalt therapy focuses on process (what is actually happening) as well as on content (what is being talked about). The emphasis is on what is being done, thought, and felt at the present moment (the phenomenology of both client and therapist), rather than on what was, might be, could be, or should have been.
- Gestalt therapy is a method of awareness practice (also called *mindfulness* in other clinical domains), by which perceiving, feeling, and acting are understood to be conducive to interpreting, explaining, and conceptualizing (the hermeneutics of experience). This distinction between direct experience and indirect or secondary interpretation is developed in the process of therapy. The client learns to become aware of what he or she is doing and that triggers the ability to risk a shift or change (Wikipedia).
- I have had firsthand experience with Gestalt in small intimate forums where experienced entrepreneurs share personal experience on problems faced by members of their group. This sharing results in a rapid awareness of the issues and possible ways forward and often sets the basis for valuable dialogue.
- A dialogue leader is useful to keep people from devolving into sharing opinions rather than actual experience. It is a methodology that stresses presence, which you will by now have identified as my most important of the five attributes of effective dialogists.

Group Coaching

- www.coachfederation.org/about-icf/.
- The International Coach Federation (ICF) defines coaching as "partnering with clients in a thought-provoking and creative process that inspires them to maximize their personal and professional potential."

- I believe coaching to be a popular form of dialogue and dialogue gap to be one of the contributing factors that has led to the growth of the coaching industry.
- Group coaching is the same as regular coaching but instead of one-on-one sessions, meetings consist of several people, typically one coach and three to four coachees.
- Group coaching is growing in popularity because it provides a more economical way to extend the benefits of coaching to more people.
- I attended the global ICF conference in Montreal several years ago and was impressed with the quality of senior professionals leading the industry. Executives still need to be wary of the wide spectrum of people who call themselves coaches. I have found myself invited into situations where the previous consultants simply couldn't handle the difficult situations they were hired to resolve.

Happy Hours

- As we grew into the 1980s the Friday drinks, long lunches, and happy hours that were common and useful for dialogue slowly gave way to a growing awareness of diet and the intensity of longer working hours. Although people continue to enjoy happy hours around the world, their usefulness for dialogue has become interrupted by the fact that not everyone participates.
- Happy hours are rightly perceived by some as strictly alcoholic events but more adventurous types have found it perfectly acceptable to join happy hours without drinking alcohol. My work with Asians in Australia and Muslims in the Middle East reminds me of the value of nonalcohol fueled happy hours to generate dialogue.
- Some of my clients in the city of London and in Sydney, Australia sponsor end-of-week drinks in their office to promote dialogue in an informal relaxed way.
- Organizations looking for a good dialogue opportunity need not look any further than happy hour, but at the same time it is useful to have someone managing the dialogue opportunity to ensure that everyone is included and comfortable.
- In Korea one of my clients assigns someone (on a rational basis) to purposefully stay sober during these happy hours and collect as

much information as possible from their suppliers and clients who are present.

Indaba

- Indaba is a Zulu word for a gathering for purposeful discussion and is both a process and method of engagement, and offers a way of listening to one another concerning challenges that face the group. The term comes from a Zulu language word meaning "business" or "matter."

- An indaba is an important conference held by the izinDuna (principal men) of the Zulu and Xhosa peoples of South Africa. (Such meetings are also practiced by the Swazi, who refer to them using the close cognate indzaba.) These indabas may include only the izinDuna of a particular community or may be held with representatives of other communities.

- The term has found widespread use throughout Southern Africa and often simply means *gathering* or *meeting*. It is also used in the Scouting movement. The World Scout Indaba was a gathering of Scout leaders (Wikipedia).

Indaba in the Anglican Communion

- www.lambethconference.org/lc2008/news/news.cfm/2008/7/4/From-Indaba-to-Reflections.

- In April 2008 the Archbishop of Canterbury, Rowan Williams, used the expression when he announced a move away from plenary meetings voting on formal resolutions for bishops attending the 2008 Lambeth Conference. He introduced "middle-sized groups for discussion of larger issues," saying: "We have given these the African name of indaba groups, groups where in traditional African culture, people get together to sort out the problems that affect them all, where everyone has a voice and where there is an attempt to find a common mind or a common story that everyone is able to tell when they go away from it. This is how we approached it. This is what we heard. This is where we arrived as we prayed and thought and talked together."

- A few years ago I was invited by the Archbishop of Hong Kong to write to the Archbishop of Canterbury and suggest dialogic solutions for reconciling the current divide among the 70 million members of the Anglican communion. Recognizing the challenge of training dialogue leaders around the world and coordinating a dialogue in so many languages and settings I proposed the church consider using existing trained mediators who were members of the church and who could manage the dialogue for local congregations around the world.

- The Archbishop has thus far chosen to use the indaba process instead. In his letter to members in 2008 he wrote: "Among the desired outcomes anticipated by this diverse group from across the Communion was not so much debates, position papers, votes and resolutions but participation on an equal footing, listening as well as speaking and the emergence of wisdom and a common mind."
- The Primate of Cape Town, the Most Rev'd Thabo Makgoba, proposed to the Lambeth Design Group (LDG) and Archbishop of Canterbury Rowan Williams, the concept of indaba, which was readily adopted by Archbishop Williams.
- Each indaba group nominates one of their group whom they believe to be most capable of carrying their views and the fruit of their discussion into the reflections process. Their Listener joins a Listening Group who, "Working with the summaries of the fruit of Indaba arising from each group, it is their duty to generate a common text which reflects authentically the Indaba."
- The text must reflect the mind of the people attending the conference. The intention is that the Listening Group meets in four open sessions. Here all bishops can comment on the developing text. It is envisaged that in this way every bishop attending the conference will be given the opportunity to "shape the Reflections" from what emerges.
- The process permits the development of a Reflections Document, which aims to meet the objectives set out for it, and be available on the last day of the conference to be received as an authentic account of the engagement of the bishops together in the service of Christ.
- At the time of writing this entry for my book it appears the indaba process has evolved into international dialogues bringing together representatives of three countries in each group to further dialogue on the major issues facing the Anglican Communion. Time will

tell if this particular process is able to achieve optimal outcomes for its stakeholders.

Inquiry-Based Learning

- Inquiry-based learning describes a range of philosophical, curricular, and pedagogical approaches to teaching. Its core premises include the requirement that learning should be based on student questions. Pedagogy and curriculum requires students to work independently to solve problems rather than receiving direct instructions on what to do from the teacher. Teachers are viewed as facilitators of learning rather than vessels of knowledge. The teacher's job in an inquiry-learning environment is not to provide knowledge, but to help students along the process of discovering knowledge themselves (Wikipedia).

Insight Dialogue

- www.metta.org/index.php?option=com_content&view=article&id=30&Itemid=9.
- One of the more valuable books I discovered in writing this list of dialogue approaches, methods, and processes is entitled *Insight Dialogue* by Gregory Kramer.[7] Kramer's years of experience leading valuable dialogues following a group mindfulness approach within the Buddhist context has much to offer non-Buddhists interested in improving their dialogues at work, at home, and in the wider society. Kramer suggests that dialogue should follow the following steps and suggests several ways to improve results at each step of the way. I list the steps and use my own words to describe these.
- Pause—Slow down and take the time for dialogue.
- Relax—Take a deep breath and recognize that your emotional state will influence the dialogue.
- Open—Become wholly aware and absorb the verbal and non-verbal messages that influence your situation at the moment.
- Trust emergence—Understand that what emerges from the stakeholders in the dialogue is the beginning of the solution and the jewels to which you must attend.
- Listen deeply—Listen not only to others but to how these messages are influencing you.

- Speak the truth—Express yourself truthfully stating thoughts and emotions diplomatically, recognizing the impact your messages are having on others.
- Kramer also lists, based on his experience, some of the most common causes for dialogues to become stuck and as such dialogue leaders must beware. The six most common causes of insight dialogue blockages are:
  1. When people get stuck identifying and talking (only) about their emotions.
  2. When people are stuck talking (only) about superficial niceties.
  3. When people are stuck talking (only) about concepts, ideas, thoughts.
  4. When people feel a need to teach others or be a student to others.
  5. When people are stuck in silence.
  6. When people are stuck craving for the experience of dialogue rather than the outcomes.

Interfaith Dialogue

- The terms interfaith or interfaith dialogue refer to cooperative and positive interaction between people of different religious traditions and spiritual or humanistic beliefs, at both the individual and institutional level with the aim of deriving a common ground in belief through a concentration on similarities between faiths, understanding of values, and commitment to the world.
- Interfaith dialogue is distinct from syncretism or alternative religion, in that dialogue often involves promoting understanding between different religions to increase acceptance of others, rather than to synthesize new beliefs. There is a view that the history of religion shows that conflict has been more the state of affairs than dialogue (Wikipedia).

Interfaith Dialogue at the World Council of Churches

- www.oikoumene.org/en/who-are-we.html.
- The World Council of Churches (WCC) brings together 349 churches, denominations, and church fellowships in more than 110 countries and territories throughout the world, representing more than 560 million Christians and including most of the

world's Orthodox churches, scores of Anglican, Baptist, Lutheran, Methodist, and Reformed churches, as well as many United and Independent churches.

- The world's largest Christian body, the Roman Catholic Church, is not a member of the WCC, but has worked closely with the Council for more than four decades and sends representatives to all major WCC conferences as well as to its Central Committee meetings and the assemblies.
- For its member churches, the WCC is a unique space: one in which they can reflect, speak, act, worship, and work together, challenge and support each other, share and debate with each other.
- The goal of the World Council of Churches is not to build a global "super-church," nor to standardize styles of worship, but rather to deepen the fellowship of Christian churches and communities so that they may see in one another authentic expressions of the "one holy, catholic and apostolic church."
- The governing bodies established by the WCC's constitution are the means of ensuring that the activities undertaken by the council as an institution are attuned to the needs and concerns of its member churches and ecumenical partners. They should function in ways that:
  - Ensure maximum representation and participation by the member churches, with policies set and decisions made in a transparent way.
  - Listen to the voices of all, not just to those whose culture, language, education, or experience give them special advantages in the setting of a global organization.
  - Give priority to reflection and deliberation on the key issues facing the churches in the world today, rather than being dominated by institutional concerns.
  - Pay constant attention to the theological coherence and coordination of the WCC's activities, rather than being a place where particular interests and agendas lobby.
  - Establish and deepen relations with churches that are not WCC members but are open to ecumenical fellowship.
  - Stimulate those with leadership responsibilities in member churches to take up ecumenical concerns locally and to act ecumenically in their immediate context.

Learning Organizations

- www.solonline.org/aboutsol/.
- Peter Senge, author of the seminal text *The Fifth Discipline* is one of the best-known proponents of systems thinking and is famous for his concept of learning organizations.[8] According to Senge, "'learning organizations' are those organizations where people continually expand their capacity to create the results they truly desire, where new and expansive patterns of thinking are nurtured, where collective aspiration is set free, and where people are continually learning to see the whole together."
- Senge argues that only those organizations that are able to adapt quickly and effectively will be able to excel in their field or market. In order to be a learning organization there must be two conditions present at all times.
  1. The first is the ability to design the organization to match the intended or desired outcomes.
  2. The ability to recognize when the initial direction of the organization is different from the desired outcome and follow the necessary steps to correct this mismatch. Organizations that are able to do this are exemplary (Wikipedia).
- I met Peter Senge when he spoke at the ICF conference in Montreal a few years ago and I first came to know of his work several years before that when I was working with the international engineering firm called ABB in Australia. ABB had adopted several of the best practices described in Senge's *Fifth Discipline Fieldbook* and looked to me to reinforce these practices (e.g., ladder of inference by Chris Argyris) in my negotiation work with them.[9]
- Learning organizations succeed because of the dialogue that is at the heart of their learning. If the quality of their dialogue diminishes, so does their learning.

Lego Serious Play

- www.seriousplay.com/.
- LEGO® SERIOUS PLAY® is an innovative, experiential process designed to enhance innovation and business performance. Based on research that shows that this kind of hands-on, minds-on learning produces a deeper, more meaningful understanding of the world

and its possibilities, LEGO® SERIOUS PLAY® deepens the reflection process and supports an **effective dialogue**—for everyone in the organization.

- I have used Lego building blocks several times with organizations and it has always been successful. First the participants love to play with the blocks, adults often returning to their childhood to find their favorite pieces and fit them together into something creative.

- I usually ask participants to team up and produce something that represents the organization today and something that represents the organization as you'd like it to be. The resulting dialogue as groups describe their creations creates valuable insights that are fun, meaningful, and lasting because the creations can be kept and referred to in future sessions as a form of measure on how things are progressing, or not.

- My favorite Lego creation produced by a financial services team is one I carry with me everywhere I work with teams. Newer editions of Lego have innovative pieces including a skateboard and a shark. This particular team simply put the shark on top of the skateboard to represent management. "They move back and forth with no real strategy except to open their mouth and eat up whomever is in the way." Needless to say this particular creation led to some serious reflection by the team management following the discussion.

Mind Mapping

- www.thinkbuzan.com/intl/home.
- A mind map is a diagram used to represent words, ideas, tasks, or other items linked to and arranged around a central key word or idea. Mind maps are used to generate, visualize, structure, and classify ideas, and as an aid to studying and organizing information, solving problems, making decisions, and writing.
- The elements of a given mind map are arranged intuitively according to the importance of the concepts, and are classified into groupings, branches, or areas, with the goal of representing semantic or other connections between portions of information. Mind maps may also aid recall of existing memories.
- By presenting ideas in a radial, graphical, nonlinear manner, mind maps encourage a brainstorming approach to planning and

organizational tasks. Though the branches of a mind map represent hierarchical tree structures, their radial arrangement disrupts the prioritizing of concepts typically associated with hierarchies presented with more linear visual cues. This orientation toward brainstorming encourages users to enumerate and connect concepts without a tendency to begin within a particular conceptual framework (Wikipedia).

- I have been using mind maps since the 1980s when they were first introduced to me as part of the Evelyn Wood speed reading training (www.ewrd.com/ewrd/EvelynWood_aboutus.asp). Since that time mind mapping has become synonymous with Tony Buzan, author of various mind mapping books and now producer of related software.
- In my experience mind maps are useful for individuals and groups to organize thoughts as they emerge; for example, writing an outline for a document, organizing existing concepts, memorizing information for use or for taking notes when listening to presentations.
- Mind maps can help dialogue by helping people structure their expressions, helping listeners capture what they hear and helping groups capture ideas as they flow out of the dialogue with the jewels of the dialogue hanging on every branch like balls on a Christmas tree.

Occupy Wall Street People's Assemblies
- www.takethesquare.net.
- Occupy Wall Street (OWS) is further evidence of the dialogue gap in society today.
- OWS spread from its inception on September 17, 2011, in New York City's Zucotti Park to nearly 1,000 sites and 100 countries in just three months.
- While each location operates slightly differently, the OWS consensus process is managed by moderators who ensure every issue considered to be important is discussed before reaching agreement.
- Through a fairly well-defined process and the use of hand signals this leaderless process does do a good job of involving a large number of people in relatively effective dialogue.
- Each proposal put before the general assembly must clearly state what it is, why it is being proposed, and how it can be carried out if consensus is achieved.

- A proposal is accepted when there is no outright opposition to it. If opposition exists then the moderators help the assembly achieve consensus using the following steps:
  1. Moderator asks the assembly to prepare and present three arguments for and three arguments against the proposal. Rules exist to ensure all ideas are heard and minority groups are represented.
  2. If after step 1 a consensus is still not achieved, the moderator asks the assembly to sit and discuss the issues for and against the proposal in small groups.
  3. If after step 2 a consensus is still not achieved, the moderator refers the proposal to a working group who studies it and returns with a revised proposal at a later date.
- OWS refer to their process as What, Why, How, and deal only with practical issues, not ideological issues. They stress people must be peaceful and leave their prejudices and ideology at home.

Open Space Technology
- www.openspaceworld.org.
- Open Space Technology (OST), developed initially by Harrison Owen, enables all kinds of people, in any kind of organization, to create inspired meetings and events. It is used, often very productively, to harness collective wisdom when addressing complex issues for which nobody has an answer. It is a self-organizing process for decision making. OST operates with a simple set of guidelines.
  - The four principles:
    1. Whoever comes are the right people.
    2. Whatever happens is the only thing that could have.
    3. When it starts is the right time.
    4. When it's over it's over.
  - The law of two feet: If you find yourself in a situation where you are neither learning nor contributing, move somewhere where you can. This is a law like the Law of Gravity. You can choose to notice it or not, but it's safer just to notice it.
- Open space has devoted followers around the world who have seen it produce wonderful results in diverse settings. For some the process may feel too open and too loose. These people prefer to follow a more clearly defined path to a more clearly defined goal.

- Experienced practitioners tend to like the liberating aspects of open space and realize that this freedom is often what participants need to achieve optimal outcomes.
- When choosing a dialogue process, practitioners need to consider how directive a process the dialogue participants and sponsors will accept. In assessing this you should consider professional background, corporate and ethnic culture.

Parliamentary Systems

- A parliamentary system is a system of government characterized by no clear-cut separation of powers between the executive and legislative branches, leading to a different set of checks and balances compared to those found in presidential systems (Wikipedia).
- One of the original concepts of Socrates was that civil society was based on the quality of the dialogue that took place among society's leaders. Parliamentary systems originate from this era and the inherent checks and balances force dialogue in the chamber in order to air the different issues of importance prior to passing laws affecting society.
- As outlined early in my description of the effects of dialogue gap on society, political leaders, whether they find themselves in parliamentary, presidential, or other systems need to remember that the quality of their decisions is based on the quality of their dialogues and that partisan behavior, which limits the proper airing of views, leads to suboptimal decision making.

Performance Appraisals

- Lots of people dislike the performance appraisal system in their organizations for a variety of reasons but this doesn't stop the process from creating one of the most valuable and sometimes the only opportunity for dialogue between an organization and its employees. If handled well, performance appraisals can generate valuable ideas for personal and organizational growth. If handled poorly they are nothing more than communication of rating and salary adjustments.
- Performance management dialogues achieve the best results when both the appraiser and appraisee have received guidance on how the meeting(s) will be conducted and what to do when various sensitive

topics arise. Performance appraisal meetings work well when they follow a pre-agreed-on agenda, which normally includes:

- *Preparation*—Specifics about appraisee.
- *Start dialogue*—Set relaxed atmosphere, agree on agenda.
- *Update situation*—Discuss what went well and what to improve.
- *Handle reactions*—Use Ma-Ma questioning to understand each other, focus on what is important, use "I-statements" to explain specifically how you feel or think as a result of the observed actions of the appraisee, for example, "I am pleased when I see you put in overtime to meet customer deadlines."
- *Synchronize future expectations*—Both appraiser and appraisee will have ideas of what will result from the appraisal meetings and it is best to dialogue about these expectations so that they are synchronized.
- *Agree on next steps*—Bring the meeting to a close once you have agreed on together what will happen next.
- An important part of the performance appraisal process is the selection of people for promotion. This part of the performance management process also leads to considerable dialogue but it doesn't always lead to optimal outcomes because people often put personal or organizational goals ahead of the goals of the candidate or other options available for this person's career development.

John was a senior associate in a large international law firm. John's mentor and senior partner in the firm wanted to promote John to partner but his promotion prospects created considerable dialogue inside the partnership. Edward, another influential partner at the firm felt that if John was promoted to partnership then his associate should also be promoted. Some disagreed that Edward's associate should be promoted citing a relative lack of experience. The debate dragged on over more than a year and John was aware of the situation he found himself in at the firm. As a result John accepted an offer from a competing firm and resigned. Edward's associate meanwhile was promoted to partner. Did this dialogue lead to an optimal outcome? Far from it. John was sought after for his much needed skills and the fact he was headhunted away by a competing firm hurt the firm he left and contributed to still more conflict within the partnership.

Positive Deviance

- www.positivedeviance.org/.
- Positive deviance (PD) is based on the observation that in every community there are certain individuals or groups (the positive deviants), whose uncommon but successful behaviors or strategies enable them to find better solutions to a problem than their peers. These individuals or groups have access to exactly the same resources and face the same challenges and obstacles as their peers.
- The PD approach is a strength-based, problem-solving approach for behavior and social change. The approach enables the community to discover existing solutions to complex problems within the community.
- The PD approach differs from traditional "needs-based" or problem-solving approaches in that it does not focus primarily on identification of needs and the external inputs necessary to meet those needs or solve problems. A unique process invites the community to identify and optimize existing, sustainable solutions from within the community, which speeds up innovation.
- The PD approach has been used to address issues as diverse as childhood malnutrition, neonatal mortality, girl trafficking, school drop-out, female genital cutting, hospital acquired infections, and HIV/AIDS.
- What I like best about this dialogue process is that it spots success, generates dialogue about what caused the success, and then extends the dialogue to find ways to spread the isolated success to the rest of the community that can benefit. When I suggest the solution is in the dialogue, this approach finds solutions and then uses dialogue to define and spread these solutions to a wider audience.
- For further information I encourage you to read the recent book *The Power of Positive Deviance: How Unlikely Innovators Solve the World's Toughest Problems*, Richard Pascale, Jerry Sternin, and Monique Sternin, Harvard Business Press, 2010.

Quiet Time

- Quiet time, in my experience, is an important process to engender dialogue because by imposing a time of quiet or even silence is like an interval in a sports match, which allows the players to perform even better after the pause.

- When working with groups and teams, leaders and facilitators often overlook the value of the quiet time. Some participants will resist "wasting their time sitting together doing nothing" so it is useful that you assign a reflection for individual consideration during the quiet time, for example, two minutes. Dialogue leaders will need to police the quiet time as some participants will prefer to fill in the silence sooner than others thus robbing the others of their rare chance for quiet reflection.

Robert's Rules of Order

- www.robertsrules.com.
- The first edition of the book, whose full title was *Pocket Manual of Rules of Order for Deliberative Assemblies*, was published in February 1876 by then U.S. Army Brigadier General Henry Martyn Robert (1837–1923) with the short title *Robert's Rules of Order* placed on its cover. The procedures prescribed by the book were loosely modeled after those used in the United States House of Representatives, with such adaptations as Robert saw fit for use in ordinary societies.
- The author's interest in parliamentary procedure began in 1863 when he was chosen to preside over a church meeting and, although he accepted the task, he felt that he did not have the necessary knowledge of proper procedure. In his later work as an active member of several organizations, he discovered that members from different areas of the country had different views regarding what the proper parliamentary rules were, and these conflicting views hampered the organizations in their work. He eventually became convinced of the need for a new manual on the subject, one that would enable many organizations to adopt the same set of rules.
- Robert's traditional meeting rules for meetings, which originated in the nineteenth century seem not to have made it into the less formal and digitally connected era in which we live today. Despite this element, Robert's rules are still found wherever meetings are formally chaired and minutes taken.

- In my experience the more formal the meeting the less dialogue that takes place and although I am in favor of Robert's Rules for procedure I again stress the importance of creating **TIME for dialogue** within the regular communication agenda.

Scenario Planning

- Scenario planning is a straightforward dialogue based on competing views of the future. Once competing views are established the stakeholders dialogue the likelihood of their happening in whole or in part and then plan accordingly.
- Scenario planning is attributed to the pioneering work of Paul J. H. Schoemaker at Royal Dutch Shell.
- Scenario planning starts by dividing knowledge into two broad domains: (1) things we believe we know something about, and (2) elements we consider uncertain or unknowable.
  - The first component—trends—casts the past forward, recognizing that our world possesses considerable momentum and continuity. For example, we can safely make assumptions about demographic shifts and, perhaps, substitution effects for certain new technologies.
  - The second component—true uncertainties—involves indeterminables such as future interest rates, outcomes of political elections, rates of innovation, fads and fashions in markets.
- The art of scenario planning lies in blending the known and the unknown into a limited number of internally consistent views of the future that span a wide range of possibilities.
- Numerous organizations have applied scenario planning to a broad range of issues, from relatively simple, tactical decisions to the complex process of strategic planning and vision building.
- The power of scenario planning for business was originally established by Royal Dutch/Shell, which has used scenarios since the early 1970s as part of a process for generating and evaluating its strategic options. Shell has been consistently better in its oil forecasts than other major oil companies, and saw the overcapacity in the tanker business and Europe's petrochemicals earlier than its competitors (Wikipedia).

Six Thinking Hats

- www.debonogroup.com/parallel_thinking.htm.
- The six thinking hats method is attributed to Dr. Edward de Bono and is the subject of his book, *Six Thinking Hats*. It is a thinking tool for group discussion and individual thinking. Combined with the idea of parallel thinking it provides a means for groups to think together more effectively, and a means to plan thinking processes in a detailed and cohesive way.
- Parallel thinking is defined as a thinking process where focus is split in specific directions. When done in a group it effectively avoids the consequences of the adversarial approach (as used in courts).
- In adversarial debate the objective is to prove or disprove statements put forward by the parties (normally two). This is also known as the dialectic approach.
- In parallel thinking practitioners put forward as many statements as possible in several (preferably more than two) parallel tracks. This leads to *exploration* of a subject where all participants can contribute, in parallel, with knowledge, facts, feelings, and so on.
- Crucial to the method is that the process is done in a disciplined manner and that all participants play along and contribute in parallel. Thus each participant must stick to the specific track (Wikipedia).
- The six distinct thinking states are identified and assigned a color:
  1. Questions (White)—Considering purely what information is available, what are the facts?
  2. Emotions (Red)—Instinctive gut reaction or statements of emotional feeling (but not any justification).
  3. Bad points judgment (Black)—Logic applied to identifying flaws or barriers, seeking mismatch.
  4. Good points judgment (Yellow)—Logic applied to identifying benefits, seeking harmony.
  5. Creativity (Green)—Statements of provocation and investigation, seeing where a thought goes.
  6. Thinking (Blue)—Thinking about thinking.
- I like this approach because it helps dialogue leaders ensure the completeness of the issues covered in their dialogues; however, my clients who have experienced the process seem to have done so more as a

training event rather than as a tool to continually improve the quality of their dialogic outcomes.

- Like all of these approaches the success rests on the dialogue leader to ensure the outcomes are optimized using whatever it takes.

Sunday Brunch

- Families looking to sustain dialogue need not look any further than the traditional Sunday brunch. If you can manage to get key family members seated around the table for a meal at least once a week then you will be creating a space for dialogue to take place.
- At the table dialogue leaders should do their best to keep the dialogue positive and yet focused, covering the successes and challenges of the people present. Once participants are used to the quality of the dialogue that arises from useful questions and following a process, which gives everyone a voice and a chance to help each other, then getting people to attend again becomes quite easy.
- Sometimes the family meal devolves into a platform for the most expressive participant to tell others something addressing his or her personal needs. When this arises attempts should be made to regain the opportunity for dialogue because when lost it is often another week before the family reunites with the opportunity to dialogue.

Technology of Participation (ToP)

- www.ica-usa.org/index.php?pr=whatistop.
- The Technology of Participation teaches team members how to collaborate on projects and group facilitators how to effectively lead their team. ToP® provides methods that:
  - Recognize and honor contributions of all.
  - Let a group deal with more data in less time.
  - Pool individual contributions into larger more informative patterns.
  - Welcome diversity while minimizing polarization and conflict.
- The ToP approach was developed by the Institute of Cultural Affairs (ICA) from the late 1950s to the mid-1970s with some development after that.
- This approach is currently being applied in corporations, communities, organizations at the grassroots level, and in board rooms around the world.

- I was first introduced to the work of the ICA in Hong Kong in the early 1990s and have been a fan of the process ever since. One of the strong benefits is how everyone gets involved in having an active dialogue on subjects that matter.

Theatrical Skits

- Earlier mention of experiential learning, play, and song would not be complete without separate mention of skits that are common features in at work, at home, and in society and that are great sources of dialogue.
- Theatrical productions are dialogues in themselves and playwrights are intent on setting up the dialogue to communicate the messages they do. Likewise the plays generate dialogue among the spectators and harnessing these opportunities is a great way to help achieve optimal outcomes for the people involved.
- Theater is often a good way to express issues that can be told through a third party but that might be deemed too sensitive to address head-on.

Theory U

- www.presencing.com/presencing-theoryu/.
- Theory U, created by Otto Scharmer at MIT, offers both a new theoretical perspective and a practical social technology.[10]
  - As a theoretical perspective, Theory U suggests that the way in which we attend to a situation determines how a situation unfolds: *I attend this way, therefore it emerges that way.*
  - As a practical social technology, Theory U offers a set of principles and practices for collectively creating the future that wants to emerge (following the movements of co-initiating, co-sensing, co-inspiring, co-creating, and co-evolving).
- "Presencing," a blend of the words "presence" and "sensing," refers to the ability to sense and bring into the present one's highest future potential—as an individual and as a group.
- Theory U explores a whole new territory of scientific research and personal leadership. By moving through the U we learn to connect to our originating self. We travel down the left side of the U to find ourselves in the realm of presencing, where we learn to sense the future that is seeking to emerge.

- Fundamental problems, as Einstein once noted, cannot be solved at the same level of thought that created them. Learning to pay attention to our attention and to illuminate the blind spot, according to Scharmer, is the key leverage point to bring forth the profound systemic changes in business, society, and in science so needed now.
- I learned of Scharmer's work through my focus on presence in dialogue. I have yet to experience it firsthand but look forward to doing so as soon as the opportunity arises because clearly optimal outcomes need presence and Scharmer's work is proving to create a valuable connection between the stakeholders and the outcomes awaiting their co-creation.

Town Halls

- A town hall meeting is a name given to a secular and informal public meeting. All people in a town community are invited to attend, not always to voice their opinions, but to hear the responses from public figures and (if applicable) elected officials about shared subjects of interest.
- There are no specific rules or guidelines for holding a town hall meeting. If the turnout is large, and in a particular case the objective is to give as many people as possible an opportunity to speak, then the group can be broken down into smaller discussion groups. Each group in that case appoints someone to summarize discussion of the group (Wikipedia).
- Town hall meetings have come back into favor thanks to the Internet, which means that dialogue leaders can meet people locally and remotely and thereby greatly widen the reach and importance of the dialogue.
- Town hall meetings are a Western tradition building on older traditions from around the world when local residents would assemble in the commons to dialogue key issues of the day. These dialogues can be so significant that in countries like China, groups need government approval to assemble.
- In order for town hall sessions to be effective it is important the space be well equipped in terms of equipment so all people can express themselves and absorb the messages of others. It is also

important that dialogue leaders ensure that large group issues also are addressed, for example, managing conflicts, grouping of ideas, and like-minded people.

Truth and Reconciliation Commissions

- A truth commission or truth and reconciliation commission is a commission tasked with discovering and revealing past wrongdoing by a government (or, depending on the circumstances, nonstate actors, also), in the hope of resolving conflict left over from the past. They are, under various names, occasionally set up by states emerging from periods of internal unrest, civil war, or dictatorship.
- South Africa's Truth and Reconciliation Commission, established by President Nelson Mandela after apartheid, is one of the most well-known Truth Commissions but others exist as well (Wikipedia).
- Truth commissions create a carefully managed space for dialogue and truth to emerge so that the stakeholders can make known the truth and as a result move forward into the future in greater harmony.
- Due to the nature of truth commissions and despite the quality of their dialogue and the truth they surface, there are proponents and detractors.
- While people appreciate they can provide proof against historical revisionism of state terrorism and other crimes and human rights abuses, they are sometimes criticized for allowing crimes to go unpunished, and creating impunity for serious human rights abusers.

Truth and reconciliation in Canada

- www.trc.ca/websites/trcinstitution/index.php?p=3.
- The truth telling and reconciliation process is part of an overall holistic and comprehensive response to the Indian Residential School legacy and a sincere indication and acknowledgment of the injustices and harms experienced by Aboriginal people and the need for continued healing.
- This is a profound commitment to establishing new relationships embedded in mutual recognition and respect that will forge a brighter future. The truth of our common experiences will help set our spirits free and pave the way to reconciliation.

- The Canadian Truth and Reconciliation Commission will build upon the "Statement of Reconciliation" dated January 7, 1998, and the principles developed by the Working Group on Truth and Reconciliation and of the Exploratory Dialogues (1998–1999).
- These principles are: accessible; victim-centered; confidentiality (if required by the former student); do no harm; health and safety of participants; representative; public/transparent; accountable; open and honorable process; comprehensive; inclusive, educational, holistic, just and fair; respectful; voluntary; flexible; and forward looking in terms of rebuilding and renewing Aboriginal relationships and the relationship between Aboriginal and non–Aboriginal Canadians.
- Reconciliation is an ongoing individual and collective process, and will require commitment from all those affected including First Nations, Inuit and Métis former Indian Residential School (IRS) students, their families, communities, religious entities, former school employees, government, and the people of Canada.
- Reconciliation may occur between any of the previous groups.[11]

United Nations

- www.un.org/en/.
- The future of the world rests in the multilateral organizations that our political leaders have established over the years including the UN, the World Bank, the IMF WTO, G8, and G20. The success of all of these organizations rests on the quality of the dialogue inside their chambers and among their members. Sadly, in my experience, the quality of the dialogue is often lacking and perhaps that is part of the dialogue gap we face today at the start of the twenty-first century.
- The UN Charter as written is surprisingly silent on the importance of effective dialogue. Perhaps those who drafted the Charter thought any form of dialogue was better than none at all, knowing that without dialogue the United Nations need not exist. Readers can consider whether explicit mention of effective dialogue and how to achieve it is needed to amend the UN Charter. It would appear that many leaders today have a different understanding of "by peaceful means" and could use some training in dialogue.
- The United Nations is an international organization founded in 1945 after World War II by 51 countries committed to maintaining international peace and security, developing friendly relations

among nations, and promoting social progress, better living standards, and human rights.

- Due to its unique international character, and the powers vested in its founding Charter, the Organization can take action on a wide range of issues, and provide a forum for its 192 Member States to express their views, through the General Assembly, the Security Council, the Economic and Social Council, and other bodies and committees.

- All Members shall settle their international disputes **by peaceful means** in such a manner that international peace and security, and justice, are not endangered.

- All Members shall refrain in their international relations from the threat or use of force against the territorial integrity or political independence of any state, or in any other manner inconsistent with the Purposes of the United Nations.

- All Members shall give the United Nations every assistance in any action it takes in accordance with the present Charter, and shall refrain from giving assistance to any state against which the United Nations is taking preventive or enforcement action.

- The Organization shall ensure that states which are not Members of the United Nations act in accordance with these Principles so far as may be necessary for the maintenance of international peace and security.

- Nothing contained in the present Charter shall authorize the United Nations to intervene in matters which are essentially within the domestic jurisdiction of any state or shall require the Members to submit such matters to settlement under the present Charter.[12]

Videos

- Another dialogue process that I have found useful is video clips or full-length movies that are professionally produced and that stimulate thoughts and feelings for subsequent dialogue.

- All readers will have experienced videos so well produced they create a space ideal for dialogue and rich in emotional and intellectual content. As a dialogue leader you should consider using videos or movie clips to stimulate and prime your stakeholders for an effective dialogue.

- Some groups have found it useful to video themselves or similar groups and share these video clips accordingly.

World Café
- www.theworldcafe.com/.
- World Café is a conversational process based on a set of integrated design principles that reveal a deeper living network pattern through which participants co-evolve their collective future. The integrated design principles include:
  - Set the Context
  - Create Hospitable Space
  - Explore Questions that Matter
  - Encourage Everyone's Contribution
  - Connect Diverse Perspectives
  - Listen Together and Notice Patterns
  - Share Collective Discoveries
- My experience with World Café is positive for a number or reasons. It allows for an informal environment, it anchors people to subjects that matter to them, it allows for freedom of movement between subjects, it is self-regulating with people spending as much or as little time on each subject as they wish.
- The value of using this process is to enable participants to focus on a particular issue through going deeply into the fundamental questions at the core of the matter. Once this happens the means to address the issue becomes clear.
- The story of the World Café and its unfolding during the first decade of its life are told in *The World Café: Shaping Our Futures Through Conversations That Matter*, co-authored by Juanita Brown, David Isaacs, and the World Café Community, and published by Berrett-Koehler in 2005.

Dialogue Processes Not Included in the Preceding List
Readers will wonder why some of their favorite approaches, methods, and processes are not included in the preceding list. For the most part I have included all those that, in my experience, were effective and widely used or worthy of being exposed to a wider audience. There are two that I purposefully excluded from the list: Business Process Reengineering (BPR) and Six Sigma.

1. BPR creates considerable dialogue but experience shows that it doesn't always lead to optimal outcomes because the outcome is often a fait accompli and BPR is simply used to figure out how to achieve this goal sometimes by excluding some of the key stakeholders from the dialogue. For example, BPR is considered one of the leading contributors to the United States, outsourcing much of its manufacturing and service industry to lower-cost jurisdictions. Although this might have been good for investors and overseas employees who have been hired, it has not always been appreciated by on-shore employees and local customers. Can better solutions be achieved? The solution is in the dialogue.

2. Six Sigma is a quality improvement program that generates considerable dialogue but which has also led to considerable criticism. I have worked in many organizations that have implemented Six Sigma to eliminate defective or variable quality manufacturing or service, but the overwhelming response to the program is not one of dialogue but rather statistical analysis and reporting. Motorola invented Six Sigma in 1986 with the intent of business improvement and it is shared with the world through its Motorola University where I did some work in the early 1990s. If the emphasis was more on dialogue than on measuring then I would have happily included Six Sigma in the list of dialogic solutions. Considering the number of clients that have shared their complaints with me about the way Six Sigma was implemented in their markets, dialogue is the one thing missing.

Where Else to Turn to Sustain Dialogue

Look inside yourself—Dialogue leaders know that sometimes what is preventing dialogue is caused by the selfish desires, craving, attachment, and lack of emotional regulation in the stakeholders themselves. It is useful to keep track of these things in the stakeholders you work with and in yourself because these emotions and how you regulate them will influence your ability to achieve optimal outcomes.

Look to professionals—Dialogue leaders need not make mistakes as they learn how to achieve optimal outcomes because there are many experts available to help. People who are experts in managing dialogue in different contexts include facilitators (www.iaf-world.org/i4a/pages/index.cfm?pageid=1), counselors, coaches (www.coachfederation.org/), consultants, psychiatrists, religious leaders, family members, and mentors.

Look online—Increasingly solutions are being created online through social networks like Facebook (www.facebook.com/) and LinkedIn (www.linkedin.com/), and broadband services like Tele-Presence (www.cisco.com/en/US/netsol/ns669/networking_solutions_solution_segment_home.html).

A good description of online dialogue solutions being created to address the problems facing the twenty-first century are described in MacroWikinomics as examples of collaborative innovation, the underlying basis of which is effective dialogue (www.macrowikinomics.com/).[13]

Look for training—Another good source of solutions exists in the growing list of dialogue- or conversation-training programs available. Although most of these originate in the United States or are local in nature, two programs are beginning to spread internationally and in so doing becoming even more valuable as they incorporate more of the cultural differences affecting dialogue around the world.

- Crucial Conversations—www.vitalsmarts.com/crucialconversations_book.aspx.
- Fierce Conversations—www.fierceinc.com/index.php?page=book.

Readers interested in training options related to this book can choose one of the options listed at the back of this book and step forward as a dialogue leader without delay. The world needs more dialogic leaders prepared to push for optimal outcomes at work, at home, and in society. This book represents the underlying philosophy of training courses including the Star Negotiator© and the Dialogic Selling Workshop©.[14]

Look to silence, music, and dreams—Other sources of solutions reside in places you might not associate with dialogue. In times of silence our soul or intuition speaks to us and if we are listening we can pick up signals to move us toward optimal outcomes. Similar to mindfulness practices for some music and natural sounds like bird song can inspire dialogic improvements toward achieving optimal outcomes. Finally some readers will look to their dreams for a door to inner dialogue, which can lead to the achievement of optimal outcomes.

Sustaining Dialogue—A Final Word

I speak to many people who are working their way through the problems of dialogue gap and life beyond the digital tipping point where poor results are typical and the stakeholders involved have lost hope. For you and for dialogue leaders who simply find the going tough I encourage you to remember and recite like I do these well-known lines to help you through the tough times:

Tough Times Never Last but Tough People Do

—Robert Schuller

Never, Never, Never Give Up

—Winston Churchill

Keep your head when others lose theirs and blame it on you.

—Unknown

You never get a rainbow without a storm.

—Unknown

Extreme pressure makes diamonds.

—Unknown

Notes

1. *The Concise Oxford Dictionary*, Oxford University Press, 1990.
2. Alex F. Osborn, *Applied Imagination: Principles and Procedures of Creative Problem-Solving*, 3rd edition, Creative Education Foundation; 3rd rev. edition, February 1993.
3. Parker J. Palmer, *A Hidden Wholeness* (Hoboken, NJ: John Wiley & Sons, 2004).
4. www.united-church.ca/organization/moderator/tindal.

5. http://en.wikipedia.org/wiki/Paulo_Freire.

6. Robin Stuart-Kotze, *Performance: The Secrets of Successful Behaviour* (FT Prentice Hall, 2006).

7. Gregory Kramer, *Insight Dialogue* (Boston: Shambhala, 2007).

8. Peter Senge, *The Fifth Discipline* (New York: Doubleday, 1990).

9. Peter Senge, Kleiner, Roberts, Ross, and Smith, *The Fifth Discipline Fieldbook* (New York: Doubleday, 1994).

10. C. Otto Scharmer, *Theory U* (SoL, 2007).

11. www.trc.ca/websites/trcinstitution/index.php?p=3.

12. Sourced from www.UN.org/en/ where readers can access the full charter.

13. Don Tapscott and Anthony Williams, *Macrowikinomics* (Portfolio, 2010).

14. The Star Negotiator Workshop is the basis of the book *Negotiation: Mastering Business in Asia*, Peter Nixon, John Wiley & Sons, 2005.

Chapter 8

Dialogic Leadership

One good conversation can shift the direction of change forever.

—Linda Lambert[1]

What Do Dialogic Leaders Know That Others Don't?

The future prospects for humanity diverge greatly depending on what sort of values guide the 21st century.

—Majid Tehranian[2]

In this final chapter I challenge you to become a *dialogic leader* and in so doing make the world a better place, not just at work but even more importantly at home and in society.

- Dialogic leaders **realize that the solution is in the dialogue** and don't exclude people or issues from inclusion in the dialogue.

- Dialogic leaders **know when to dialogue and when to communicate** and are effective at both.
- Dialogic leaders **aim to achieve optimal outcomes** by leveraging their understanding of the dialogue puzzle and are not satisfied with "good enough" outcomes.
- Dialogic leaders **protect against the negative effects of the digital tipping point at work** by bringing key stakeholders together face-to-face to dialogue in the right way on key issues whenever necessary.
- Dialogic leaders **at home and in society put in place, reinforce, and respect dialogic behaviors**, approaches, methodologies, and processes that systematically encourage dialogue and minimize the effects of dialogue gap and life beyond the digital tipping point.
- Dialogic leaders **have compassion for nondialogic leaders** who don't yet recognize that the solution is in the dialogue and/or lack the requisite skills and experience outlined in this and other books that offer them the optimal outcomes they require.
- Dialogic leaders **focus on and develop their presence, respect, and expression while suspending their assumptions and beliefs and fully absorb the messages being shared by others** with a goal of fully understanding the current situation and taking optimal decisions as a result.
- Dialogic leaders **recognize that we live in a dynamic world making it necessary to stay in dialogue**, that is, to "stay in touch" and "keep touching base" with key stakeholders over time.
- Dialogic leaders know that **it is getting harder to engage people in dialogue** and work hard to create times and spaces for dialogue to happen regularly.
- Dialogic leaders say no to silence and violence at work, at home, and in society knowing that **our interdependent futures are built on our ability to dialogue effectively together.**

When my knowledge is helpful to the various practitioners in the field—that is the moment when I know that I know.

—Ed Schein[3]

It takes considerable confidence to be a dialogic leader especially in the face of conflict and other leaders who prefer to take a unilateral decision and move on. Nondialogic leadership masquerades as leadership in the short term but leaves organizations short of the optimal outcomes that are needed to survive the complex and threatening environment we are living in today.

Do we have a choice? As John Denver said, "Now for the first time this could be the last time." At work, at home, and in society we are facing unprecedented peril around the world and we need to learn to dialogue not just to survive but to thrive and enjoy the outstanding opportunities that await us.

Globalization requires a new type of Universalism, a theory and practice that begins with the acknowledgment of similarities before it starts to negotiate through dialogue the differences.

—Majid Tehranian[4]

If dialogue gets better we all win. Our home life will become more invigorating and happy, our businesses will become more successful and motivating as places to work, and society will become significantly more sustainable, peaceful, and enjoyable for more and more people.

As Gandhi has reminded us, "Be the change you wish to see in the world," become the dialogic leader you expect of others so they can learn from your behaviors and emulate your success. As dialogue leaders I believe we need to take a stand and that it is not enough to simply talk about the importance of dialogue; we need to make space for dialogue to take place in our lives at work, at home, and in society. As a result I suggest five things to help create momentum for a dialogic future at home, at work, and in society from this point forward.

We cannot afford to be ordinary human beings any more. It was all right at one time. You cannot afford to be an ordinary, mediocre, dull, stupid, human being any more.

The challenge is too immense. You will have to do something.

—J. Krishnamurti[6]

How to Improve Dialogue @ Home

> *Great ideas usually appear in such times of political and moral crisis.*
>   —Majid Tehranian[5]

Everything begins and ends at home and it is the basis on which we are able to perform at work and in society effectively, so I suggest the following changes in our home lives.

These are recommendations and need to be implemented according to your own situations but nonetheless the purpose and intent is clear—to create space for optimal outcomes to arise through dialogue:

- Couples and families should eat together at least once a week and preferably every night for up to two hours during which time there should be *no* digital gadgets allowed (that means no TV, iPods, iPads), although stimulating music is okay.
- Each participant should be asked about the highs and lows of the day. Time should be equally distributed and not allocated on just one person.
- Couples and family members should aim to **spend 10 to 20 minutes one-to-one in dialogue with each other every day**, during which time they should practice their presence and effective dialogue. Again this means 100 percent focused time, fully present, no ear phones hanging down, no Facebook pinging in the background, no TV.
- Each of you should **complete Potential's *Individual Dialogue Assessment*** and if you wish, ask others to complete the assessment on you so that you can identify those specific dialogue behaviors you need to improve.
- Stop using all digital gadgets when it is time for dialogue or sleep.
- Don't think that it is normal to be half-focused on your laptop while you are with someone else. Close your laptop, put away your phone, take the earplugs out, and turn off the TV and focus 100 percent on the person you are with.
- People addicted to their "crackberries," PC games, and Facebook will interrupt their sleep. Turn them off, put them on the table outside your bedroom, and eliminate any digital gadgets (other

than your alarm clock) that will prevent you from sleeping soundly all night long. Your brain (and body) need to synchronize and rejuvenate overnight from your busy day.

- If your daytime schedule at work or school is lived beyond the digital tipping point it is important you rebalance your life by minimizing your use of digital gadgets outside of work or school.
- **Devote more time reconnecting with yourself and others in person**. This will make all the difference to your relationships, happiness, and presence.

How to Improve Dialogue @ Work

Without dialogue, we will have to walk in the darkness of self-righteousness.
—Majid Tehranian[7]

We spend most of our waking hours at work (or school) and many of us now live our lives beyond the digital tipping point and our organizations need us to achieve optimal outcomes to survive and thrive in the complex markets we now face, so I suggest the following changes in our work lives.

These are recommendations and need to be implemented according to your own situations but nonetheless the purpose and intent is clear—to create space for optimal outcomes to arise through dialogue:

- Leaders should **dialogue daily for 5 to 10 minutes with each of your direct reports** during which time you should practice effective dialogue, especially focusing on your presence, suspending your assumptions, and absorbing the accurate and complete message being expressed to you regardless of how effective it is shared.
- **Insert dialogue into the agenda of your regular meetings** and if you don't have regular meetings start doing so (e.g., weekly team meetings of 40 to 60 minutes) because the solution is in the dialogue.
  - Ensure that the meetings cover the important communication issues but include time for dialogue as well on matters of importance to the team.

- These meetings should be face-to-face but if people are traveling or are located overseas or across town do all you can to connect using audio and video so that you can see each other during the dialogue.
- Ensure that future meetings double back on topics discussed at previous meetings so that people know what has come of their previous dialogues.
- Effective dialogue leads to optimal outcomes and sharing these wins motivates stakeholders to even more dialogue. Not sharing the outcomes of previous meetings demotivates stakeholders from sharing, cuts off dialogue, and prevents future wins.
- **Complete Potential's** *Organization Dialogue Assessment* and discuss the results with your colleagues to devise ways to improve dialogue among the stakeholders.
- Make dialogic leadership a key competence in your organization by doing the following:
  - Institute dialogue training in your organization to ensure that people understand the difference between communication and dialogue and to ensure that people know how to dialogue effectively in sales, sourcing, performance management, priority account, service, and other mission-critical situations that if done well lead to success for the organization and if done poorly lead eventually to bankruptcy.
  - Insert effective dialogue into your performance appraisal system to spotlight where dialogue problems exist in your organization so that you can give help to the individuals involved and divert problems from happening before it becomes too late.
  - Stop rewarding nondialogic leadership that creates conflict and unsustainable suboptimal outcomes via unilateral decisions taken without consulting the key stakeholders.
- **Appoint a dialogue referee every time you meet** to ensure that someone is keeping an eye on the dialogue process needed to achieve optimal outcomes.
  - Dialogue referees should assess and comment on the quality of the dialogue in real time to ensure that corrections are made midstream.

- Dialogue referees should refer to the simple formula that Right Outcomes = Right People dialoguing on the Right Issues in the Right Way and at the Right Time and in the Right Space.
- Dialogue referees should have gravitas sufficient to be respected and listened to by the others involved in the dialogue.

Improve Your Meetings

Most dialogue at work takes place in the context of meetings so there are several do's and don'ts that you can put in place to improve the quality of your meetings. Consider which of these relate to the meetings you lead and attend:

	DO'S
INFORMATION	• Clearly state the purpose of the meeting • Meet as soon as necessary • Take notes yourself • Share agenda before meeting • Agree on agenda at start of meeting • Order agenda specifically • Send information for reading before meeting
PEOPLE	• Recognize language differences • Keep up momentum after the meeting • Adjust output according to audience • Ensure everyone knows what's expected of them • Ensure key people are included • Excuse people if they are not needed • Select the right chairperson • Include everyone
TIMING	• Allocate sufficient time for preparation • Maintain focus on the deadline • Match duration to participant needs • Share time zone differences • Handle interruptions effectively
MOOD	• Do all you can to reinforce required mood • Gather details about conflict • Match style to output required • Agree on conflict resolution process in advance • Manage existing and new conflicts arising
PLACE	• Realize allies sit together • Ask others for input on place • Match location to output required • Consider using a facilitator • Make group's work visible to all

DONT'S

INFORMATION	• Assume people have done their homework • Meet unless you need to • Underestimate importance of simply airing the issues • Underestimate externally communicating meeting output • Hand out material without referring to it specifically • Leave without an agreed action plan • Overlook the need to market decisions made
PEOPLE	• Start without knowing who's coming • Assume people will walk away committed • Mismanage people's personal agendas • Underestimate people's desire for a good chairperson • Misstep cultural nuances • Take silence – no comment • Overlook body language • Let negative behavior derail the meeting
TIMING	• Start or run late • Underestimate time required/available • Assume others will respect deadline • Expect your time to take priority • Book people at last minute
MOOD	• Overlook current feelings • Forget choosing level of formality • Limit your style flexibility • Assume "they'll get over it" • Assume no conflict
PLACE	• Overlook personal reasons linked to place • Assume technology will work • Choose wrong place • Meet in the same place all the time • Use equipment not supporting output desired

How to Improve Dialogue in Society

When the forms of an old culture are dying, the new culture is created by a few people who are not afraid to be insecure.

—Rudolph Bahro[8]

Our biggest challenge involves how to live an environmentally sustainable, socially just, and spiritually fulfilling human presence on earth. All the conflicts we face raising our families, running our businesses, and living together on this small earth require dialogue, not silence and violence, to find ways to overcome them. We need to find ways to insert effective dialogue back into the center of our collective lives and for all of these reasons I suggest the following changes in society.

These are recommendations and need to be implemented according to local culture and priority but nonetheless the purpose and intent is clear—to create space for optimal outcomes to arise through dialogue:

We need a twenty-first-century upgrade on the seemingly failed systems of capitalism and communism. I propose Potentialism, which I define as our duty to realize our potential while helping others realize theirs.

By putting the realization of potential (personal, organizational, societal) at the center of our endeavors rather than the accumulation of capital or working for the commune, we will stimulate the dialogue needed to survive and thrive in our fragile and increasingly crowded world (I continue this theme next).

The more complex societies get and the more complex the networks of interdependence within and beyond community and national borders get, the more people are forced in their own interests to find non-zero-sum solutions.[9] That is, win–win solutions instead of win–lose solutions. . . . Because we find as our interdependence increases that, on the whole, we do better when other people do better as well—so we have to find ways that we can all win, we have to accommodate each other.

—Bill Clinton[10]

- We should **insert dialogue training into school curriculums everywhere**. Education started as a dialogic process and the best education remains a dialogic process between teacher and student but sadly most education is strictly communication with the best marks going to the students that can re-communicate the teacher's communication from his/her lectures or books.
  - This requires teaching teachers how to dialogue and how to train students in dialogue.
  - This also requires creating time and space in schools for dialogue because the classroom setup is typically seats facing the front, not each other, and schools' curriculums are built around communicating knowledge, not dialoguing about topics of importance.
  - If we need dialogic leadership today we need to ensure our leaders of tomorrow are well prepared for the challenges that await them.

> *Learn from the people*
> *Plan with the people*
> *Begin with what they have*
> *Build on what they know*
> *Of the best leaders*
> *When the task is accomplished*
> *The people all remark*
> *We have done it ourselves*
>
> —Lao-Tzu[11]

- Coffee shops, fast food restaurants, bars, and other suitable **public places should create dialogue tables where people can sit and engage in dialogue with strangers** knowing certain minimum standards will be kept, including:
  - Polite language.
  - No solicitation of any kind.
  - No obligation to continue if people don't wish to.
  - No hostility.
  - Practice effective dialogue on matters of the day using PRESA (presence, respect, expression, suspending, absorbing).

> *Potential stands in need of you in order to be born.*
>
> —Martin Buber[12]

- Parliaments, legislatures, town halls, and other public gatherings should **employ dialogue referees** whose job it is to keep dialogue participants focused on optimal outcomes and alert to shortcomings in individual and group dialogue effectiveness.

> *The United Nations decided to begin the new millennium by dedicating the year 2001 to a "dialogue of civilizations" to build a culture of peace. But in order to dialogue, civilizations need to be embodied in gifted individuals.*
>
> —David W. Chappell[13]

- **Online ratings of the dialogue effectiveness of our leaders** to begin to weed out nondialogic leaders and promote the importance of dialogic leadership in our public institutions.
  - Only dialogic leadership will allow us to attain the social future we expect our leaders to push for and only through exposing good and bad practices can we begin to identify the impartial dialogic leaders we need to take us sustainably into the future together.
  - Online dialogic leadership ratings of leaders would have highlighted, for example, the wrongheaded ways of the Tunisian, Egyptian, and other Arab leaders who were clearly not achieving optimal outcomes in their countries and whose citizens had long ago lost hope of their leaders engaging them in the dialogue about their future.
  - Online ratings can send specific feedback to leaders while they are still in office so they can correct and improve their behavior and thereby prevent the revolutionary changes that also cause suboptimal outcomes.

As kill/hit ratios have advanced with weapons of mass destruction, there has not developed a comparable moral or institutional restraint on the use of violence for settling international disputes. And, in war, human beings turn into true barbarians, discarding most codes of civilized behavior.

—Majid Tehranian[14]

Effective Dialogue versus Silence and Violence

Potentialism

The lethargy and apathy that so many people experience comes from lack of confidence in and conviction about the greatness of human potential.

—Daisaku Ikeda[15]

My idea for a patch or an upgrade to twentieth-century capitalism and communism is directly linked to where I started this book, saying that optimal outcomes require finding what's best for you and the other party (Nash's Nobel-winning economics). Given that war between the capitalist countries didn't make sense now that these same countries are among the capitalist countries' leading trade partners; and given that both communism and capitalism have proven to have serious failings (consider the bankruptcy and break-up of the Soviet Union in 1989 and the near bankruptcy of major Western economies in 2008 to 2009); and given the twenty-first-century economy is so intricately connected that we need to work together simply to survive, our economic system needs to also make sense.

There is enough in the world for everyone's need; there is not enough for everyone's greed.

— Gandhi[16]

Building on Nash's economics I propose that by putting the attainment of potential at the center of our sociopolitical systems will give emphasis to what matters most and provide an easy benchmark against which our policies can be considered. Potentialism suggests that, "We have a duty to realize our potential while helping others realize theirs." The system has to work in tandem and here are a few suggestions on what that might mean in practice.

To realize our potential while helping others realize theirs, dialogue leaders need to engage stakeholders in their communities to focus on the following topics:

- **Interdependent living**—We must accept that we are all interdependent and will win or lose together.
- **Dialogic leadership**—We must train people young and old to dialogue and create space for effective dialogue to solve the problems we face.
- **Environmental protection**—We must protect our environment by producing and consuming sustainably.
- **Bureaucracy free**—We must eliminate the bureaucracy that wastes time and money and stands in the way of people realizing their potential.

- **Efficient infrastructure**—We must provide efficient and effective transport, communication, water and sewage systems pollution-free.
- **Quality education**—We must provide quality education at the start and middle of life to develop people's potential in response to societal needs.
- **Compassionate community**—We must provide safe, healthy, nurturing communities where people can interact freely and productively.
- **Quality health care**—We must provide health and social services that support people in need and provide a mutually agreed minimum level of wellness.
- **Minimum taxation**—We must govern efficiently and effectively and ensure taxes not exceeding 20 percent of income are sufficient to balance budgets and eliminate debt.
- **Give charity**—We must devote 20 percent of our time and resources (fully tax deductible) helping others in need.
- **Corruption free**—We must eliminate corruption and ensure transparent governance prevents theft and greed and undue enrichment.
- **Enforced human rights**—We must enforce the protection of human rights and freedoms including the protection of language and culture.

Finding Courage—The Role of Communications Professionals

The starting point for a better world is the belief that it is possible.

—Norman Cousins[17]

Readers might think that it is the job of their communications departments to sort out what is not quite right in terms of communication inside their organizations, but in my experience working with leading communications professionals whether the leaders of their organizations are good or bad at dialogue is outside of their control and they must only deal with the consequences.[18]

I encourage people in the communications industry to make yourselves available to improve dialogue inside your organizations and between your organization and your customers, suppliers, shareholders, and other key stakeholders. You might want to evolve your title from directors and managers of communication to directors and managers of dialogue. Likewise I encourage "C" suite leaders to empower your communications professionals to focus on the issue of dialogue gap in your organizations and explore ways to improve dialogue especially in the key areas of sales, sourcing, project management, key account management, performance management, and so on.

We must become a new kind of institute for "a new kind of world."
  By "a new kind of world," I mean a world endowed with expanding channels of communication yet sorely in need of dialogue.
                                                          —Majid Tehranian[19]

Dialogue Leader Training

As mentioned in the outset to this book I stumbled on the difference between communication and dialogue as a result of my work in negotiation. What evolved has become an important element of our internationally acclaimed *Star Negotiator Workshop*, a one-day event that normally is twinned with our *Dialogue Leadership Workshop* where participants learn the important aspects of dialogue covered in this book. Our foundation training also includes our *Dialogic Selling Workshop,* which has also now spawned our *Dialogic Sourcing Workshop,* which simply covers the opposite side of the table but incorporates key challenges faced by the buy-side of the transaction. The fourth leg of our foundation workshops is our *Conflict Dialogues Workshop* where we consider the sources of conflict, how to use dialogue, and other methods to de-escalate the conflict and move the parties toward optimal outcomes. From these foundational workshops we have been asked by clients around the world to develop and deliver specifically applied workshops in the following areas:

- Dialogic Leadership in Health Care
- Dialogic Leadership in Education
- Dialogic Auditing

- Dialogic Membership Development
- Dialogic Trade Development
- Dialogic Fund-Raising
- Dialogic Customer Service
- Dialogic Talent Development
- Corporate Governance Dialogues
- Trainer, Leader, and Facilitator Development

I encourage you to incorporate dialogue training with whatever you are already doing to manage the key areas where dialogue makes the difference between success and failure. Overlooking the importance of dialogue gap is a lead indicator to a lower share price, decline in sales, lost value for money in procurement, and wasted resources in project, people, and asset management.

Be a Dialogue Leader

Finally, I encourage you to join me in being a dialogue leader yourself and in helping introduce dialogue training into school and corporate curriculums around the world. We will all be better off as a result. The solution is in the dialogue.

Dialogue Cases for Consideration

Right Way

On the importance of persisting three times to get what you want, a story contributed by Bryan, owner and CEO of an international business based in the United States—"In the way of sharing something with you I wanted to remind you of a story. Do you remember when we were in Tokyo at the airport and you were trying to get us on an earlier flight with JAL? I have taken that experience of how you posed the same question to that lady three different times and applied it countless times in my world since then with marvelous results. Thanks for creating that experience for me. I am sure my travels will push me through your fair city soon. Until then take care and please keep me on your list."

Organization Development Dialogues

An international financial services company with large market share in some countries and small market share in others found it important that the country managers find a way to share ideas in developing markets to grow their respective markets. The corporate culture, however, placed heavy emphasis on compliance and financial reporting requiring every request for capital to need several levels of approval even after the project had been agreed to and approved in the annual plan and budget. Although the message was continuously being expressed, the regional and global heads did little to absorb and respond to their messages so eventually the desire to improve things diminished and the company fell into a slow stable growth rate, which seemed "good enough" to most but far from optimal to others.

Notes

1. As quoted in Alan Stewart, *The Conversing Company: Its Culture, Power and Potential*, 2nd ed. (Adelaide: Multimind Solutions, 2009).

2. Daisaku Ikeda and Majid Tehranian, *Global Civilization* (London: British Academic Press, 2004), 85.

3. As quoted in C. Otto Scharmer, *Theory U* (Cambridge: Society for Organizational Learning, 2007), 56.

4. Ikeda and Tehranian, *Global Civilization*, 34.

5. Ibid., 29.

6. *Can Humanity Change?* (Boston: Shambhala Publications, 2003), 193.

7. Ikeda and Tehranian, *Global Civilization*, 9.

8. As quoted in Ikeda and Tehranian, *Global Civilization*, 157.

9. It has been theorized by Robert Wright in his book *Nonzero: The Logic of Human Destiny*, that society becomes increasingly non-zero-sum as it becomes more complex, specialized, and interdependent.

10. *Wired* interview, December 2000.

11. As quoted in Richard T. Pascale, Jerry Sternin, and Monique Sternin, *The Power of Positive Deviance* (Boston: Harvard Business Press, 2010), 193.

12. As quoted in P. Senge, C. O. Scharmer, J. Jaworski, and B. S. Flowers, *Presence* (New York: Doubleday/Currency, 2005), 221.

13. As quoted in Ikeda and Tehranian, *Global*, vii.

14. Ikeda and Tehranian, *Global Civilization*, 76.

15. Ibid., 103.

16. Quoted in Ikeda and Tehranian, *Global Civilization* (London: British Academic Press, 2004), 108.

17. As quoted in Ikeda and Tehranian, *Global Civilization*, 176.

18. I have addressed the leaders and members of the International Association of Business Communicators (IABC) and heard from them overwhelming agreement about the importance of improving dialogue (versus communication) in their organizations. www.iabc.com/wc/.

19. Ikeda and Tehranian, *Global Civilization*, 7.

Conclusion

I believe that the moment you claim to have found the truth, you have lost it because that stops you from seeking further for knowledge and wisdom, which itself requires you to negotiate with other people in the common search for truth. In my mind, that would be tantamount to renouncing dialogue. My truth is therefore the search for truth through dialogue.

—*Majid Tehranian*[1]

This book was offered in three parts. Following the introduction, which set the tone and placed conversing into the eight steps of dialogue, Part I shares my discovery of dialogue gap, how it arose, and the impact it is having at work, at home, and in society. I hope you now recognize dialogue gap and are sufficiently concerned about its effects to want to make improvements fast.

Part II provides you with my recommendations on how to improve dialogue and explain how to achieve optimal outcomes by getting the right people talking about the right issues in the right way, at the right time, and in the right space.

Part III challenges you to become a dialogic leader and invites you to assess your strengths and weaknesses and put in place ways to improve your dialogue leadership and achieve the optimal outcomes you deserve.

My goal in writing this book is to highlight to the world the challenge of dialogue gap, to stress the need to regain our human gift of dialogue, and to offer ways for us to do that, at work, at home, and in society in order for us to achieve the optimal outcomes we need.

As I put the finishing touches on this book, examples abound of the negative effects of dialogue gap at work, at home, and in society. May I therefore conclude my story of dialogue gap by challenging you to become a dialogic leader and help others do the same. Your willingness to adopt this challenge is important for your career, and you will realize your potential if you do so. Becoming a dialogue leader is also important if you are to help your family members achieve their optimal outcomes and help society (large and small) make this world a better place.

Dialogic leadership is needed if we are to achieve the environmentally sustainable, socially just, and spiritually fulfilling world everyone deserves.[2]

If readers are wondering where things are headed post the Arab Spring and Occupy Wall Street movements, I suggest dialogue leaders consider embracing Potentialism (our duty to realize our potential while helping others realize theirs) while actively eliminating dialogue gaps at work, at home, and throughout society. Only once we have done so will all 7 billion of us realize our full potential together in an environmentally sustainable, socially just, and spiritually fulfilling way.

See a problem or challenge in front of you? The solution is in the dialogue. Go fix it.☺

Choose dialogue;
For at the two crossroads of life,
Once we part,
We may never meet again.

—Hafez[3]

Now that you have finished the book the dialogue continues online and face-to-face.

The team at Potential Dialogue wants you to continue the dialogue on which this book and our related workshops are generating around the world. If you'd like to organize Dialogue Cafés or specific dialogues in your organization or community let us know. If you want to continue online, here are a few more ideas to get you started:

- **Business Communicators Dialogue**

Join Jennifer Frahm's interesting IABC blog on dialogue gap, which can be found at: http://jenniferfrahmcollaborations.x.iabc .com/2010/06/27/lets-touch-base-and-dialogue.

- **Project Managers Dialogue**

Follow the developing discussion on APM's website entitled "Why Project Management Dialogues are Getting Harder": www.apm.org.uk/ news/dialogue-gap-why-project-management-getting-harder.

Other discussion groups will be notified on our social media sites, so stay tuned on any of the following:

- **Twitter**
  http://twitter.com/StarNegotiator
- **Facebook, Potential Dialogue**
- **LinkedIn**
  www.linkedin.com/pub/peter-nixon/18/b82/50a
- **Website**
  www.potentialdialogue.com/public/en/home.php

Notes

1. Daisaku Ikeda and Majid Tehranian, *Global Civilization* (London: British Academic Press, 2004), 147.

2. www.awakeningthedreamer.org.

3. As quoted in Ikeda and Tehranian, *Global Civilization*, xv.

Appendix A

What Prevents
Effective Dialogue?

Main Dialogue Blockers© v1.8

Name: _____

Organization: _____

Date/Location: _____

Stress Meter

Effective Dialogue   0   4   Silence Violence

Presence Problems

Identify in the following what prevents or diminishes your presence and how severe these causes are

The main reasons preventing me from being 100 percent present when in dialogue with others include:	Top Blockers	Severity *High* *Medium* *Low*
1 My cell phone keeps ringing.		
2 I have big problems to worry about.		
3 They interrupt me at the wrong time.		
4 I have trouble turning off.		
5 My e-mail keeps alerting me.		
6 Nonstop interruptions.		
7 Simultaneous crisis.		
8 I can't relax.		
9 Stress takes a while to subside.		
10 One problem tips the scale and I'm lost in my thoughts again.		
11 I don't practice presence.		
12 I never learned how to be present.		
13 People don't look me in the eye.		
14 People don't show they care.		
15 People are doing something else when I want to talk to them.		
16 The history between us overpowers the present moment.		
17 I don't see any future in this relationship.		
18 I'd rather be doing something else.		
19 I'm waiting to start something else.		
20 I'm unable to respect, suspend, listen, talk for reasons previously listed.		
21 They are not present with me.		
22 A lot of work awaits me so the faster I get things done the better and presence slows me down.		
23 My constant digital connections have reduced my ability to focus.		

Respect Problems

Identify in the following what causes you to lack respect and how severe these causes are

I struggle to respect people. . .	Top Blockers	Severity *High* *Medium* *Low*
. . .who clearly don't know what they are talking about.		
. . .whose opinions are not based on real-life experience.		
. . .who haven't followed a normal career path.		
. . .who haven't had to work for everything they have.		
. . .who take the easy road out and avoid conflict.		
. . .who never take a stand on their beliefs.		
. . .who have no principles.		
. . .who have no religious grounding.		
. . .who can't articulate things well.		
. . .who lack a formal education.		
. . .who haven't worked for the right organizations.		
. . .who haven't attained a certain level of seniority.		
. . .of a different gender, race, age, nationality, sexuality.		
. . .who have made moral mistakes.		
. . .who have nothing to say.		
. . .who keep changing their minds.		
. . .who have no opinion.		
. . .who want to make people happy at any cost.		
. . .who don't understand the value of $$.		
. . .who are unwilling to take risks.		
. . .who aren't interested in results.		
. . .who don't want to consider the details.		
. . .who can't handle complexity.		
. . .who don't have the time to get involved.		
. . .who don't remember me/my name.		
. . .who don't look me in the eye.		
. . .who haven't gone to the right schools.		
. . .who don't live in the right part of town, go to the right clubs, or have the right friends.		
. . .who don't have a similar economic standing as me.		

Expression Problems

Identify in the following the reasons you don't express yourself as well as you should and the severity of these reasons

Reasons why I don't speak to or express myself to others:	Top Blockers	Severity *High* *Medium* *Low*
I remain silent because time or place is not right for talking.		
I am afraid of being wrong or showing ignorance.		
I wish to avoid retaliation/rebuttal.		
I lack experience in giving feedback.		
I lack skill or experience talking.		
I am afraid of offending the other party.		
I am shy.		
I can't find the words.		
I have little experience expressing emotions.		
I don't have enough time.		
I wish to remain silent for a reason, for example, to be mysterious, hard to read, avoid accountability/guilt, no good news, only bad news.		
I need more time to think about the subject before speaking my mind.		
I am daydreaming.		
I do not understand the subject.		
I can't contain my emotions if I speak on the subject.		
I can't express myself in the language used.		
I won't speak unless asked to do so by others (can be a sign of humility or cultural upbringing).		
I believe if there is nothing good to say it is better to say nothing.		
The more I say the more risk I bear having things held against me.		
I want to avoid conflict that will erupt if I speak on the subject at hand, for example, I don't want to hear their complaints.		

Reasons why I don't speak to or express myself to others:	Top Blockers	Severity High Medium Low
I fear rejection by the listener.		
I believe my comments will have little impact and therefore prefer to save time and energy.		
I am scared of or apprehensive of the listener (e.g., can't outsmart them and prefer not to try).		
I lack ease talking to people with whom I do not normally converse, for example, different grade or culture.		
Listener has previously punished me for talking.		
Listener provides no reward to me for speaking (not even a thank you).		
Listener never asked me to talk.		
Listener is not listening and I can see that.		
Listener doesn't trust me.		
Listener doesn't speak my language.		
Listener presumes to know what I am going to say.		

Suspend Problems

Identify in the following what prevents you from suspending your beliefs and assumptions and the severity of these causes

Reasons why I have trouble suspending my thoughts, feelings, emotions, assumptions, beliefs, ego include:	Top Blockers	Severity High Medium Low
I have done it like this a thousand times and this is how it works.		
I have fully analyzed the situation.		
My feelings are impossible to disregard.		
Hiding my emotion would be untruthful.		

(Continued)

Reasons why I have trouble suspending my thoughts, feelings, emotions, assumptions, beliefs, ego include:	Top Blockers	Severity *High* *Medium* *Low*
My assumptions are what make me successful.		
Everyone agrees with my feelings.		
Everyone agrees with my thoughts.		
I know I am right.		
I am being misunderstood.		
I'm being attacked or framed.		
I'm stubborn.		
I suspect the other party (suspicion).		
This is a matter of principal.		
I want to win the point.		
I'm impatient.		
I think the other party is either stupid or wrong.		

Absorbing Problems

Identify in the following what prevents you from absorbing the messages others are sending and the severity of these causes

Reasons I don't listen and absorb messages from others include:	Top Blockers	Severity *High* *Medium* *Low*
I made a mistake affecting the speaker and don't want to hear about it again/now.		
I am lacking time to listen.		
I am lacking motivation to listen.		
I have something else on my mind.		
I am biased or prejudiced in some way.		
I am angry or another emotion is getting in way.		
I am bored.		

Reasons I don't listen and absorb messages from others include:	Top Blockers	Severity *High* *Medium* *Low*
I am worried.		
I feel time has passed and it's too late to make a difference.		
I am taking no risk in not listening.		
I am not familiar with the subject.		
I don't like what the speaker has to say.		
I am not interested in the subject.		
I have heard it all before.		
I don't want to accept as true what is being said.		
I don't care about or respect the speaker.		
I consider the speaker inferior in thought/experience.		
I am turned off by the words, tone, expressions, accent, slang, or dialect of the speaker.		
I don't like the speaker's motivation for speaking.		
I simply need a break.		
I don't trust the other party.		
I don't understand the language they are speaking.		
I presume to know what they are going to say.		
Speaker is not addressing the subject.		
Speaker is boring.		
Speaker is not clear.		

Current Version: This list was created over many years with input from hundreds of executives who shared their reasons for poor dialogue as well as ideas to make improvements. This is a living document. We welcome you to add your own barriers to dialogue and solutions for overcoming these and then to let us know so we can share your ideas with other leaders. The solution is in the dialogue.

Appendix B

Organizational Dialogue Assessment

v3.0

Your Name _____

Your Organization _____

Your Department _____

Your Location _____

Today's Date _____

Recognizing *the solution is in the dialogue,* we have prepared this *Organization Dialogue Assessment* to help assess and improve the level of effective dialogue within your organization.

This assessment is divided into the following sections:

Right People—Are all stakeholders involved in decisions affecting them?

Right Issues—Are all the key issues included in the discussion?

Right Way—Is the way people dialogue in your organization leading to optimal outcomes?

Right Time—Are issues raised and people involved in a timely way?

Right Space—Is dialogue conducted in the right space?

Right Decisions—Is your organization making optimal decisions?

Instructions

Please write your name and so forth on the first page. This questionnaire covers all of the preceding categories. Each question asks you to consider the issue from both a quantitative (e.g., frequency) and qualitative (e.g., effectiveness) perspective and to then add your comments. To ensure that we make best use of your input please answer all three parts of each question. The scale used for the quantitative and qualitative responses is 0 to 10. Please *circle the number rating* that you consider *most appropriate* in your organization and then add your comments in response to the question asked. If you have difficulty completing this questionnaire please ask the administrator. Thank you.

Right People—Are All Stakeholders Involved in Decisions Affecting Them?

1. How often does your *immediate boss* make a decision affecting you or your colleagues without asking for input from you and/or your colleagues?

Frequency—Percentage of boss's decisions taken without input from direct reports

Not at All	0	10	20	30	40.	50	60	70	80	90	100	All the Time

Effectiveness—How effective are your boss's decisions when lacking input from direct reports?

Not at All	0	10	20	30	40	50	60	70	80	90	100	Yes, Totally

What topics affecting you does your boss not invite you to dialogue on?

_____

_____

2. How often does your *boss's boss* make a decision affecting you or your colleagues without asking for input from you or your colleagues?

Frequency—How often does your boss decide without your input?

Not at All	0	10	20	30	40	50	60	70	80	90	100	All the Time

Effectiveness—How effective are the resulting decisions?

Not at All	0	10	20	30	40	50	60	70	80	90	100	Yes, Totally

Which topics affecting you do more senior management keep for themselves?

_____

_____

3. Do you have the opportunity to exchange ideas (i.e., communicate) with *top management* in your organization?

Frequency—How often can you exchange feedback?

Not at All	0	10	20	30	40	50	60	70	80	90	100	All the Time

Effectiveness—How effective is the exchange when it happens?

Not at All	0	10	20	30	40	50	60	70	80	90	100	Yes, Totally

If not, why not?

_____

_____

4. Are there groups of people in your organization that you know are excluded from dialogues even though the related decisions affect them?

Frequency—What % of the workforce is excluded from dialogue?

Not at All	0	10	20	30	40	50	60	70	80	90	100	Every-one

Effectiveness—How effective are the decisions where people are excluded?

Not at All	0	10	20	30	40	50	60	70	80	90	100	Yes, Totally

Which groups of people do you think are regularly excluded?

_____

_____

Right Issues—Are All the Key Issues Included in the Discussion?

5. Are all the issues considered important included in the dialogue?

Frequency—How often are important issues **voluntarily** excluded from the dialogue?

Not at All	0	10	20	30	40	50	60	70	80	90	100	All the Time

Effectiveness—How effective are decisions where issues have been voluntarily excluded?

Not at All	0	10	20	30	40	50	60	70	80	90	100	Yes, Totally

Which issues are commonly omitted from the agenda that should be included?

_____

_____

6. Some issues are overlooked involuntarily simply because the people involved do not recognize the importance of the issues at the time of the dialogue.

Frequency—How often are key issues **involuntarily** excluded from the dialogue?

Not at All	0	10	20	30	40	50	60	70	80	90	100	All the Time

Effectiveness—How effective are decisions where issues have been involuntarily excluded?

Not at All	0	10	20	30	40	50	60	70	80	90	100	Yes, Totally

What should we do to better prepare people for dialogue in your organization?

_____

_____

7. Is the complexity of the issues limiting the ability of some of the stakeholders to effectively dialogue and take decisions?

Frequency—How often does complexity limit dialogue?

Not at All	0	10	20	30	40	50	60	70	80	90	100	All the Time

Effectiveness—How effective is dialogue when complexity exceeds understanding?

Not at All	0	10	20	30	40	50	60	70	80	90	100	Yes, Totally

Which issues require more understanding?

_____

_____

8. Is decision making jeopardized in your organization because some issues are given undue importance over other issues (e.g., cost over quality) causing the resulting dialogue to produce less than optimal outcomes?

Frequency—How often does this occur?

Not at All	0	10	20	30	40	50	60	70	80	90	100	All the Time

Effectiveness—How effective is decision making when this occurs?

Not at All	0	10	20	30	40	50	60	70	80	90	100	Yes, Totally

What are the conflicting issues in your organization?

_____

_____

Right Way—Is the Way People Dialogue in Your Organization Leading to Optimal Outcomes?

9. Voicing—Do people in your organization readily put forward their opinion when it differs from that of their boss or colleagues?

Frequency—How often do people do this?

Not at All	0	10	20	30	40	50	60	70	80	90	100	All the Time

Effectiveness—How effective are decisions when differing opinions are not discussed?

Not at All	0	10	20	30	40	50	60	70	80	90	100	Yes, Totally

Why do some people not want to share their differing opinions?

_____

_____

10. Listening—Please rate *how often* your *immediate boss* listens to what you have to say and how effective he or she is at listening to you.

Frequency—How often does your boss listen to you?

Not at All	0	10	20	30	40	50	60	70	80	90	100	All the Time

Effectiveness—How effective is your boss at listening?

Not at All	0	10	20	30	40	50	60	70	80	90	100	Yes, Totally

What prevents your boss from listening better?

_____

_____

11. Suspend and Respect—How often and how effective are your peers and superiors able to suspend their views and respect diverse opinions when considering how best to realize the potential of the organization?

Frequency—What % of time do they suspend their beliefs and respect others?

Not at All	0	10	20	30	40	50	60	70	80	90	100	All the Time

Effectiveness—How effective are they at suspending their beliefs and respecting others?

Not at All	0	10	20	30	40	50	60	70	80	90	100	Yes, Totally

If there is a problem with suspension and respect in your organization, what is the cause?

_____

_____

12. Presence—How often are the people you work with 100% present when in dialogue with you and for those people who are less than 100% present how effective are they at work?

Frequency—How often are people 100% present in dialogue with you?

Not at All	0	10	20	30	40	50	60	70	80	90	100	All the Time

Effectiveness—How effective at work are people who are less than 100% present?

Not at All	0	10	20	30	40	50	60	70	80	90	100	Yes, Totally

What should people do to improve their presence?

_____

_____

13. Do leaders in your organization reward effective dialogue and intervene to improve ineffective dialogues?

Frequency of reward and intervention

Not at All	0	10	20	30	40	50	60	70	80	90	100	All the Time

Effectiveness of reward and intervention

Not at All	0	10	20	30	40	50	60	70	80	90	100	Yes, Totally

How?

_____

_____

14. How often do people use communication when they should really be using dialogue and when they use communication instead of dialogue how effective is their resulting decision making?

Frequency—How often do people communicate when they should dialogue?												
Not at All	0	10	20	30	40	50	60	70	80	90	100	All the Time

Effectiveness—How effective are decisions based on communication instead of dialogue?												
Not at All	0	10	20	30	40	50	60	70	80	90	100	Yes, Totally

What causes people to communicate when in fact they should dialogue?

_____

_____

Right Time—Are Issues Raised and People Involved in a Timely Way?

15. Are issues discussed at the right time in your organization?

Frequency—How often are issues discussed at the **WRONG** time?												
Not at All	0	10	20	30	40	50	60	70	80	90	100	All the Time

Effectiveness—How effective are decisions when issues are discussed at the wrong time?												
Not at All	0	10	20	30	40	50	60	70	80	90	100	Yes, Totally

If dialogues are either absent, too early, or too late (please specify) what is the reason?

_____

_____

16. Do meetings last long enough to properly cover all the issues allowing optimal decisions to be made?

Frequency—How often do meetings last long enough to cover all the issues?											
Not at All	0	10	20	30	40	50	60	70	80	90	100	All the Time

Effectiveness—How effective are meetings that *do not* last long enough?											
Not at All	0	10	20	30	40	50	60	70	80	90	100	Yes, Totally

What can we do to match the time available to the issues needing dialogue?

_____

_____

17. How often and effectively are deadlines imposed on dialogues in your organization?

Frequency—How often do people have to impose deadlines to end meetings?											
Not at All	0	10	20	30	40	50	60	70	80	90	100	All the Time

Effectiveness—How effective are the decisions when deadlines are imposed?											
Not at All	0	10	20	30	40	50	60	70	80	90	100	Yes, Totally

What is the most common reason for imposed deadlines in your organization?

_____

_____

Right Space—Is Dialogue Conducted in the Right Space?

18. Are *internal dialogues* (e.g., management, staff, and colleagues) conducted in the right place to achieve optimal outcomes?

Frequency—How often are **internal** dialogues conducted in the **WRONG** place?

Not at All	0	10	20	30	40	50	60	70	80	90	100	All the Time

Effectiveness—How effective are **internal** dialogues conducted in the **wrong** place?

Not at All	0	10	20	30	40	50	60	70	80	90	100	Yes, Totally

If not, what needs changing?

_____

_____

19. Are *external dialogues* (e.g., clients, partners, suppliers) conducted in the right place to achieve optimal outcomes?

Frequency—How often are **external** dialogues conducted in the **wrong** place?

Not at All	0	10	20	30	40	50	60	70	80	90	100	All the Time

Effectiveness—How effective are **external** dialogues conducted in the **wrong** place?

Not at All	0	10	20	30	40	50	60	70	80	90	100	Yes, Totally

If not, what needs changing?

_____

_____

20. Is the spirit and atmosphere associated with the meeting venues selected for dialogue by your organization conducive to open, honest, and reflective dialogue?

Frequency—How often is the spirit and atmosphere just right?

Not at All	0	10	20	30	40	50	60	70	80	90	100	All the Time

Effectiveness—How effective is leadership in this organization at getting the spirit in meetings just right?

Not at All	0	10	20	30	40	50	60	70	80	90	100	Yes, Totally

What limits the spirit and atmosphere in the meeting venues selected by your organization?

_____

_____

21. Do the size, physical layout, and equipment available in your meeting venues cater to both communication and dialogue?

Frequency—How many of your venues are good for **both** communication **and** dialogue?

Not at All	0	10	20	30	40	50	60	70	80	90	100	All the Time

Effectiveness—How effective are your meeting venues **for dialogue**?

Not at All	0	10	20	30	40	50	60	70	80	90	100	Yes, Totally

What limits dialogue in your meeting venues?

_____

_____

Right Decisions—Are We Getting Things Right?

22. How often are optimal decisions made by people in your organization and how optimal are the decisions taken? (Optimal means that no one party can improve its situation without hurting the position of another party.)

Frequency—How often are "optimal" decisions made by people in your organization?

Not at All	0	10	20	30	40	50	60	70	80	90	100	All the Time

Effectiveness—How "optimal" are the decisions taken in your organization?

Not at All	0	10	20	30	40	50	60	70	80	90	100	Yes, Totally

What do you think should be done to improve decision making in this organization?

_____

_____

Typical Dialogue Spaces

23. The following is a list of opportunities for dialogue that are used by organizations to generate solutions and enhance their ability to realize their potential. Please identify which ones your organization makes use of and whether they are used primarily for communication or dialogue.

Opportunity	Used or not by my organization?		Is opportunity primarily used for communication or dialogue?	
	USED	NOT USED	Communication	Dialogue
A. Employee focus groups				
B. Skip level meetings				
C. Town hall meetings				
D. Financial results announcements				
E. Lunch with the boss				
F. Employee appraisal meetings				
G. Employee development plans				

(Continued)

Opportunity	Used or not by my organization?		Is opportunity primarily used for communication or dialogue?	
	USED	NOT USED	Communication	Dialogue
H. Career development path sharing days				
I. Women's interest network				
J. Brown bag lunch talks				
K. Customer appreciation days				
L. Staff appreciation days				
M. Birthdays and anniversaries				
N. React to the news sessions				
O. Periodic departmental meetings				
P. Quarterly and annual dinner				
Q. Annual strategy sessions and updates				
R. Leadership development workshops				
S. Regular training workshops				
T. Local working together meetings				
U. Appraisal sessions				
V. Award presentations and celebrations				
W. One to one with direct reports				
X. Other—please specify				

Thank you for completing this assessment. ©Potential Dialogue, Research Office, Suite 9D, Sunrise, Discovery Bay, Hong Kong, Phone +852 2987 2433, www.PotentialDialogue.com.

Appendix C

Dialogue Skill
Practice Activities

Skill # 1—Presence (100 Percent Focused)

Dialogue Skill	Activity to Clarify Dialogue Weakness	Activity to Improve Dialogue Behavior
Control your emotions to enhance your situation rather than hinder it.	Make a list of times recently when your emotional reaction or that of others led to a less than an optimal outcome. Note that conflict avoidance seldom leads to optimal outcomes.	The sequence is: event – impulse – reaction – result. Working with a coach or close friend, begin categorizing your levels of response to problems that arise at work, at home, or in society. The levels of response include: Untrained—You react *without thinking* and pick up the pieces Trained—You think *while you react* and minimize the impact of your reaction Advanced—You think *before you react* and limit the impact Master—You *don't react* and have no impact to deal with
Don't multitask when in dialogue with others.	Watch people around you and find who manages to do the most things while in talking to others (commonly on the phone).	In pairs, sit down facing the person with whom you are in dialogue, switch your phone to mute, ask them to speak for 2 minutes on something important to them, during which time all you do is look at them and listen. Resist the impulse to nod or speak or smile. Just create the space with your presence so they can talk. Once you have been the listener, switch roles and experience what it feels like to be the speaker when you are with someone who is 100 percent present. Discuss how it felt to experience this exercise.
Recognize and listen to your gut feelings (inner knowing) and those of others.	Similar to the exercise above where you write down the emotions you spot in others while they speak, try identifying your inner feelings on issues of importance and jot	After your decisions have been made and the consequences known review your diary to see if your head and heart were aligned and if not, which seemed to get it right on the topic at hand. In preparing for and debriefing important decisions, for example, strategic and high-value decisions, ask people to take a moment to reflect on their gut feelings and discuss why they are not following their gut feeling

these down for later review. It is especially helpful to listen to your inner feelings where decisions are required.		when this is the case. The solution is in the dialogue and bringing gut feelings to the table is like bringing an experienced consultant into the dialogue and giving them a voice. You don't have to ultimately agree with them but their perspective will always be valuable.
Meditate regularly to develop and strengthen your mindfulness.	Ask people on your team to share their experience with prayer, meditation, yoga, quiet times, or reflective practices and you will be surprised to see who does and who does not include this activity in their daily (or weekly) lives.	Some say dialogue is a form of meditation but the form of meditation we are suggesting here is something as simple as silently concentrating on your breath for a period of 5 minutes during which time you keep your eyes closed and you keep returning to your breath as thoughts come and go from your mind much like clouds moving through the sky. As you wish you can extend the duration and frequency of your meditation sessions. Alternatives include focusing on nature, instrumental music, footsteps.
Interact regularly with different people to open your mind to new perspectives.	Make a list of the people you spend most of your time with in a typical week and prioritize the list in terms of amount of time spent.	Look at your list and answer the following questions: Are these the right people I should be spending my time with? Am I spending the right amount of time with the right people? How can I widen my network and interact with a greater variety of perspectives on the things that are most important to me?
Show genuine curiosity in exploring what others have to say.	Honestly assess whether you are genuinely interested in the views of all the stakeholder groups involved in your priority projects.	If you identify groups of stakeholders whose views don't interest you, delegate someone to collect their views for you or fix a meeting where you can practice your dialogue skills and maybe learn something you need to know at the same time. This genuine curiosity in others is often cited as a trait of a great leader.

Skill # 2—Respect (Yourself and Others)

Dialogue Skill	Activity to Clarify Dialogue Weakness	Activity to Improve Dialogue Behavior
Be inclusive of others regardless of what diversity separates you.	List a few people with whom you work (or know as extended family members) and with whom you consider yourself to share few if any values, interests, or beliefs in common.	Call one or more of the people on your list to address a project you have in common and tell them you are seeking their views on the project because you believe they will bring original and valuable thinking to the dialogue. Practice your suspending and listening skills as they share their thoughts with you.
Be diplomatic and don't criticize or use judgmental labels.	Ask someone close to you, someone you trust, to give you a few examples of when you were not diplomatic or when you labeled people in your discussion with or about them. Write down the words that you used in these situations.	Using the examples you have gathered from your close trusted friend (or from your own self-dialogue) write down a more positive or diplomatic way of saying the same thing. For example, you accuse someone of being *aggressive and confrontational*. A more diplomatic way of saying this is *assertive and expressive*. While you are still labeling people respond nicely to positive labels but dialogue tends to shut down when negative labels are used.
Be sincere, honest, and dialogue with proper motives.	The key here is intent so ask yourself: What is your intent in saying what you have just said, or intend to say. Another question I regularly ask in watching dialogues is "Whose needs are being addressed by what is being said." Generally if you are addressing your needs instead of the needs of	Ask an observer to shadow you in your dialogues with others and to write down (à la Peter Senge, *Fifth Discipline*) what you say in the left-hand column and why they think you said it on the right-hand column. After your dialogue is completed debrief with your observer/coach to see what you can do to eliminate any mixed messages you might be giving others, for example, "Have you stopped eating desserts?" The intent might be to correct your health and the needs are yours but the wording really suggests, "You should stop eating sweets." A better question

	the other party then you are unlikely to achieve optimal outcomes.	might be, "How are you controlling your sugar intake?" This item is brought to life through voicing and expression so refer to those specific skills for some more ideas.
Involve all key stakeholders in the dialogue.	Think about a recent problem at work and list all the stakeholders affected by the problem. Using a red pen circle the stakeholders on your list who were *not* involved in the dialogues *preceding* the problem. Now using a red pen circle the stakeholders on your list who were not involved in the *problem resolution* dialogues.	Involve all key stakeholders in your important dialogues going forward and when a problem crops up, ask yourself whose perspective you are missing—which stakeholders if any are missing or which stakeholders if any have changed their view and not yet shared it with you. Problems of changing perspectives highlight the reality that everything changes all the time and that sustaining dialogue is needed for effective leadership.
Accept that you need your opponents' perspectives to make optimal decisions.	Using your list of unrepresented stakeholders from the exercise above write down what you think might be the important bits of information that you could gain from dialoguing with these stakeholders and which you would not have known without involving them.	Working with your team members focus on an important and current project and list all the stakeholders involved. Circle the stakeholders not currently involved in your dialogues and brainstorm the information these stakeholders might have that could make or break your project. Go talk to these stakeholders to test your assumptions. This step is really about risk management, getting value for money, and defining good leadership.
Recognize that you'll need each other either now or later and explore why.	Continuing with your list of unrepresented stakeholders, identify why you need each other either now or in the future.	If you have not already done so (e.g., future stakeholder whose perspectives aren't currently existent) and if it is appropriate in the situation, dialogue with these stakeholders to solicit *the direction of their thinking* on the project or issue you are managing.

Skill # 3—Expression (Voicing and Writing Messages)

Dialogue Skill	Activity to Clarify Dialogue Weakness	Activity to Improve Dialogue Behavior
Speak your mind and share your feelings without rage, anger, or lecturing.	List the times recently where you either verbally or in writing (e.g., in e-mail): stopped expressing your views because you felt it best to shut up; expressed your views but did so emotively.	• Role-play a dialogue on an emotionally charged subject and try to express yourself without using emotion-charged words and descriptors. Just state facts, not emotions. • Complete and discuss the dialogue assessment, which in part identifies why people don't talk and what people don't listen. • Review a flaming e-mail and rewrite the contents more professionally.
Inquire appreciatively of others by asking engaging questions (based on your experience) without causing bad feelings.	The goal here is to inquire appreciatively and when you do ask questions to look carefully at the way you ask your questions of others. Don't ask questions to solve the situation, ask questions to understand the situation.	Clearness committees and circles of courage and renewal—requires advanced facilitator. Coaching can also provide guidance to improve this skill.
Don't wait to know it all or get it right before you speak up.	Ask people in your group to share examples of times when they held back from talking because they didn't feel confident they had the whole picture or the time to prepare a coherent statement or position paper.	Challenge map exercise with regular interruption to reinforce the many times ideas and perspectives emerge in the dialogue that were not known to be present before the commencement of the dialogue.

Use "I-messages" to talk about patterns of behavior rather than one-off events.	Write I-messages to tell the persons involved how you feel. For example, "I notice you spend considerable time either watching TV or doing your e-mail when I get home from work. I feel this takes away from the little time we have to talk together during the week"; "I had to chase you for the last three items you had agreed to look after. I feel that if I have to chase you then you aren't really looking after it."
List *recurring* behaviors demonstrated by specific people around you who either delight or irritate you but about which you have not said anything much so far. Look for recurring behaviors, not one-off events.	
State the mutual purpose and focus on the common ground.	At the start of your project and team meetings state what you see as the common goals and ask people to comment, add, or delete from the list. Once the list is agreed on keep it visible for all subsequent project/team meetings.
Consider the stakeholders involved in one of your current projects. Write down all the goals and objectives that you think all the stakeholders have in common.	
State what you mean and what you don't mean to leave no doubt in the other's mind.	Identify the people for whom you need clarification and ask them to state what they mean and what they don't mean. You might have to encourage them to expand on what they don't mean because they probably haven't given it that much thought. For example, "I am in favor of offshore drilling but I don't mean that we should proceed without relief wells and emergency caps being ready so that blowouts can be fixed in hours or days instead of weeks or months."
On currently important projects think about the positions of key stakeholders and ask yourself if you are clear what they mean and don't mean with regard to their positions.	

365

Skill # 4—Suspend (Beliefs, Judgments, and Ego)

Dialogue Skill	Activity to Clarify Dialogue Weakness	Activity to Improve Dialogue Behavior
Be equal in mind and not beholden to others (egalitarian).	Working alone and thinking about people with whom you interact regularly make four lists of people: (1) people senior to you, (2) people junior to you, (3) people to whom you owe something, and (4) people who owe you something.	Share your list with others and discuss things you do now that reinforces the hierarchy as well as things you might do to reinforce egalitarianism. Ideas such as speaking with confidence and authority to people more senior or slowing down and taking time for people more junior are examples of things you can do to reinforce egalitarianism.
Avoid either/or choices and looking at the world as black and white.	In groups make a list of current examples of dualistic thinking in your company, for example "You work at the office or you don't work at all."	Continuing with the same group of people and your same list of examples of dualistic thinking, try to identify a third road to break the dualistic thinking for each of the examples listed, for example, "Actually I work on my laptop and it doesn't matter where I plug in my laptop. Furthermore since I log onto the company intranet from my laptop you have proof I am connected over 10 hours each day regardless of where I am physically located."
Find compassion for others and accept everything is interconnected.	List a few examples where people have messed up recently at work or at home.	For each example on your list brainstorm mitigating conditions that might have contributed to their emotional turbulence; for example, she was very badly behaved at work because her husband was being treated for brain cancer; he showed favoritism toward his daughter–in–law because out of his three he was unlikely to see her again for a year possibly even forever.

Demonstrate openness to new ideas and interest for subjects not your own.	Ask colleagues to propose wild ideas to improve the situation at work and practice remaining completely neutral about the ideas, speaking only to ask honest open questions so they can clarify what they mean by their ideas. If necessary assign someone as your observer and ask that he or she give you feedback whenever you lose your neutrality or begin shutting down the idea.
	Think of one to two examples where you had a new idea and the people you shared it with chopped it up or didn't even care to listen. What did they do that prevented your ideas from seeing the light of day or getting crafted?
Investigate and understand your assumptions.	Go engage in dialogue with people to test your assumptions. If they are true then they are not assumptions, they are facts. If they are not true then you need to correct your understanding accordingly. For example, you assume your client will remain in place for the life of the project—test this assumption by asking them what might cause them to stop working on the project and what is the likelihood of that happening. If you doubt their answers ask a second person who should know.
	Take a look at the list of common assumptions, identify any that might apply to you, and then add your own additional assumptions to the list.
Suspend your opinions about other people's opinions.	When the time is right ask to speak to the opinion leader you have identified. Explain that you have learned the importance of suspending your opinions of other people's opinions in order to allow for a better way of knowing. Express your opinion of their opinion in a friendly way and ask them what you must be missing in your understanding. For example, "I'm concerned you will sell the division without clearly understanding the value that exists. How have you assessed the value of the division if you have never visited it physically?"
	Think of highly opinionated people close to you, possibly thought leaders in the company, pick one and list their most obvious opinions (e.g., this division should be sold, it will never make money). Next to each of their opinions clearly state your opinion of their opinion (e.g., he doesn't know what he's talking about, he's never stepped foot in the division in all the years he's the boss).

Skill # 5—Absorb (Listen to and Read Messages)

Dialogue Skill	Activity to Clarify Dialogue Weakness	Activity to Improve Dialogue Behavior
Watch people's body language to check if it validates what they are thinking.	Facilitate a dialogue with the group about the body movements and facial expressions that people recognize and discuss what these might mean (e.g., stroking hair can mean nervousness).	Watch Ekman video or conduct Facial Expressions Test to train people how to enhance what they notice of others' behavior—remember, "Body language never stops talking."
Mirror what others say and ask a related question to deepen your understanding.	Ma-Ma technique. Using a live dialogue, ask an observer to count and record how many times you use a mirror question and how many times you ask an open question.	In three's ask respondent to answer while questioner only uses Ma-Ma. Observer's role is to keep questioner in check for proper mirroring and asking.
Recognize feedback as a gift regardless of how nicely it is wrapped.	Make a list of feedback statements you have received lately and identify if you were ☺ ☺ ☺ for each one.	For each of the pieces of feedback on your list identify what the real gift of the feedback is for you, what value can it really give you now or into the future?
Listen to others' feelings to understand their perspective and uncover their intent.	Review a fuller list of emotions with members of your team and discuss situations where people have identified emotions that caused dialogue to either diminish or disappear altogether.	In dialogue with others, either in role-play or live, practice using the Ma-Ma technique to express the identification of emotions as they arise either in yourself or in the other party. For example, you mentioned the recession hurt and at that moment I remembered the fear I felt when the large project was canceled. For example, "You say you are confident you will find a job but as you say it your eyes dilate as if you are in fear."

After your dialogue is completed and if the dialogue space allows for it and if the person is willing, go back over your notes together and assess how accurate your thoughts were on the motivations people had in telling you the things they said.

Practice I.ve in your daily discussions to open the dialogue box and use questions to search for the dialogue jewels that await your discovery. When you do uncover some piece of value make a note in your diary of the question that led to its discovery. You will be regularly surprised at the value created by interrupting your own talking to ask a question and get the other party talking instead. I suspect it will so surprise you that you will greatly increase the # and quality of your questions going forward.

Make notes on the needs you think are being addressed by what people are telling you in your dialogues with them.

List the people you will be in dialogue with during the coming week and mark down an open question (starting with what or how) that will uncover the most important information this person could share with you if asked.

Think about why they said what they did before you ask them.

Recognize effective dialogue results from good questions rather than good answers.

Acknowledgments

To be granted the time and insights sufficient to write a book on dialogue is truly a gift. This gift was entrusted to me by the thousands of people who entered my life in the past several years and who by sharing their lives with me, asking questions, listening, and providing feedback have given me the chance to offer what you now have in your hands. I can only hope that I have repaid your kindness in some way by transcribing what you have given to me in a meaningful way.

Over the years some special people have believed in me enough to include me in their dialogues and have given me the time and opportunity to create and refine the ideas and insights included in this book. Principal among these have been my clients, many of whom have become lifelong friends. They not only have allowed me to pay my bills, they have also entrusted me with their staff and colleagues while sharing their commercial and personal challenges. Some of these clients believe so much in dialogic leadership as to contribute immensely to the ideas in these pages. I wish to thank in particular Bernard at Quam; James, Warren, Laura, and Kok Sin at Standard Chartered; Loretta at HKR; Mike in IOM; Anson at KPMG; Gerry and Mike at EY;

Ian, Cliff, Martin, Tas, and Chris at Western Union; Therese at the Peninsula; John and Nick at White & Case; Doris, Terence, and Wing at Hang Seng; David at Manulife; Ron at Johnson Electric; Melina at HKU; Chris at Savills; Vishy and Olivier at CA-CIB; Sunil and Paul at Scotia Capital; Zeph at Expedia; Rochelle at CSL; John and Richard at Deloitte; Simon at InvestHK; Susan and the HR team at Barcap; Grant and the Council at DBIS; John at UNICEF; Dittmar at Bayer; Peggy at SIM; YB at Uncle Russ; Peter at HK Police; and the many executives I have had the privilege of coaching around the world. You are all exemplary dialogue leaders.

I also wish to thank all the organizers who have invited me to speak to their members over the years. There is no better deadline than standing in front of a room full of discerning senior executives. Although I speak often, there are a few groups that stand out from the others in terms of contributing to the value of this book. These include EO, IABC, YPO-WPO, APM, ISACA, and the outstanding Chambers of Commerce in Hong Kong. Let's continue the dialogue.

Another group to have contributed significantly to this book are my team members without whom I could not fulfill my work. Special thanks to Vivienne, Andrew, Tomas, Philip, and Herman at Potential; Ivor at Hippo; Tim at Personal Strengths; Kelly at FCM; Wreath at my favorite bookshop; and the many great consultants with whom I have co-facilitated over the years.

I am also indebted to those of you who have inspired me along the way, many perhaps not even aware that you were doing so at the time, either through words of encouragement or guidance or by laying the groundwork on which I was able to build. In the order in which you have graced me with your help I thank my former colleagues at Coopers & Lybrand, consultants and authors David West, Robin Stuart-Kotze, Henri-Claude de Bettignies, Michael Hudson, Leo Hawkins, Min Basadur, Matthieu Ricard, Peter Senge, His Holiness the 14th Dalai Lama, Thich Nhat Hanh, Alan Stewart, Mark Rogers, Henry Mintzberg, and many others.

None of this would have been possible without the ongoing support of the team at John Wiley & Sons and the thousands of readers of my first book on negotiation whom together contributed to the belief in the market for this book. Of note through the ups and downs of the great recession and the upheavals still being felt in the publishing industry I wish to thank: Nick W, CJ, Nick M, Cynthia, and the editors, especially Kimberly Bernard, Todd Tedesco, and Andrew Willis, all of whom have stuck with me and made writing a labor of love.

Finally I wish to reserve the most special thanks for my family members in Hong Kong and Canada. You bravely tolerate living with an accountant who decided to do something different and agree that we all have a duty to realize our potential. If we are ever to truly realize our potential it will be because those living with us want this as much as we do. To the Nixons and Marchands in Canada, dialogues with you are the reasons we travel around the world every year. To Marie, Ni Si, Long Tim, and Jean-Pierre, thanks for constantly reminding me (even when as a father or husband I forget) that the solution is in the dialogue.

—Peter Nixon
Discovery Bay
Hong Kong

About the Author

*D*ialogue Gap was discovered to exist by Peter Nixon while advising senior executives negotiating buy, sell, change, and conflict situations in more than 50 countries. The more that Peter observed the challenges faced by his clients, the more he realized our need to regain the human gift of dialogue.

Since the start of time, when faced with a problem we have sat in circles in caves to dialogue until a solution was found. It is only since the turn of the century that we have significantly reduced our time spent in dialogue (i.e., thinking together) and replaced it with communication (i.e., sending information through e-mail, slides, documents, instant messages). The solution however is found in dialogue, not in communication. They are both important but not the same.

Peter inspires leaders and entrepreneurs to go beyond getting a simple yes to achieving the optimal outcomes signaled to exist by John Nash's Nobel Prize–winning economics. Peter gets the right people to discuss the right issues in the right way and at the right time and space.

Originally from the French Canadian city of Montreal, Peter began his international career working as an auditor with Coopers & Lybrand, one of the world's leading audit firms. Peter qualified as a chartered accountant in Montreal before transferring to Geneva and Hong Kong where he deferred an invitation to partnership and instead chose to launch his own consultancy allowing more time with both clients and family.

Peter has traveled extensively and worked with a wide variety of public and private organizations. He counts among his client base leading banks, professional firms, public organizations, membership organizations, and MNCs. Peter's mantra, The Solution is in the Dialogue©, has become a constant refrain among clients. Recognizing the urgent need to improve dialogue globally Peter is busy building an international network of dialogue leaders to promote effective dialogue at work (offices, schools, hospitals, government), at home, and in society. Peter has collected various university qualifications from Bishop's, McGill, U of A, Leicester, Harvard, and INSEAD. He has been a visiting lecturer at Tsinghua, Fudan, and the HKU/LBS/ Columbia Global EMBA. When not busy with clients and research, Peter enjoys family and community endeavors in the rural settings of Discovery Bay, Mt. Tremblant, and Lac des Iles.

Peter's dialogue solutions are delivered through keynote speeches, consulting, coaching, seminars, and train-the-trainer workshops. Peter's workshops include the internationally acclaimed "Star Negotiator Workshop" described in *Negotiation: Mastering Business in Asia*, John Wiley & Sons, 2005; "The Dialogue Leadership Workshop" described in *Dialogue Gap*; The Dialogic Sales & Sourcing Workshop, which focuses on the buying and selling of sophisticated services; and the "Executive Resilience Workshop," which explores stress, behavior, and decision making under pressure. Peter's workshops are often rated as the best workshops people have ever attended. Participants describe them as being fun, memorable, practical, interactive, and directly linked to participants' daily experience. Workshops feature participant workbooks, pocket cards, preparation templates, local and web-based support.

Interested parties are welcome to contact the author at Peter .Nixon@PotentialDialogue.com.

Index